Figment

RICHARD GALLUN

McGregor Publishing

Table of Contents

No writer sees himself in second place in his own memoir.

Attribution: Maybe Judith McGregor

Prologue

RECENTLY I READ an essay by George Orwell in which he explained how he became a writer. Orwell began saying, "From a very early age, perhaps five or six, I knew that when I grew up I should become a writer." His isolation as a child, he said, contributed to his developing disagreeable mannerisms that made him unpopular as a schoolboy. So he spent time making up stories and holding conversations with imaginary persons. His facility with words enabled him to create a private world that gave him the space to compensate for his failures in everyday life.

While all of these experiences find some parallel in my life, what really caught my attention was Orwell's enumeration of the four reasons he saw for a person to write prose. Those reasons are: sheer egoism, aesthetic enthusiasm (the love of words), historical impulse (preserving the facts for posterity), and political purpose (the desire to influence others).

I am a little like George Orwell, except that from my earliest days, I had no talent for writing. My writing skills did not improve much even with a superior secondary and college education, maybe a little when confronted with the vaunted "Written Analysis of Cases" at Harvard Business School. Even so, today writing is what I do, and I want to do it well. Motivation, you ask? It's ego, I guess; but also the love of words, at least my own words, when they sing a song that touches me and resonates with my reader. It is too a historical appreciation, not necessarily relating to consequential events, but an appreciation for the humorous and sometimes defining moments of my life. I have a desire to share these moments, if only for the exhilaration that springs from touching the nerve of another person. And again, like Orwell, I have had a lifelong interest in politics, a consuming concern that motivates me to want to contribute to the molding of political thought.

Of these desires, the strongest, by far, is ego. Ego is a component of each of my motives, but it is not egoism that drives me. Mostly, it is that that I have something to say.

I am eighty-three years old, and I have learned that life is about letting go of the things you love and finding new things to care about. I have had to do that with a handful of my closest friends, with my favorite sports and avocations, and with several careers, and with significant women in my life. After all these material changes, I am stuck on writing, not perhaps as the most crucial part of my life, because that part is my immediate family, including a dear wife and four dogs. Nevertheless, writing is of great import to me, and it has become my most consuming diversion.

As a child and as a young adult, I showed neither interest nor promise in writing. Even at Williams College, where I was offered a superior liberal arts education, I developed only pedestrian writing skills. I was strong in math and science, but I had little ability to grasp the abstractions of poetry or the arts. Besides, I went to Williams to play hockey. Nevertheless, I did get an adequate education, and finally, in business school, I developed writing skills that would prove useful in my diverse careers. Today, with a lifetime of such experience and an incipient talent for creative writing, I fear that I still lack the ability to write from the heart, writing, rather, according to my own perceived formula for creativity.

Despite this deficiency, I still think I have stuff I want to write about, and I find that I gain insight as I struggle to put it in prose. With barely adequate humility I am proud to have lived a multifarious life that allowed me to tread my own path, all the time being close to interesting and successful people, but people who wore their human frailty on their sleeves. I am not unique, probably not even unusual, in my exposure to the comedy stage of life, but I think I am more sensitive than most to the absurdity that hides in the normal course of events.

Some think that life is a journey. I suppose they are not wrong, but I, if this metaphor is apt, have come to think of it as a succession of side trips, a collection of pursuits that often lead down blind alleys but every so often out into the sunlight. Or, there may be no journey at all. We just stay at home, perhaps adventuring out a bit from time to time. If we're lucky, we evolve, and then we die. I recall Kurt Vonnegut concluding that life was really about amusing oneself. I agree with that.

This book is about how I amused myself for the last seventy-five years or so. It is about the happenings and adventures that I valued, or at least that amused me. It is not in any way an autobiography. It hits the high points and does not attempt to conceal the lows. But looking back at what might have been the nadirs, I begin to understand that I was able to turn most lows into amusing adventures, amusing, at least, to me. That may have been something of a skill of mine, but it may have resulted more from the forgiving nature of the time in which I have lived than from my expertise at living.

One of my wife Judith's mother's favorite aphorisms was "Into every life a little rain must fall," and in this, she was groping with and understating her own reality. The problem, though, is not a little rain . . . it is the monsoon. Some people face many tragedies in their lives and undergo inordinate pain and sadness. Much of the bad experiences, though not by any means all, is in life, events that fall outside of the normal order, as in children dying before their parents, friends dying in the bloom of their lives, or incidental tragedies that destroy life's natural rhythms. Until recently, I experienced almost none of these. Then there are the life-interrupting debilitating illnesses, injuries, and destructive circumstances like wars, earthquakes, and economic collapse. I did not face any of these catastrophes in any personal way during my lifetime. It is a fact that, if you were born in 1935 and avoided the incidental hazards of living, you had an extraordinary opportunity to live a long and satisfying life. Of course, there was, even during this golden age, a human talent that I shared, for screwing things up by creating interpersonal tragedies, like divorce and other dysfunctional personal decisions. Nevertheless, even with a few poor hands that I dealt myself, the issue for me was not how bad were the cards but how well did I play them.

The writing of this book may be just another side trip, another opportunity for personal amusement. As my physical and mental prowess declines, evident to me in the ability of younger and younger grandchildren to beat me in NASTAR races, the game "Stratego," and even in argumentation, I decided I had to make better use of my mind to enjoy the rest of the voyage. That's when I decided to take up writing.

When I first found a course on the Internet called "Creative Nonfiction," I laughed out loud at the very idea. It's sort of like making up the truth. Even so, as I set about writing with the smattering of direction provided in the early lectures in this course, I began to perceive the nebulous border and the interaction between reality and fiction. That is how I come to my story of *Sardanapalus*.

That story began for me sixty-some years ago while I was attending Williams College. At the time, I was a hockey player aspiring to become a Renaissance man, even though I had no idea what a Renaissance man was. An athlete at Williams then had a better-than-average chance of achieving such a distinction because he was inclined to invest his academic opportunities and capabilities in courses like art, philosophy, music, and other seemingly soft disciplines. These courses were viewed as "guts" and seemed like a good route for the athlete to maintain an adequate grade point while pursuing his "raison d' être," in my case, hockey. They were not as easy as one hoped.

My first and only art course, aptly dubbed Art 1, exposed me to a broad survey of the art of many cultures with only a modest bias toward Western civilizations. Here, I was first introduced to what was to become my favorite painting, *The Death of Sardanapalus*. It is a large painting of the Caliph of the title name seemingly lying on his deathbed with a couple of nubile slaves preparing to accede to his wishes. I liked the painting for what I saw as blatant hedonism and greed for life's pleasures. It was my perception that my hero was about to take his last shot at earthly gratification, a culminating side trip, so to speak. What a guy!

It is a fact that I did not take great notes, and perhaps I wasn't always paying close attention to what our lecturer was saying. (That was probably the reason I was lucky to get a "Gentleman's C" in the course.) In any case, I walked away from Art 1, believing that Sardanapalus was trying to warm his body with the heat from the release of terminal sexual energy.

Some years later, I was vacationing with my wife Kathy in Paris, and we devoted a day to the Louvre. Kathy, who had been an art major at Smith College, did not seem to have as good a memory for artistic parlance as did I. At least, so I thought as I described the significance and the stories behind many of the easily recognized pieces to be found in this great museum. I was impressed with myself for my recollections from my limited art education, and for much of the day, I regaled Kathy with my impressive inventory of artistic and historical facts.

Then in the great central hall where the really huge and impressive French paintings hang, I came face-to-face with my old icon of French painting, Delacroix's *Death of Sardanapalus*, much bigger and grander than I had imagined. When my recollection of the story of this painting burst into my forebrain, I felt obligated to share this information with my wife. I held forth, and she believed. Full of confidence in my disquisition, I failed to notice that, even in the painting's vast dimensions and with plenty of time to explore the details of the painting, the harem girls in the painting were not in bed warming our hero; rather, they were being held brutally by well-muscled eunuchs. Neither Kathy nor I gained much real insight into that painting on that occasion.

Some thirty-five years later, I returned to Paris with my new wife, Judy. Of course, we visited the Louvre and not by accident found ourselves standing in front of this iconic painting. I went through my harangue on *Sardanapalus*. Judy, who was probably tired of absorbing my wisdom, took it all in without comment. We both left with the same interpretation of Sardanapalus' death with which I had arrived.

Fast-forward about fifteen years to the more recent past. Judy and I were at home, nestling in front of the fire with our three and a half Weimaraner dogs. (One of them, the half, was a Shih Tzu mix but had come to believe he was a Weimaraner.) As older people might do, we were bantering lightly about plans for our funerals. Judy said she did not want any funeral. She would prefer, no, she would *insist* on a fireworks display to accompany the departure of her cremated remains as a hot air balloon carried them off. After only a little thought, I opined that I would like to go out like Sardanapalus with a couple of virgins in my bed during the final hours. Discussion led to a minor modification of this plan which would put me in a posed photograph of this scene—that is, I in bed with a couple of virgins. This picture would be the centerpiece at my wake. We laughed about that, and then Judy commented that it might be hard to find virgins who would pose with me; in fact, it might be difficult to find any virgins at all. Judy looked at our two spayed female Weimaraners and asked what would be wrong with them, as we are certain that they would qualify as virgins. We joked about hiring William Wegman, the artist who poses his Weimaraners as people, to create the proposed composition.

Until this point, our dialogue was just banter between spouses who were joking about funerals because they don't want to face the reality of the other's death, followed by the prospect of living life alone. However, I put *Sardanapalus* on my story list for Creative Nonfiction, thinking that I could make a story out of the idea of imitating this painting as the focus for my own funeral, then writing about the reactions of the funeral guests. Even among Judy's and my friends, the responses to such a picture would probably run the gamut, ranging from outrage at the sacrilege of such a presentation at a serious ritual to outrageous enjoyment of this final spoof.

To the end of accuracy in a nonfictional story, I did a little research on the subject painting. In the process of freshening my facts, I learned that I had the story all wrong. Sardanapalus wasn't dying, but he was about to die. His army had just lost a crucial battle, and he was soon to croak at the hands of the victors. While sulking over his losses, he had all of his assets, including his sex slaves, brought before him to be destroyed to deprive his enemies of their spoils. The female slaves were not preparing for coitus but were begging for their lives. All this information is apparent in the painting. I wonder how I missed it till now. Was it possible that my interest in Sardanapalus was a waste of time?

Even so, this episode gave me insight into the value of the fanciful side of life to the diminution of the distinction between reality and imagination. The facts may not be as important as the enjoyment of one's own illusions. That is to say that perception trumps harsh reality; in fact, perception almost certainly is the only reality we know. A true disciple of Vonnegut can believe that Sardanapalus went out in style.

This insight has led me to the task of writing my memoirs. My life has consisted of a great number of side trips, many of which have provided me with life-enriching amusement and only a few that penalized me with sadness and regret. For the most part, these exploits, while entertaining to me, have, like most personal experience, no reality except in my own recollection. I have noticed in discussing some of these stories with persons who played important roles in them that those other participants frequently do not share my recollection of events. That deviation is not a function of recall deficiency on my part, purposeful creativity, or even of "gilding the lily"; it reflects, rather, the uniqueness of the prism through which each of us comprehends his being.

Rather than a record of accomplishments, this memoir, then, is an effort to preserve for a time a succession of amusing detours in the excursion of my life. Having a passing interest in some level of immortality, I have endeavored to record here the best and worst vignettes of my life, hoping that I tell them well enough to engage the interest of my reader.

The Family Fugue

In my still-evolving sense of reality, people are family only if they are part of our lives in the present or, if they lived earlier, a fragment of our understanding of who we are and how we drew from their lives. Looking back at those ancestors who lived before I was born, I think that to be family, these shadowy figures need to hold a place in our memory, remembered not only for their successes but for their vulnerabilities and idiosyncrasies. Unless we understand their humanity, there is no tangible family among barely remembered progenitors. For them to be authentic family members, we need to know what they believed, how they felt, what they fought for, and, when they did, how they failed. In the old days, we got that information from oral histories that went back many, maybe tens of generations, sometimes even more. Of late, we Americans haven't done very well with our family histories; we have not continued the art of storytelling.

In my family we have not cultivated the art of listening, nor have we taken a genuine interest in our origins. Our lack of attention to family background may arise from our failure to comprehend just how much the even minor decisions of our ancestors shaped the course of events that influenced the quality of our lives, even our very existence. Alternatively, our indifference may derive from the perception of the remoteness, even unreality, that a century or two of metamorphosis can impart in a world evolving at warp speed. Possibly, though, we spend so much time trying to improve the quality of our own lives that there is little time even to live in the present, let alone to remember our forebears.

In this chapter, I hope to add to the family memory, recording important or just intriguing events that colored the itineraries of our progenitors.

THE FIRST GALLUN showed up in Germany around 1590, soon after the ruin of the Spanish Armada; and although there is no evidence that any Armada wreckage was found on continental Europe, the timing of their surfacing in Germany has given rise to the conjecture that the Galluns were originally Spanish. In any case, at least one "Galluninun" settled in northern Germany about this time and took up the trade of leather making near the middle part of the seventeenth century. For the next two and one-half centuries, the Galluns prospered well enough so that eventually a town by the name of Gallun emerged in this region. They lived peaceably until the middle part of the nineteenth century, having benefited rather than suffered from the Napoleonic wars, which allowed them a French market for leather military clothing. With this history in mind my parents opined that we Galluns had tanned Napoleon's pants.

My first truly identifiable antecedent (by identifiable, I mean that we know something interesting about him beyond the basic data of birth and death), August Friedrick Gallun, was born in Osterwieck, Germany, and lived there until 1854, his twentieth year, when he migrated to the United States. He did so either because of fear of military conscription (according to my mother) or because of his attraction to the American ideal (according to a Milwaukee historian). My mother's theory has legs, in that young Gallun was of draftable age at the onsets of the German wars of revolution and the First Schleswig War, which commenced in 1848 and destabilized northern Germany for an extended period. Even as they continued for many years, those wars did not succeed in satisfying the growing thirst for individual liberty among the peasantry and the evolving middle class in Northern Europe. Recognizing that this unsatisfactory political environment existed in midcentury Germany and having found later reports in the press about August's love of liberty, his community service, and his reported attention to the Americanization of Milwaukee immigrants, I am inclined to believe that the American ideal was a more important issue to him than draft dodging.

August arrived in New York late in 1854 and found employment in nearby Yonkers, where he got his economic foot on the ground. He spent almost a year there adding to his knowledge of the leather trade before venturing to Chicago and finally settling in Milwaukee in 1855. Three years later in 1858, having accumulated sufficient capital to enter the game, he started with Albert Trostel, a tanning business that became well known as Trostel and Gallun. The business was located on the Milwaukee River just south of the North Avenue Dam, on a site that the Gallun family would continue to hold until the beginning of the twenty-first century.

By 1863, the rest of the family, including all of his eight brothers and sisters and parents, followed August to Milwaukee and settled here, some of them working for a time at the family tannery. It is noteworthy that our line of the family, while it hired some of the other Galluns as well as a few of their descendants, never seemed to maintain much of a relationship with them, that is, except for Charlotte, who got a good introduction to August's partner, whom she subsequently married, thus obtaining a ticket to continue as part of Milwaukee's emerging tanning dynasty and seemingly cementing the Trostel-Gallun partnership.

Other of the relatives cropped up occasionally in the twentieth century, like Great-Aunt Helen, who will fall into this narrative a bit later. In addition, there was Clyde Gallun in my parents' generation. He was a motorcycle cop on the East Side, but our closest relationship with him occurred when he clocked my aunt Gladys Gallun Brumder Lindsey at fifteen over on Lincoln Memorial Drive. On this occasion he was both friendly and polite, introducing himself as a cousin; then he wrote the ticket. Then there was Oscar who ran a meat market on the South Side, and Dorothy who still sells estate jewelry in Cedarburg. Being tested a few years ago for hearing loss, my second such testing, I thoroughly amazed my doctor, Bill Darling, with unlikely improvement in hearing as compared with my prior exam. A few questions enlightened us both that there was another Richard Gallun in Milwaukee, one close to my age. Through the years down to the present, there have been other sightings of Galluns all over town, Galluns that are surely our cousins but whom no one in my branch of the family ever made an effort to know. This distance arising within the family over only three generations is somewhat strange but is understandable in the context of the mathematics of reproduction, when you start with nine siblings who are used to large families. Further, it is probable that the success of our branch of the family created a significant economic separation, a gulf that led to a diverging social milieu.

Alas, the cozy situation created by the merger of the Trostel and Gallun families was not destined to endure. It did last for twenty years until 1888; then this successful partnership dissolved because of an unfortunate interpersonal conflict between these two emerging leaders of their industry. I have it on the authority of Albert Trostel IV, that after August hired an architect to build a gracious house on Jackson Street on the East Side of Milwaukee, Albert Trostel I was so impressed with the house, not only with its design but also its prominent location, that he was moved to build a house of his own in the same neighborhood and from identical plans that he had acquired surreptitiously. No one took much note when he bought the lot diagonally across the Welles cross street; the brother-in-law partners were good friends, and they were family. It wasn't until the house was well out of the ground that August saw in Albert's house distinct similarities of design to that of his own.

August slowly came to realize that the house was to be an identical twin of his, and when he did, he was so outraged at this plagiarism that he determined to end all association with Albert, both in the business and within the family. Albert Trostel was dumbfounded that his partner could take such umbrage over such a petty issue, but August could not be mollified. The company was divided at the river's edge with Albert Trostel setting up his facilities on the west side of the river, while August established his business at 1818 North Water Street, where the company would remain and expand for more than one hundred years as A F Gallun and Sons.

Both partners were destined to do well on their own, and for the next century, their descendants were to be major players in the Milwaukee industrial leadership.

All of this history was still in the future, though, when August, two of whose brothers, Herman and Frederich, had arrived on their own in 1857, financed in 1863 the emigration from Germany of the rest of the family. That exodus included not only his parents, August Gottfried Christian Gallun and Louise Christian Lakenmaker Gallun but also six more of his brothers and sisters, ranging in age then from seven to thirty-one years.

Looking back from a current perspective, it is worth noting that in the 1860s, while August Gallun and Albert Trostel were getting their business under way and August was bringing his family from Germany, the United States was in the midst of the trauma of the Civil War. Considering that August may have left Germany to avoid war and conscription, we might ponder the risks that the family faced, first traveling to this war-torn nation, then traversing the country from New York to Milwaukee, and finally the men facing the serious issue of conscription into the army of the north. Still, knowing the allure of the American dream to Europeans at the time, it is not difficult to comprehend what motivated an entire family to take such a plunge, for it was a migration that was replicated countless times during the nineteenth century.

In 1864 another important family event occurred, one about which I have only rudimentary information. August became betrothed to and married Julia Kraus, who had been brought to America by her parents as a young girl in 1849. By marrying August, she was to become the grand matriarch of the Gallun Leather family in Milwaukee. To her and August, Albert Fredrick was born the next year. In due course, Julia bore a daughter, Ella, and two more sons, Edwin A. and Arthur H. As was often the case with girls in this era, Ella's fate is unknown. Edwin died in an accident in his early twenties. Arthur served as an important partner in the business, managing all manufacturing operations until his premature death in 1921. He had married Helen Case in 1916; but he died of pneumonia five years later, leaving a large estate but doing so without issue. Arthur left his widow a substantial cash legacy, but his ownership in the company reverted to Albert. Helen Case Gallun was not heard of again until the early forties. Albert's was the line of the family that was to continue the business for the next eighty years. His children, Eleanor, Edwin, Albert Junior, and Gladys, would oversee the final prosperous years of the company and its eventual decline in the second half of the twentieth century.

In the early forties, when she was seventy-something years old, Aunt Helen Gallun visited Pine Lake at my Aunt Ellie Pritzlaff's invitation to attend a family "party." As it happened and not by chance, the entire cast of Arthur's four nieces and nephews, together with almost all of their children, attended this family celebration. This get-together was called, according to my parents, to give Aunt Helen an opportunity to determine to whom she would leave her estate.

Unfortunately for the Albert Gallun children, the center of the event was a festive "peach bola." A peach bola is a punch made from champagne pored over brandy-soaked peach sections. The peaches are steeped in brandy for several hours, and the champagne is added after the guests have gathered. My sisters and I discovered the peaches before the champagne was added, and we found them delicious. When our mischief was discovered, it turned out that our indiscretion was not just in eating the peaches, thus diluting the punch's punch, but our behavior under the influence was deemed inappropriate after the fact. The happy part of this experience was that it amused my parents. Great-Aunt Helen was not amused. We never did find out who got Aunt Helen's money.

The tanning business prospered in Milwaukee during the last half of the nineteenth century, allowing the city to become the major leather center of the world by the turn of the century. The reason for this expansion can be traced partly to the availability of hides from the Chicago and Milwaukee packing industries and the presence nearby of tamarack, hemlock, and oak forests in great abundance, from which the bark provided the major tanning agent for the leather making process. Perhaps more important, the tanneries enjoyed a plentiful source of clean water from the Milwaukee and Menominee rivers and a place to dump their effluent—back into the river from where it was flushed out to the harbor, where much of it remains today. It is interesting to note that the North Shore pumping station, now the Colectivo Coffee Emporium opposite the Yacht Club, was established to flush the tanning effluvia from the river. Fortuitously, its river outlet was sited just upstream from the Gallun tannery.

Other factors favoring Milwaukee for tanning included the access to shipping on the Great Lakes and Milwaukee's hospitality to hardworking and intelligent German immigrants. The Gallun Corporation rode the crest of the tanning boom and was destined to become, by the end of the century, along with Trostel and Pfister and Vogel, a dominant player in the tanning industry worldwide.

Young Albert was raised in an increasingly affluent environment as the firm of Trostel and Gallun grew steadily through the seventies and eighties. He attended the German-English Academy, a private school destined to become the Milwaukee University School (MUS) and eventually the University School of Milwaukee, a school that has, by 2012, outlived the Gallun Corporation and has had a hand in educating a majority of Albert's descendants. Albert came into the business after graduating from the academy in the early 1880s and learned the business from the bottom up. He learned it well enough so that he was able to run the factory immediately after the dissolution of the Trostel partnership in 1888 and to take complete charge in 1895 when his father decided to retire. He was just thirty. While the business had grown well enough under his father's aegis, having expanded to 150,000 square feet by 1995, the growth under young Albert's leadership was truly spectacular with the total space expanding to 450,000 square feet by 1910.

The physical expansion was impressive for this era, but the profitability appears to have been more so. The tannery was reconfigured from the ground up during this period and done so in impressive style as tanneries went, with cream city brick facades covering all the poured concrete walls, and with elaborate and tasteful cornices, pilasters, and arches detailing the exposures on both sides of Water Street. Furthermore, the company became an industry leader in leather-making science, embracing chemical engineering as an integral part of the management process and establishing a tanning industry research institute at Columbia University. Young Albert did well enough so that in 1915, he built the Gallun mansion on Newberry Boulevard, remodeled his newly acquired house at Pine Lake, and then took the family to Europe for six months because "he had no place to live." (Quote courtesy Albert Jr., my father, at the time aged fourteen.)

Albert the First had married Hedwig Mann, the beautiful daughter of Henry Mann of Two Rivers, Wisconsin, in 1896, a marriage that had important meaning to Kathy Zentner, whom I married in 1958. It was not until the mid-1970s that the heredity of Hedwig, or Hattie as she was called, even entered my forebrain. It took Kathy to put it there. We had been at a cocktail party earlier one evening and apparently I had told at least one Jewish joke—you know—a joke making fun of Jewish caricatures like long noses and commercial parsimony. On the ride back to Pine Lake, she chose to confront me with this issue, doing so with extreme care. The conversation went something like this:

"Dick, I want to talk with you about something that is hard for me to bring up."

This sounded big, so I shrugged and tried to act unconcerned. Kathy continued, "It's about your telling those Jewish jokes."

She paused, looking for a reaction, so I rejoined, "You didn't like them?"

Kathy, grim faced and apparently a tad nervous, went on. "Dick, I think you tell those jokes to cover up the fact that you are part Jewish."

"What in the world are you talking about?" I whined.

"I've known for a long time about your grandmother, Hattie—that she was Jewish."

"She was? What makes you think that?"

"Well, I guess it was my parents who told me right after we told them we were engaged, not that they made anything of it. They just thought I ought to know. Besides, everyone knows it."

I was amazed that Kathy had kept this secret knowledge to herself for fifteen years. It really didn't seem quite as important to me as it had been to her. Nevertheless, I did check with my mother, who could not confirm or deny; she was surprised by Kathy's information and said that my deceased father had never mentioned this subject to her. Then I checked with some of my siblings and cousins, and everyone seemed to be in the dark. There was a kind thought expressed by Kathy, a kind thought indeed: that this ancestry is probably where my Mensa brain came from.

To get a better handle on this subject, I looked into the Mann family, learning that the three brothers, Henry, Joseph, and Leopold, had all lived in Milwaukee until 1860 when they purchased Seaman and Company, a company that had rolled up several woodenware businesses in Two Rivers. Over the next forty years the Manns expanded this business, which was renamed Two Rivers Manufacturing. By the 1890s, their production of chairs and pails required more than 10,000,000 feet of lumber, and they had become the largest manufacturer of wooden pails in the country. At the time of Hedwig's betrothal to Albert Gallun, they virtually owned the town of Two Rivers. I was not able to get any wiser on their religious affiliation, but I did learn that shortly after the Manns retired from active participation in the business, around the turn of the century, the company experienced two devastating and remarkably similar fires. As they were insured losses, maybe these events are the key to my search; they could be construed as "Jewish Fire."

Albert and Hattie seemed to have it all for the next thirty-five years of their marriage. They were both good athletes, having ample time for both tennis and golf, Hattie winning many championships in both sports. Albert was a financial leader in Milwaukee as a major shareholder and director of the Marshall & Ilsley Bank. In addition, he was a civic leader and a prominent socialite. He belonged to many clubs where he was appreciated for his "genial disposition and cordial manners." His memberships included the Milwaukee, University, Wisconsin, City, and Country Clubs, but astonishingly, with all these affiliations, he was one of three founders of The Chenequa Country Club, where he later preferred to play golf during summers, which he spent with his family at Pine Lake. He was heavily involved in the incorporation of the Village of Chenequa, an effort that was concluded in 1928. But it was the house and grounds of his Pine Lake property that most engaged his imagination. He and Hattie spent a great deal of time designing, constructing, and tending the English garden and the grounds.

Hattie and Albert probably both suffered a major inversion in their graves when Judy McGregor and I despoiled the grape arbor on the west slope of Hattie's garden to replace it with our version of an aviary. Although Judy and I loved the garden, we had our own priorities and converted this border area into a large, chicken-wire enclosure containing a crude shed to protect our bevy of exotic birds, among which were Polish fighting chickens, turkeys, and peacocks. This pen gave meaning to my father's erudite assessment of the depth of the family's decline, that being to the level of "genteel squalor."

Hattie suffered an untimely death in 1932 at the age of fifty-five, having suffered for several years from dementia, later thought to be Alzheimer's. Albert, who, in 1928 had turned the management of the business over to his sons, my father, Albert Jr., and Edwin, lived in active retirement until he died in 1938. He was seventy-three.

—⚯—

Meanwhile, in Rochester, New York, my mother's family was fashioning an impressive genetic heritage for my descendants and me. My maternal grandfather, John Ralston Williams, was born on December 27, 1874, in a log cabin in Renfrew, Ontario. In 1884, after several moves, his family migrated to Rochester, New York. Despite not finishing high school, young John was determined to become a doctor. He saved his money, and he eventually was accepted at the University of Michigan at the age of twenty-five. He graduated just four years later in 1903. Armed with his medical degree, he opened an office in Rochester in 1904; and he married Ethel Rafter that same year.

While they were married for over fifty-five years, there isn't much information about Ethel, but about "Raleigh," as she called him, there is more than a plethora. The reason for this abundance became clear to me when I attended John and Ethel's fiftieth wedding anniversary party at the Oak Hill Country Club in Rochester. Even before the speech making began, I learned a great deal about the high station my grandfather had attained in the eyes of the guests that I met that night. The real eye-opener came, though, after many laudatory speeches, when Grandfather got up to address the assembled group. He talked for about twenty-five minutes, and during that entire interval, did not mention Ethel, not even once. Not as a defense of this oversight but more as a matter of fact, I would have to admit that his speech was filled with interesting anecdotes about his accomplishments. However, the immediate family (meaning his children) was offended by my grandfather's thoughtlessness, even though this performance seemed to elicit no umbrage from the attending friends. It was about five years later that Raleigh died; and when he did, all of his children saw his death as a favorable omen for Ethyl, agreeing that, having suffered under their father's domination for so long, this good woman deserved a few years of peace and an opportunity to be her own person. Unfortunately, she was sad without him and only survived him by six months. Both had attained the age of ninety-six.

As a child, a teenager, and while attending what was to become my family school (appropriately called Williams College), I visited my grandparents many times. Grandmother, as we called her, herein to be referred to as Ethyl, was a typical woman of her day. She was soft spoken, self-effacing, and completely given to service to her husband, who was more than the center of her life: he *was* her life. Ethyl became known to my offspring as "the hat lady" because of the single sepia photograph of her that I hung prominently in plain sight for many years. In it, as in life, she looked the perfect grandmother, wearing the aforementioned hat, adorned with a partial veil, and a warm smile that bespoke her personal amiability. In this picture, as in life as I remember it, she looked prematurely old, or perhaps it is that she was old when it was taken. Ethyl had a soft side that was most agreeable, but a side effect was that she was easily moved to tears. I experienced those tears only once; on that occasion, we, Ethyl, my two sisters, and I, were playing bridge at Pine Lake when Ethyl trumped her partner's trick. Barby exclaimed, perhaps a tad angrily, "Grandmother, that's *my* ace!"

Ethyl cringed, tears welled perceptibly, and she fled up the stairs to her bedroom. According to my mother, her tearfulness had been a weapon that was used on the entire family while my mother was growing up. This behavior had a great influence on Mother, who reacted by resolving never to cry in front of her children. To my knowledge, she never did, and that was her loss as well as ours.

John had completed his entire advanced education in four years, having entered medical school in 1899 and graduating at the top of his medical school class despite the lack of any college training. He was an ambitious young man, and he set out immediately to make his mark on the world. Foregoing a honeymoon (vacations of any type were not in his life plan), he went right to work from his and Ethyl's new office-residence at 388 Monroe Avenue, a place that was to be their home for the rest of their lives.

Almost immediately upon establishing his practice, John, yielding to the demands of his curious mind, began to delve into the pathology behind public health problems. One of his early successes resulted from an extensive study into the safety of milk supplies in Rochester. He found that many homes had insufficient refrigeration, and suppliers were using inefficient and ineffective methods of distribution. Although Rochester never fully adopted his suggestions, his study was influential nationally in the effort to improve refrigeration standards. He was eventually given credit for motivating General Electric and General Motors to refine their refrigeration technology.

In 1916, John became chief of medicine at Highland Hospital, a position that he held for thirty years. At Highland, he spearheaded the establishment of the first hospital division in the United States dedicated to the study of diabetes and other metabolic disorders. He worked in conjunction with Dr. Frederick Banting of the Toronto Medical School in Toronto, Ontario. It was Dr. Banting who discovered and isolated insulin in 1922, and through this association, Grandfather introduced insulin into this country. One of his famous and early diabetes patients was Frank Gannett, the creator of the newspaper empire bearing his name. Gannett, who suffered from the disease from the time of the founding of Gannett Company, attributed his survival from the mid twenties until 1957, and thus his ability to build his empire, to John Williams. When he died in 1957, Gannett included John in his will with a bequest of $10,000.

Things hadn't always gone well for Grandfather, however. Being a conservative man, he had accumulated a meaningful nest egg by the 1930s. However, his financial progress was reversed then when a brother, for whom he had cosigned a note, became insolvent. John was wiped out by this calamity and was forced to declare bankruptcy, an act that he found more distasteful than the loss of his savings. Nevertheless, even with the loss of face that he felt from this disaster, his practice remained strong, and he went on to become a major force in Rochester civic life.

In 1932, John took an interest in the then fledgling Rochester Municipal Museum. He joined and chaired the Rochester Museum Association, an organization formed to ensure the museum's survival, which was in doubt, given the severity of the Depression. By 1935, the museum was in reasonable financial shape, and John became chairman of the Municipal Museum Commission, remaining in that position for more than thirty years. The museum later became the Rochester Museum and Science Center, and he chaired the committee that oversaw the design and erection of the museum's current building on East Avenue.

It was in a totally different area that Grandfather made his most memorable contribution to Rochester. In 1921, the University of Rochester wanted to expand onto the Oak Hill Country Club's hundred-acre downtown situation on the Genesee River. To this end, the university offered in exchange a substantial cash stipend together with a much larger site near Rochester in Pittsford. Despite the bonanza paid, which would allow the club to build an impressive clubhouse, and the more than doubled acreage, the trade was far from a no-brainer. Beyond its distance from metropolitan Rochester, the land in Pittsford, sapped by many years of overfarming, held little promise for natural beauty in 1921, being treeless and possessing poor soil. Even with the creative artistry of world-famous architect Donald Ross, who designed the thirty-six-hole course, the property seemed to need something more to overcome the defects inherent in the land. It was this perception that commandeered my grandfather's attention; and when the club opened at its new location in 1926, John had an epiphany, recognizing that the barren course needed to be revegetated in a creative way. The challenge of the leached soils led him to take up botany and horticulture as a hobby, perhaps much more than a hobby, as it would engage him for the rest of his life. Over the early years, he would launch the transformation of Oak Hill into the wooded landmark that it has become; in fact, he was never to stop planting trees during his lifetime. It is difficult to believe that all the trees numbering, according to my grandfather's estimation, "about seventy-five thousand," were started from seed in his basement and small backyard garden at 388 Monroe Avenue.

In the process of his botanical education, he had learned that the land was, as the club's historical name coincidentally would have suggested, well suited to oak trees and not much else. John was quoted as saying, "The Almighty was the greatest landscape architect of all. He planned to have oaks at Oak Hill." And so my grandfather did the work of the Lord.

John went on a crusade to collect acorns from around the world, often from well-known forests and famous places. This crusade involved anyone with whom he was in contact going anywhere in the world. When I went on a honeymoon in Europe in 1958 with the former Kathy Zentner, he instructed us to bring acorns from the Black Forest of Germany, and we dutifully did so. The finding wasn't difficult. We found our acorns in the woods that abutted the autobahn; but when asked by a customs agent if we had packed any fruits, vegetables, or seeds, I lost my nerve; and as I was denying that we were carrying such contraband, I tipped over a mountain of luggage, and at that moment I could picture the two of us being led off in handcuffs. Luckily the agent didn't seem to notice, and he waved us through. Those acorns, delivered to Grandfather forthwith, went through the incubating process at 388 Monroe, and I am sure have become part of the majestic canopy at Oak Hill.

When visiting Rochester as a young boy, I found it to be a different world from what I had known. At this time, my family lived in a spacious colonial house on Wilshire Road in Whitefish Bay, and we had celebrated every Christmas Eve at my grandfather Gallun's opulent English mansion on Newberry Boulevard, this residence having been inherited by my aunt Eleanor Pritzlaff. Meanwhile, I had heard my mother refer to her family's house at 388 Monroe Avenue with such reverence that it had become to me as exotic as the Taj Mahal.

Imagine my surprise at arriving at this fading blue-gray duplex that fronted directly on a busy downtown street, crowded between adjacent commercial structures and bereft of vegetation. Next to the house was a long and narrow drive leading to the garage behind, with no room there to turn around. So that one needn't hazard backing out with a scant nine inches on either side of the car, there was a manually operated turntable tucked in between the house and the garage. In the front of the house were two doors, one, as I was to learn later, leading into my grandfather's downstairs office, the other through which we entered a narrow staircase leading to a second-floor apartment. At the top of the stairs, one entered the smallish living room that offered seating on a sofa and two stuffed chairs, all adorned with antimacassars. The shades were always partially drawn, and the room had a dingy and antiquarian feeling to it. The only other furniture was a writing table and cane chair, but in the corner recess above the staircase was an upright piano, which turned out to be a player piano. Grandfather introduced me to the secret capability of this instrument when I was nine or ten years old, seating me across the room while he artfully pretended to be the player. I, having already taken several years of piano lessons and understanding the complexity of the music he seemed to be playing, was duly impressed . . . until he arose from the piano—and the keys kept on moving.

Grandfather was a severe-looking man and was not prone to smiling, and when he did smile, his smile appeared to be a subterfuge for concealing his underlying thoughts and feelings. While formality dominated his persona, underneath his stern veneer, he possessed a viable sense of humor, given perhaps disproportionately to practical joking, for which that player piano had been a great prop. I remember his regaling me with his story of entertaining an important symphony conductor who had been fooled in the same manner that I had been, Grandfather laughing almost to the point of tears at his own joke. In this case, as with others, it seemed to me that he drew his value and identity from seeing himself as the central character in the drama that was his life. What I saw here was an egocentric characteristic, probably a genetic defect that Judith would say I inherited directly from him, and one that his descendants need to regard with respect and their spouses with fear. It represented a single unattractive aspect of an accomplished man.

On the other hand, Grandfather had a willingness to share his interests and to spend time with me. With evident pride, he showed me his office, the turntable, and his garden. He shared with me the special pleasure he drew from the tree nursery in his basement and in his small garden plot where he was still growing seedlings of all types but, of course, mostly oaks. He had an infinite variety of trees all identified in his extensive files, cross-referenced by their locations, by their Latin names, and by the place of origin of the seeds from which they had emerged. For the longest time, our visits were all about him and his interests. Later, when I was in college, he reveled in my success as a hockey player, ignoring my mediocre academic record. All in all, while these visits were brief and not very personal, they gave me some exposure to and insights into this unusual man.

These were the only grandparents that I experienced, and as I have since learned, these were disappointing relationships relative to what grandparents might provide. The distances were great, the traveling was difficult, and while they and I, as well, tried to keep up a relationship, we did not have the time that it takes to make a rewarding grandparent connection. Nevertheless, these were great people who paved the way for us, and while I am sure they reveled in the success of my mother's married family, they were probably sad that this family lived so far away.

My mother, née Elizabeth Rafter Williams, was born into this ambitious and successful family and was inculcated with a drive for perfection. Academic success was expected of all Williamses and, of course, was achieved, not only by my mother but by her brothers and sister. My mother would say that they all had a normal childhood, including friends, good public schools, summer camps, and family fun, but a clear priority was preparing them for the challenges of life. Besides, normal is whatever you decide it should be.

Mother's sister Marney married Richard Meyer, a West Point graduate who, as a colonel in World War II, was the communications officer for Creighton Abrams in the battles for France. After the war, he went on to become a major general and headed communications for NATO in Europe. One brother, John, became a successful doctor, a medical educator at the University of Rochester, and community leader, following closely in his father's footsteps. The other, George, became a prominent lawyer, banker, and civic leader.

Of the four siblings George had the most interesting and varied career. He graduated from law school in the late thirties and went to work for the then prestigious law firm of Sutherland and Sutherland in Rochester. The firm was led at the time by the elder Sutherland, Andrew, who had been a judge, and by his two sons, Andrew Jr. and Arthur. The judge and Arthur were brilliant lawyers, and Andrew Jr. was charming but "he liked to fish and rolled his own cigarettes." George was off to a good start with this firm when World War II interrupted his incipient law career. After the war, during which he served as a naval officer, he returned to Rochester and to the Sutherland firm. George quickly learned that the firm had radically changed with the retirement of Andrew Sr. and Arthur's decision to enter the academic world. Of the founding family, only the fisherman was left, and there was no rainmaker on the scene. The firm had become an empty shell with practically no business.

Concurrently, an associate, Sol Linowitz, who had, like George, served his apprenticeship with the firm before the war, returned from Washington, where he had spent the war years with the Office of Price Administration. He and George assessed the situation in which they found themselves and realized that the practice was in the final stages of rigor mortis. They both had other options, but they decided together to resuscitate the firm. Their biggest problem, and one that persisted for several years, was cash flow. The firm had expenses, fixed expenses, and no dependable income except for a large receivable which was due from an estate and was paid in periodic installments. Sol Linowitz recalled in an interview years later how he and George would take turns going to the office on Saturdays to see if any payment against this bill had come in. Forty years later, he vividly remembered receiving many calls from George: "Not today" and "It isn't in yet."

They got through this period and began to rebuild the firm's reputation and clientele. A fortuitous connection of Sol's, a friendship with a Joe Wilson who ran a small company, led to an important relationship. This company, then called Haloid Corp., had been a customer of Rochester's premier law firm, which also had Eastman Kodak as a client. Because Haloid was doing development work in electrophotography, an area where they might compete with Eastman Kodak, they decided to seek new counsel and chose the Sutherland firm because of Wilson's relationship with Linowitz. Over the next dozen years, there was considerable patent and corporate development work for Linowitz and the law firm to assume, and, in the course of affairs, he became an officer of the company in 1953 and its chairman in 1959. Haloid's electrostatic product went to market that year, and xerography became an immediate and historic success.

This success takes us back to the Williams brothers, George and John, who had bought for $500 each, a hundred shares of Haloid in the early fifties. When the newly renamed Haloid Xerox took off in 1959, John cashed in his stock immediately to buy a Lincoln Continental. George waited a year, and then he used his proceeds to build a new house. The brothers seemed to have possessed a gene, surely inherited by me and probably some of my descendants, that made us all impatient investors.

Kathy and I visited George in his new house early in the sixties, as we were returning from Harvard with our dog, Hornburg. George and his wife Helen had a get-together to welcome us. When George met us at the door, he tried to refuse the dog, using as an excuse the new white carpeting that had just been installed, but I insisted that Hornburg be allowed in, saying truthfully that he, then four years old, had never had an accident, even as a puppy. It was a big and lively party with perhaps a bit too much excitement, and as Hornburg entered, he was greeted warmly. The occasion overwhelmed him, and he headed straight for the new white sofa and let go on it as well as the carpet with a strong stream. I was in the doghouse, and Hornburg was back in the car.

Sol Linowitz was not yet through with George Williams. Sol had been on the Marine Midland board for years, and George had been a director and then president of the Rochester Marine Midland Bank. Through his connection to Linowitz and ultimately to the chairman of the Marine Midland Corporation, George became president of the western region and moved to Buffalo to head this bank division. Shortly thereafter, he was elevated to the presidency of the parent company, the Marine Midland Corporation, and relocated to New York City.

It was about this time that I graduated from Harvard Business School, and as I was returning to Milwaukee, I, as was my custom, stopped in Rochester to visit the family. George was briefly home from New York and took me to lunch. Over wine and soft-shelled crab, he talked at length about his managing this large decentralized financial organization. George was confident that he knew how. "It's really not difficult," he said. "I have an understanding throughout the company that all the difficult decisions are to be funneled up to me. That way, there are no big mistakes made in the trenches, and I don't waste time on trivia."

That approach so flagrantly defied the business school principle of empowerment and decentralized management that it was difficult for me to believe that he gave credence to such heresy. Nevertheless, I had, for once, the tact not to challenge this very confident and successful man.

George held this job for not much more than a year before he was discharged. My mother explained his firing with the fact that his boss, the chairman, had jumped out of a high-rise window at the bank headquarters building in New York, and George had lost his patron. That may have happened but may not have been the only factor in George's sacking. I attribute at least a part of this firing to the inevitable workings of Murphy's Law.

Sol Linowitz went on to a second career as a diplomat and confidant to several presidents and made a name for himself that far eclipsed his success at Xerox. Near the end of his life, he received the Presidential Medal of Freedom from President Clinton.

Another significant exposure Kathy and I had with the Williams family was in 1958 while Kathy and I were honeymooning in Europe. For almost a week we stayed with my mother's sister Marney, at her husband's post in Poitiers, France, where he commanded NATO communications. The Meyers were living in the major château of Poitiers, quarters that were grand but a bit shabby, not having been fully restored since before the beginning of the war.

This visit was particularly eye-opening to me because I got to see how the other half lived in the military. It had been only a few months since I had left my post as a PFC machine gunner in the U.S. Army, where I had been subject to the arrogant commands of shavetail lieutenants. All of a sudden, Kathy and I were thrown into social situations with the hoi palloi of an army base. On our second evening in Poitiers, my aunt, thoughtfully wanting to expose us to people our own age, invited a cadre of lieutenants for cocktails and dinner. Having been instilled with an unworldly reverence for even low-level officers, I was a bit uneasy at first, but I soon learned that, being the general's nephew, I didn't look much like an enlisted man to them. I had more in common with them than I thought. What was somewhat off-putting to me, though, was the relationship between the general's wife and the young officers, not to mention their wives. The wives pandered unmercifully to her every need, with three lighters flashing open whenever she pulled out a cigarette, sycophantic conversational gambits, and an overzealous reaction to her humor. She was treated like a queen, not gracefully but too obviously indulgently, and she encouraged this behavior. All this is not to say that the dinner party was unenjoyable; it wasn't, and it introduced me to an unfamiliar and strangely disconcerting perspective on the military social context.

Of course, my mother had been raised in the Williams family, and she, the oldest child, was also extremely intelligent and ambitious. Grandfather viewed education as critical, and he steered her on a path that led inevitably to Vassar College, without question, the premier women's college of the day. For women of ability, he believed, there were no alternative schools. Grandfather's continuing influence was confirmed many years later, when my mother had convinced my sister Carol to attend Vassar, having failed three years earlier to persuade our older sister, Barby, to do so. Mother was suffused with pleasure when Carol chose Vassar, after having been accepted at both Smith and Vassar. Unfortunately, at least from Mother's perspective, it was about midsummer that Carol came to me and confessed that she had made a mistake in this selection. What should she do, she wanted to know. I suggested that before opening the subject with Mother, she write to Smith and determine if she would still be admitted there. She did, and she was. When she confronted Mother with her unwelcome change of heart, I stood in the next room and listened at the door. Mother received the information with extreme dismay, putting her face in her hands and just sitting there evidently in agony, for a minute or so. At first, I could not understand what made Carol's change of heart such a devastating event. Then I heard her whimper despairingly, "Oh, oh God, oh God, what will I ever tell Dad?"

Mother had roomed for several years at Vassar with a Gladys Gallun from Milwaukee, Wisconsin, and the two had become, in the course of events, best friends. During their senior year, Gladys invited "Billy," as Mother had become known at college, to visit her in Milwaukee over Thanksgiving. My father, still called "Albert" at the time, picked the two of them up at the Northwestern Railway Station on the lakefront at the end of Wisconsin Avenue and drove them home along the two-lane road that later became Lincoln Memorial Drive. As they turned into the ravine road that led from the lakefront through Lake Park and onto Newberry Boulevard, Albert said, "Well, we're home," implying that this roadway was the family driveway. It appeared to be so, and, of course, the Gallun house was as impressive as the driveway, particularly to a girl from 388 Monroe Avenue. This charade was exposed immediately and drew a good laugh from Billy even as her gullibility had been exposed.

Albert was handsome and, although somewhat taciturn, quite charming, a trait that persisted throughout his life. Before she returned to Vassar, his charm had worked its magic on my mother, and Billy and Albert were an item. They were married a year later in January of 1929.

The family, which revolved around Albert Senior and Hattie at this time, was copacetic and there was no sign of the hostility that was to arise some twenty years hence. The Gallun tanning business prospered without significant interruption during the Depression, not seriously impacted by the economic malaise of the day. It was a good life as my parents settled into a colonial house with a white picket fence on Circle Drive in Whitefish Bay.

After the business, the most important part of my father's life was his sailing. He had, in 1925, won the first class "E" Inland regatta. In 1931 and 1932, he repeated this feat and for the next forty years, stood as the only three-time winner of this championship. He came close to improving on this record every year during the thirties as he recorded five second places and a third in the seven-year period. He was, according to my mother, the outstanding sailor in the Midwest in his day. Sailing was destined to be the center of his family's life for many years to come.

After Albert Senior's retirement in 1928, my uncle Ted and my father managed the tanning business—as partners, my father thought. Ted, as president, presided over finance and sales, and my father, the vice president, ran the tannery. Father thought they were equals and someone had to have the title of the president; and because Ted was the eldest, it should be he. Not because he was running the tannery but because he was the best bowler. Father was captain of the bowling team, on which another Albert participated. To differentiate between the two, the other Albert was called Al, and my father was called Al F, which promptly was shortened to "Alf." In no time, Alf became his sobriquet to the world.

In the late thirties, my father had hired a beamhouse foreman (the beamhouse is where they take the hair and flesh from the hides, indeed a smelly place), who, in short order, did not measure up to Father's standards. While Father was a gentleman who did not like to fire people, he dismissed this young man, Bill Law. A short time later, Law started his own tannery. Three years later, according to my father, the *Milwaukee Journal* published a list of the top income taxes paid in 1940 to the state of Wisconsin. It should be noted here that 1940 was not a great year for income with the Depression still dominating the business scene. In any case, the Gallun Corporation was second on this list. The William Law Tanning Company held the top spot. That didn't even seem possible to me, but my father stuck to this version of events.

A. F. Gallun and Sons prospered during the war years as leather manufacturers always had during prior wars. In 1944, the company received the "Army Navy E" for excellence in war production. That might sound like a trivial recognition until one understands that less than 4 percent of manufacturers of war equipment received this award. The company was doing fine.

The clouds, however, were beginning to gather on a foreshortened horizon. Uncle Ted had taken up sailing, and he didn't view it as a friendly sport. He and Father brushed occasionally, and unpleasantly, on the judge's stand, and for a while, the two of them competed every year for the annual season championship on Pine Lake, a prize that my father had had mostly to himself in the years prior to Ted's arrival. The sailing relationship was bad from the beginning, but what's more important, it was an omen of their changing personal relationship. In his business life, Ted had become autocratic and dictatorial, and he used his superior title to exert control over my father and to deprecate employees who reported to my father. Furthermore, both my mother and father were drinking too much; and while probably not yet alcoholics, their drinking was noticed and used against them both by all three of Father's siblings.

As the relationship with Ted became more rancorous, my father determined to confront his brother; and when he did so in 1949, the discussion led abruptly to the conclusion that the business was not big enough for both of them. With a clear presumption that the "partnership" was over, my father asked, "You don't mind if I talk to the girls?"

Ted responded casually, seemingly without a thought, "No," he said, "I already have."

About a week later, Father set his three children down on the front steps at Pine Lake and told us that he was out of a job. He did not prettify the situation, suggesting that the meaning of this schism was that we would have to tighten our belts. He would no longer have his thirty-five thousand salary to support our regal lifestyle. As I learned later, Ted had already bought half of each of the sisters' stock for a price that equaled a quarter of net quick assets, reflecting no value for the plant and machinery or, for that matter, the "going concern" value, which in 1949 still was still considerable. Not wanting to be under Ted's control and having no alternative, Father accepted the same deal from Ted for his entire quarter interest.

The battle was not yet over. There was another family corporation called Argola Corp., a real estate holding and investment company that Father had managed for years. With the two sisters still naively under Ted's influence, Ted was able to inveigle control of this business as well, and by the midfifties, Father was excised from the management of Argola. There was some discussion among the siblings about buying their brother out at a reasonable price in view of the fact that the assets were highly liquid and easily divisible, but this discussion collapsed on the persuasiveness of the "control premium" and "minority discount" arguments, which meant to Ted a 50 percent discount from realizable value.

This time, my frustrated father decided on legal action. The family's firm, Burlingame, Gibbs, and Roper, was not available for Father's action since they already represented the rest of the family. The new firm of Malcolm Whyte and Associates was developing a good reputation, particularly for litigation, so Father approached Malcolm Whyte to take up his side of the issue. Malcolm was known then as the toughest bulldog in any fight, and he definitely looked the part—of the bulldog, that is—but after a cursory review of the facts, he begged off, saying that current law did not leave any avenues for a favorable decision in court. As my father started to leave Malcolm's office, the incipient great lawyer threw out a bone for Father to chew on if he wished, "Of course, if anything changes in the law, I'll let you know."

Not much of a bone, but two years later, my father received a call from Malcolm, who offered, "I think I can take up your case now if you are still so inclined. You'll be interested to know that the legislature in Madison just passed and the governor signed a bill that suits your needs to a tee."

The bill permitted a shareholder of a family corporation that held real estate and other liquid assets and had less than five shareholders, all of whom had received their stock through inheritance, to liquidate his interest at fair market value. The law became known eventually as the Gallun law and had only one day in court.

When that day arrived two years later, the Argola lawyer, Wayne Roper, formerly my father's lawyer, began his defense by demanding that the case be thrown out because the plaintiff, Albert Gallun Jr., came to court with unclean hands. Wayne had discovered and was prepared to present evidence to back up his position that Victor Harding, an associate of Whyte's, had lobbied for the law and had done so while not registered as a lobbyist for my father, whom he had surely represented. There arose a buzz in the courtroom at this revelation, and the two reporters present ran for the telephones. When Roper finished his indictment, Malcolm asked to be heard, and he was given the floor. He promptly testified, imaginatively, that he had authorized the lobbying by Harding for the possible benefit of a number of his firm's clients, and more accurately, that Albert Gallun had never been a client of his nor of any other associate in the firm. When the dust settled, Mr. Roper was made by the judge to apologize to both my father and to Malcolm for his intemperate accusations. Roper did not gain back his composure that day, and by midafternoon, the case was resolved in Father's favor. It was a big win for my father but not really; he just got back what was his.

The resolution of the Argola issue did not bring the brothers any closer together. The hostility between my father and his brother reigned for the rest of my parents' life. While I only heard my parents' side of the conflict, I did have verification of my father's worth from many ex-employees of the tannery. Everyone knew that Father had a drinking problem, even as early as the forties, but he had never embarrassed himself or the company and was always held in high esteem. He was known to understand all aspects of the tannery operation and showed sensitive interpersonal skills, which began with a respectful attitude toward his fellow workers.

On the other hand, I learned of Ted's reputation for arrogance and downright meanness. One story had him ordering the fish at a company dinner, while the top salesman of the day, sitting across the table, ordered the beef. When the food came, Ted sniffed at his fish, looked at the salesman's beef, and said, as he switched the plates, "I should have ordered the beef."

I got a deeper look into Ted's personality from his son Ned. Ned had disappointed his father by not being willing to stay with another of his father's businesses, Perfex

Corp. Ned left a promising position at Perfex and went into consulting for a few years; then he bought a small metal forming company in Mayville. The business, which he renamed Metalcraft of Mayville, was touch-and-go for several years, but by the late seventies had finally become a significant business. Ned decided to try to patch things up with his father, who had turned his back on him since Ned had left Perfex. It had seemed a good sign to Ned that his father had come to Mayville; and after a tour of the factory when they came back to Ned's office, Ned was feeling good, proud of what his father had seen and glad that his father had been willing to look at what he, Ned, had accomplished. As Ned closed his office door, expecting his father to initiate a rapprochement, Ted said without apparent emotion, "Don't say anything. I know why I'm here."

He paused briefly and then continued, "Understand this and hear me well! I will not invest in this business. I will not lend you money. I think bankruptcy is what you should do."

Then he turned and left unceremoniously. Ned was heartbroken.

Ned was an interesting relative with just a tad of downside. His flaw was that he is a somewhat puritanical Christian. "Somewhat" may not give him enough credit. He has strongly held and consistent views of right and wrong. In 1970, he was an initial investor in Quadgraphics, and its founder, Harry Quadracci, asked him to be a director of this start-up company. It was well known that Ned was intolerant of pornography, and it was well known that a then important business of Quadgraphics at that time was printing the *Playboy* centerfold; actually *Playboy* was their most important account. In fact, Harry Quadracci, in his day, pasted all the centerfolds he had printed on the back of and behind his office door. He kept the door open most of the time, a position that totally concealed his erotic display. When appropriate, he proudly closed the door to display his gallery, but that was only when pressed by those, like me, who possessed a prurient interest. What was surprising was that Ned knew none of this. When he found out that *Playboy* was a major customer, he went to Harry and resigned from the board. Then he asked Harry to buy back his Quadgraphics stock. With the *Playboy* account growing fast and the business developing profitably, Harry said, "Of course, and you will have a nice profit."

Ned countered, "I don't want a profit. I just want my money back."

That was Ned Gallun.

I liked my relationship with my father. He was a thoughtful man and was good to me. The first time I sailed with him, I was six years old and was the fifth crew on a four-man boat. It was windy, and for three rounds, I was scared because the boat tipped so far. Finally, I convinced myself that I was safe because my father was the best sailor in the whole country. Reinforcing this view was the fact that we were winning the race by a lot. Then all of a sudden, we capsized, and I was clinging to the side stay with the boat on its side. My father hastened to attend to my fears, but I had accommodated to the situation and was no longer afraid. I remember that event clearly because, for the rest of the summer, I was taunted mercilessly by a neighbor friend, Julie Quarles, with the false claim that I had clung to the rigging screaming, "Daddy, save me!" Deny this story as I would, Julie saw to it that it clung to me like the scent of a skunk. I survived this unfair onslaught, and at the end of the summer, I was invited to go to the Commodore's Table with the rest of the crew to receive our championship trophy. That was a proud moment for me.

Sailing was big in the family, and it was the most important thing in my young life. As a child, I waited for the chance to have my own boat and lucked out at age twelve when Carol passed on her chance to inherit the cub boat from Barby, who, at sixteen, had passed the age limit for the junior class. It only took half the summer for me to figure out how to compete. After consistently having come in at the tail end of the fleet, I, during a watershed race, lost myself in concentrating on maintaining the right angle to the wind on a windward leg. Suddenly, and to my amazement, I was in second place. I finished second that day, never to see the rear of the fleet again. I had discovered one "Columbus Egg" secret to sailing that of concentration on the relationship of the boat and the sails to the wind.

Sailing the boat fast is only one facet of sailing. My parents expected their children, even as they first started to sail, to know the right of way rules from A to Z. That may sound like a tall order, but in the ILYA rule book, which was a hundred and fifty pages long, the right of way rules spanned only ten pages or so, but knowing these rules was the key to most racing tactics, a fact that many of my lifelong competitors never discovered. We also were required to read and absorb my father's library covering all aspects of sailing. Manfred Currie's *Racing Tactics* was the closest thing to a Bible to be found in our house.

Father's emphasis on sailing was not without rewards for him. A three-time ILYA class "E" champion himself, he lived to see his daughter Barbara come within a hair of that championship herself, a feat that has never been achieved by a woman, and later earn a second place in the Adams Cup, the Woman's National Championship. Carol had rethought her original disinterest in sailing and went on to win the ILYA Junior Championship. Then, in 1955, sailing as a substitute for Barby, who, after qualifying a second time for the Adams Cup finals, had contracted polio in the last year of that scourge, Carol finished in third place in this prestigious contest.

It was the next year, 1956, that the Pine Lake Yacht Club rented the Chi Psi house in Madison for the Inland Regatta. Late one evening, long after I had gone to bed, the oldsters were drinking their nightcaps in the living room when an intruder appeared. Later, we learned that the intruder was a Chi Psi from Minnesota and an

All-American football player of the previous season. My father tried to dissuade him from entering, but this guy knew his rights as a member of the fraternity. My father tried to block his entry, and the intruder dispatched him with a blow to the face that rendered him immediately unconscious with a broken nose and two black eyes with which he would suffer for many days. My mother watched this spectacle with horror, and as a woman of action, she walked right up to the perpetrator and smashed her heavy cocktail glass on the crown of his head. He went down in a heap, not to move until the police arrived and took him off.

Drinking became an increasing problem with both of my parents as they aged. After my freshman and sophomore years at Williams, there were many elaborate debut parties in Milwaukee to which I was invited. Often, when I came home from these parties, arriving at the lake with the rising sun, I would find my father, an early riser, in the garden with a glass of dark liquid in his hand. At first I thought it was coffee, but it quickly became apparent that Father's morning eye-opener was scotch. At the time, this habit did not greatly bother me. Father always had had control over his conduct and rarely showed any signs of inebriation except occasionally late in the evening. On mornings that I ran into him in the garden, he was an amiable companion. We had a good time just being together even with divergent perceptions of appropriate early-morning activities.

Nevertheless, his lifestyle was clearly unhealthy. About this time father's doctor, Fred Madison, had persuaded him to give up drinking under a certain sentence of death from cirrhosis if he did not. For at least several years he was on the wagon, and I thought that he was out of the clutch of this devil. Then at my bachelor's party before my marriage to Kathy in 1958, I saw him with a drink and confronted him. He responded that I shouldn't worry, it was just one drink, and he just had to have one to celebrate his son's marriage.

Of course, it didn't work out that way. He was back drinking hard in no time at all. His health went into a decline, and this time, he occasionally showed signs of incoherence, though, for the most part, he was still a good companion.

A couple of years later, I got recalled into the army during the Berlin Wall crisis. While that confrontation looks benign in retrospect, at the time, it seemed like Armageddon. When Father learned that I was to drive out alone to Fort Lewis in Tacoma, he insisted on driving with me, believing, I think, that I was going into real danger. In any case, despite his deteriorating health exacerbated by a serious case of gout, he accompanied me on this odyssey and was a good companion for me. We stopped in Aspen to visit my sister, Carol, and then went on to Jackson Hole, where we spent the next night at a good hotel, eating well and drinking together conservatively. The next day, we entered Yellowstone Park, a shortcut for us that would save about a hundred miles versus the alternative route that circumvented the park. We took some notice of the sign indicating that the park was closed for the season, but, while the weather was hazy, it was only mildly threatening. We drove for an hour before it began to snow and then another half hour before it was really snowing with an inch of snow already accumulated on the ground. At this point, we admitted to ourselves that we might be in some danger, and deciding that discretion was the better part of valor, we turned around and retraced our entry route. It was slow going on the return, and by the time we got back to the park gate, there were five inches of snow on the ground, and the road had no definition. The adventure was a good piece of stupidity, and I enjoyed committing it with my father. That night at a lodge near the park, basking in the warmth and flickering light of the hearth, we had a poignantly intimate time reliving our close call.

We got to Fort Lewis the day before Thanksgiving, and after reporting for duty, I was given the weekend off. At the time, my father was interested in the new phenomenon of regional shopping malls and was aware of a big one in Portland. "Besides," he said, "I have an old friend who lives there, and maybe we could have Thanksgiving dinner with her."

With her? I thought, but let it pass and agreed. So we went to Portland, visited the mall, and had dinner with "Ginny" who greeted us warmly, embracing both of us and then treating us with gracious hospitality. She was an attractive, midfifties woman and obviously liked my father a lot. It was not apparent to me from their interaction what their relationship had been, but it clearly *hadn't* been business. That visit was to me another step in my father's letting me see who he was, and I appreciated the growing intimacy of our relationship. I, an insensitive male at the time, did not give any thought to what this tryst would have meant to my mother.

A half-dozen years later, Father contracted cancer of the throat. After a two-year hiatus during which he undertook the reasonable steps to deal with this scourge, he succumbed to the disease. When it was apparent that the end was near, Father asked a favor of me. After he died, he wanted me to confront Dr. Fred Madison with the error of his prognosis. I was to remind the doctor that he had told Father that if he continued to drink in the sixties, he would surely die of cirrhosis—and, of course, my father was dying of cancer.

A month or so after Father's death, I ran into Dr. Madison with whom I had always had a cordial and pleasant relationship. I threw out my father's pitch just the way he had given it to me. As I was getting to the punch line, I could see the color rising from the doctor's throat, spreading all the way to the top of his balding head. For a moment, I thought he was having apoplexy, and indeed, maybe he did because, in the next instant, he virtually exploded at me in an emotional fit of vituperation.

"Young man," he roared, "I told your father that he was committing suicide if he had another drink! And that stubborn man didn't listen. He killed himself by drinking, as surely as he could have with a gun. Cancer of the throat only happens to people who drink and smoke heavily, and what's more, it's genetic! And I know about you! You are a smoker, and I've heard you are something of a boozer too, so watch *your* step."

With that, he turned on his heel and stomped off. Boy, some people just can't take a joke, even from the hereafter.

In the years after my father died, I had experiences that gave me further insight into my father's character. These perceptions arose first from my activities running the Aspen office building that he had rebuilt in the mid-fifties from the ashes of an earlier fire. The building, first called the Gallun Building and later renamed the Woods Building, became an architectural icon of the combination of Victorian with modern architecture. Barby and I inherited this property subject to a mortgage equaling the value of the building. The rental income fell short by almost $20,000 of meeting the cash costs of running the building. I drew the short straw and became the responsible party to deal with the tenants. While all the rents were too low, it was a beautiful blonde who ran the restaurant in the basement, who had conned my father into renting the space for practically nothing. Fortunately, her lease expired about this time, and after failing to renegotiate a reasonable lease with her, I was able to get a new tenant who made up more than half of our operating deficit. Nevertheless, it took several years to get the building into the black. My experience with the tenants illustrated to me that my father was not only a bit too sympathetic with the problems of his renters, but equally important, he was soft on blondes.

It was twenty years later that I was shopping at Sendicks on Downer when I was paged to the phone at the checkout counter. When I completed my call, there in front of me stood Sal Balistreri, the Sendicks owner. He asked me who my father was. When I told him that it was Albert, he became effusive with gratitude for my family. Apparently, Father had owned the Sendicks' building in the thirties, when Sal's father did not have money to pay the rent. When he informed Father of this situation, my father said, "I am sure you will pay me when you can." Sal told me that that decision saved the Sendicks' business. I felt proud of my heredity that day.

My parents, together, shared many common interests; among them was farming, an activity that was important early in their married lives. It was in the late thirties that they began to travel to the southwest for their vacations taken without the children. Their modus operandi was to engage a realtor who was to show them ranches within a reasonable distance from the realtor's office, say one hundred miles, which might have been in Tucson, Phoenix, or Albuquerque, for that matter. Indeed, they looked at ranches in all these locations. On these trips, the realtor would provide many services, including meals, horses to ride while looking, and most important, a close-up view of the southwest. It looked for many years like they were taking advantage of their hosts, but they were not; they were serious buyers. In fact, shortly after the war (World War II), they did sign a contract with a seller to buy a 50,000-acre ranch in Springerville, Arizona, south of Phoenix, and according to the realtor, whom I met in the eighties, it was the seller that backed out of what would have been a good deal for my parents. I learned from her then that the price was approximately one dollar per acre, and the ranch covered three and one-half counties. It was one of those ranches that when traveling to it, you ask, "When are we going to get to the ranch?"

The answer comes back, "We've been on the ranch for the last hour."

Mother and Father's agricultural bent had begun to take substance when, in 1940, they bought a dairy farm in Wisconsin and began to raise registered Holstein cows. With my mother at the helm in this endeavor, they embarked on a herd improvement journey, which eventually had them breeding championship dairy cows and bulls with ostentatious names like "Wisconsin Admiral Pabst Burke Lad." This dairy-farming venture continued until the early fifties. Mother planned the breeding, kept the production records on all the cows, and attended auctions all over the state. When she was done, she had a herd that produced considerably more milk per cow than when she arrived and one where the value per cow had more than trebled as the cow generations unfolded and the new genes were absorbed.

The proceeds from the dairy farm, about $50,000, were immediately redeployed to buy a small cattle ranch in Brush Creek near Aspen. The ostensible reason for this purchase was that all of us children had become inveterate skiers, and it looked to the parents as though a ranch near a ski area, one that we all revered, was an attraction to keep us coming home for the holidays. If that was the plan, it worked well, as my sisters and I all developed a lifelong attachment to this iconic resort.

Soon after he made this investment, my father was offered a stretch of land lying across the Brush Creek-Snowmass Pass. The offering price was $25,000, but the land was largely untillable forests and steeply sloping open spaces. Father said that he really liked the property, but he had enough of a commitment to this area. This stretch of land totaling a quarter section, ultimately bought by Doug Ziegler, became immensely valuable twenty years later when it became adjacent to downtown Snowmass.

During the Aspen years, Mother acquired a Guernsey cow overcoat that became a major component of her wardrobe for the rest of her life. For her, this coat was in season except in the hottest part of summer no matter whether she was in Milwaukee or Aspen or even New York or Paris, and Williamstown, for that matter.

My mother lived another dozen years after my father's death. She had taken up painting late in life and was talented and generous with her pictures, of which many which were prominently hung in Kathy's and my house. I was excited, more for her than for me, when I was offered by Bob Manegold $1,000 for one of her paintings, a picture to which I had no particular affinity; and thinking that she would be proud of the value that Manegold had put on it, I asked her for permission to sell it. She neither was at all appreciative of my request or impressed by the valuation, and she threatened never to give me another picture if I sold it.

I still have the painting.

One memory of her that stands out in my recollection starts with the formality of the names assigned to all relations in the family. My parents were Mother and Father; Mother's parents were Grandmother and Grandfather to us and Mother and Father, even to my father. My mother had even had called her mother-in-law, Mrs. Gallun until the time of Hattie's death, and still referred to her that way. After Kathy and I had been married for five or even ten years, Kathy admitted to me that she had never known what to call my parents and for all those years, she had never called them anything, believing that she couldn't be too familiar, but she just could not call them Mother and Father or Mr. and Mrs. Gallun, as some of the siblings and siblings-in-law did. As she said, "I already have a mother and father."

So, Kathy bearded the lioness in her den, saying honestly but warmly, "I think we have been family for a long time. I have never been comfortable calling you Mr. and Mrs. Gallun; would you think it's all right if I called you Billy and Alf?"

Mother mused for only a second and came back with a Billy Gallun comment. "I don't know about Father, but no pipsqueak is going to call me Billy!"

Despite her precipitate abruptness, Mother did put some thought into resolving this issue. After considerable musing, she announced to Kathy that henceforth, Kathy should call my parents by their given names, Elizabeth and Albert. The issue was finally resolved.

Mother had been very clever about introducing the family to new foods. When I was about eight, she decided to acquaint the three of us children with eggplant . . . not just eggplant, but *fried* eggplant, this disgusting vegetable in its most revolting form. She knew that we all loved Jones Sausage patties, and given their similarity in appearance to fried eggplant, she encouraged us to eat by telling us that we were to eat Jones Sausage. I, gullible Gus, dove right in and came up spitting, not quite upchucking, but it was a close thing. I hated eggplant immediately; and after being told they had to try it, so did the girls. Mother compounded her error by forcing us to have several forkfuls. Then she went geometric with the issue, and she had our gardener start eggplant in the greenhouse to have it as a summer vegetable. As the plant grew to transplanting size, I took matters into my own hands, sneaking into the greenhouse and ripping out every last plant. Of course, I was the number one suspect when this indignity was discovered and was soon persuaded to confess. I was severely punished, but there was no eggplant that summer and not ever again while any of us children lived at home. I became a modest hero to my sisters.

When I was in high school, Mother was impressive to my friends. She was a large woman, almost six feet tall, and at this time in her life, she was still winning tennis and golf tournaments. I, knowing that she had been a competitive shot-putter at Camp Aerie when in her teens, began to spoof my friends with the idea that she had been an Olympic shot-putter in the 1930 Olympics. My Milwaukee friends never really believed it, but the gullible Harry Drake, who went to Williams College with me, carried the story with him and to my fraternity, the Delta Upsilon House. The fraternity brothers were a bit dubious, even as I supported the story that Harry told, but when Mother arrived, and they saw her in the flesh (and in her cow coat), to a man, they became believers!

Mother wasn't a great companion for me during her later years, but she was valued importantly by a group of widows who were her friends. Through the years and after her death, many of these women shared with me their memories of my mother's kindness. She didn't know how to be a mother to me, but she had a good heart underneath a rather gruff exterior. She was a smart and once-beautiful woman who lost a good part of the second half of her life to alcoholism.

On Christmas night just before her death in 1980, Mother drove herself to our house and celebrated the season by playing poker with us, playing with Rich's new poker chips. It was not a high stakes game, but she walked out the big winner and drove herself home. The next morning she drove to the hospital and checked herself in, having a variety of symptoms. She went downhill quickly and died a week later. She had been a tough hombre but had had enough. She went out as she lived, a very independent and self-reliant woman.

A hallmark of my mother's identity in her waning years was her 1976 Lincoln Continental. It was a great green, four-door sedan with a yellowish vinyl top. It was that vinyl top that distinguished it and set it apart from other Lincolns of almost acceptable taste. In any case, you could always tell when Mother was in attendance at Chenequa, because her car dominated the front entrance. A good place to find this car was in the circle immediately in front of the club, a location that was marked well with no parking signs. In the early years of this Lincoln, 1977 and '78, there was considerable gnashing of teeth over this defiance of the rules, but by 1979 this carping had ceased; no one had the nerve to confront Billy. For the next several years until her death, she parked there with impunity.

After she died and we children started divvying up the personal assets, Barby took the Ming vases, Carol took the piano, but, I, the sentimentalist, took the Lincoln, certainly not for its financial value, quite a bit for its sentimental value, but what's more important, I had a plan for it. Before putting it to use, however, I replaced the vinyl top with a finish that mirrored the rest of the car and had then a beautiful car, subsequently named by my children as "The Boat" and frequently found with a large hawser attached disrespectfully to the bow. In putting this iconic car to use, I occasionally parked it in mother's parking place at Chenequa, one that was identified by a sign that stated clearly "NO PARKING." The ghost of Billy seemed to carry enough weight so that no one ever asked me to move it. Members of the club would occasionally comment about seeing the car there and getting an eerie feeling that Billy was back. Just as I had hoped, Mother's parking place ran with the car. I had inherited it.

It was some years after my mother died that I married Judy McGregor, and to get me onto the straight and narrow, Judy took me to a couple's adjustment course called "Pairs." This course ran to a hundred hours over ten weeks and dealt importantly with the baggage that each of the sixteen participants brought with him (her). I was a bit bored with the whole idea of baggage from one's past, believing quite soberly that I hadn't brought any baggage. I had come from an ordinary family, albeit an economically privileged one, and my relationships ran a normal gambit. It was not until we got deep into family mapping that I began to understand that my family may have been normal, but normal may include quite a few abnormalities.

I became aware of my potential baggage when we began to identify with squiggly lines dysfunctional (as in unpleasant) relationships. My neat and lightly lined family map became darkened by the additional ink required just to make those lines squiggle, but that change was modest next to the pinkish aura that emerged when the red was added to highlight the names of alcoholics.

While my lineage may not have been exemplary in every respect, our forebears did lead intriguing and mostly very successful lives: and while my upbringing may not have been ordinary, who wants ordinary anyway? It was an ancient Chinese curse that wished upon those being cursed, "May you live in interesting times." While it may not seem so to us, the Chinese would have viewed the span of time covered by this brief history as relatively uninteresting. Over the last century and a half the Gallun family brought to life that old Chinese curse, but rather than just living in ordinary times, our forebears made ordinary times interesting.

CHAPTER II

An Introduction to Matilda Hinch

In the journey of my life, I begin and end my story with a spirit represented by the Matildas of my life, one my childhood caretaker, the other my final dog. These Matildas personify for me the essential nature of intimate relationships. It is true that my relationships with women and dogs have had for me a value that is way beyond reasonable. It may seem an untenable juxtaposition of ideas, but it is not beyond the pale to believe, as I do, that both women and dogs can be of comparable value in our emotional lives. Both amuse us, accept our attention, and give us the love we require, and of the two, only the love coming from a dog is unconditional and lifetime guaranteed.

MY RELATIONSHIP WITH Matilda Hinch began right after my parents brought me home from the hospital. Because of a then recent illness, my mother was not able to take care of me, so my parents hired a baby nurse. Enter Matilda Hinch.

Over the next ten years, Matilda was to become my surrogate mother. Her stern and outwardly gruff demeanor occasionally obfuscated the fact that she possessed substantial maternal skills. While her physical characteristics made no impression on me at the time, I was later able to recognize that Matilda was no beauty. Matilda was about four feet eleven with stats of something like 38-38-38. She wore an unhealthy pallor, and her whitish skin was a mottled blend of age spots that had arrived well ahead of their time. Her upper lip and chin offered a vestigial memory of a porcupine. Her graying hair was usually secured in a bun and added little to the composition. Nevertheless, even with these physical imperfections, Matilda was the archetypical woman to me. She knew about love, and she knew how to hand it out tough as well as soft. That is to say that, while she didn't truck bullshit, she was a Florence Nightingale over even the smallest of hurts, especially those that were of the heart.

Her life started in 1901 near Hamburg, Germany, where she was born prematurely to a poor family. According to Matilda, she weighed two pounds at birth, and, given the circumstances of her family, had had a poor chance for survival. Matilda often recounted, with only small variations, the story of how her parents took care of her. Having no crib, they placed her in a shoebox and kept her in the warming oven of the wood stove, on which they cooked their food and heated their house. This part of her narrative has been passed along to several generations of my family. It is a favorite story, one that has been retold many times in creative detail, and, while there are skeptics in the family who disbelieve it, the core version is generally accepted as true. I, for one, have never doubted it.

Surprisingly, Matilda survived and thrived, and eventually was trained as a nurse. Then she came to America, found her way to Milwaukee, and found a better life as a baby nurse than as a medical nurse. She joined my family in 1936 and stayed for almost ten years, possibly because she couldn't leave her "Dickie." (That was me.) This tenure ended in a memorable confrontation with my mother, when Matilda, quite perturbed over whatever had just transpired between them, threw a kitchen knife on the floor, narrowly missing my mother's foot, exclaiming, "I kvit!"

There was no undoing of this clash, even though my sister, Carol, and I begged both my mother and Matilda to rethink this hasty decision. Neither relented. Matilda was soon gone in an emotional departure. Even my mother was saddened, but she said of the event, "Maybe it was about time."

Matilda went back to Milwaukee and her trade as a baby nurse, but she stayed close with my siblings and me. It was not long before she was again a regular at birthdays and holidays, having a mixed role as a valued friend and a quasi-retainer, often doing the cooking and taking charge of the kitchen. Eventually, even my mother recognized that Matilda had a permanent place in the family. Then our babies came, and she was there for all of them. She stayed on for years with my sister Carol, who lived on a ranch in Colorado.

While seeming to be an independent but somewhat lonely person, Matilda always talked of an elusive boyfriend whose name was Edmund. When my sisters or I visited her apartment, as we occasionally did, we saw no evidence of him, not even a photograph. After many years of hearing about him but never seeing him, we were doubtful that he existed. I came to realize too late that we were Matilda's family, and we had been, for most of it, the anchor in her life.

By the mideighties I saw Matilda only occasionally. My life had become complicated by a girlfriend, a divorce, and then girlfriend problems. One day in the midst of problems born of my own self-indulgence, Matilda called. I conversed briefly and got rid of her saying, "I'm awfully busy right now. Let me call you back tomorrow when I have a little time."

A week later I still had not called her back. Then I got a call: Matilda had died the previous night. My callous inattention to this dear woman will haunt me to the end of my life.

———∝∞———

I have had many dogs during my lifetime, but they all came to me as eight-week-old puppies or sometimes older. This one we got to watch on video from the day she was born. From first sight, something was special about this dog, and both Judith and I loved her right off. We had had many discussions about names, but when we thought of the Matilda of this story, our decision was easy.

For Judith and me Matilda Hinch is a perfect name for a beloved dog.

CHAPTER III

The Weather and Me

Since my earliest memories of Pine Lake, the phenomena of weather have always fascinated me. Having been raised in a sailing family, I grew up with an awareness of the influence that climatic instability has on our daily lives. Even with its changeability, the weather usually was benevolent, and I treasured the days in the sun. Sailing exposed me to a range of weather that, even at its worst, did not pose much danger because our lake environment was benign, and as children, we were carefully supervised by our elders.

While this memoir deals with my fascination with violent weather, an interest that came to me early in life, it is the effect of ordinary and extraordinary changes in climate and how these nuances influenced my life that is a persistent theme herein. But it was the storms I remember from my earliest days that captivate me still today. Even as Judith and I lived for many years in this same house and with the same perspective over the lake, the nocturnal storms of this later era did not generate the emotional impact that did those storms of my childhood. While one might speculate that maturity and experience have mitigated my excitement at extreme weather, I would argue that they just don't make 'em like they used to, at least in the places I have lived.

WHAT ATTRACTED ME most of all was the excitement of violent weather, the raw power of nighttime storms that I experienced from the safety of my family's summer home. At Pine Lake, we lived in a big and solid house that gave me a sense of sanctuary. From the favored vantage point of my bedroom, which looked out onto the lake to the south and west, the direction from which the summer storms approached, I would notice with equanimity the signs of the approaching tempest.

The big storms often came at night, always after a sultry day that sucked moisture into the towering thunderheads accumulating in the sky beyond the western shore. On such days, one could sense the coming of destructive weather in the heaviness of the atmosphere and the ominous calm of the early evening. As the day faded, flashes of yellow and orange flickered on the horizon. We called it heat lightning because there was no thunder nor evidence of a storm. Yet if one paid close attention to his senses, he might detect the rumble of an approaching storm, feeling rather than hearing it. As the darkness deepened, the receding glow in the western sky would become obscured by the advancing cloud cover. The big storms did not arrive until well after we children were in bed, probably at eleven or twelve, when I would awaken to the sound of the wind intruding into the house.

Before the wind arrived, there was an ominous period of calm, a stillness heavy with anticipation, so absent of sound and movement that it screamed its message of foreboding. The audible rumble of distant thunder eventually broke the unearthly silence of this phase. As the storm drew nearer, the thunder became louder, and I would feel the first gust of wind sweeping into the house, suddenly cool against my sweat-dampened skin. I recall the sounds of wind-driven doors slamming noisily against their jambs, my mother yelling at my father to shut the bedroom windows, and then suddenly, the drumming staccato of first raindrops splattering hard against the windows. These experiences were not at all unpleasant or disturbing to me. Confident in the security of the house, I savored the sense of danger and potential destruction that was represented by the storm, its power to wreak damage, and the awe-inspiring drama of Zeus' light show. The lightning, if striking nearby, would be accompanied by rolling peals of thunder that reached a crescendo as the center of the storm made its closest pass. The house would respond to the nearby strikes with shaking that generated additional noise from within its depths. Then, if the lightning had been close, the pungent smell and taste of cordite lingered in the air, reminding me of the deadly power of this natural phenomenon.

As quickly as the big storms arrived, they passed on, and the former stillness returned. Sometimes after the storm had passed, there was damage to evaluate and boats to secure. The first assessment would take place immediately after the storm passed, and I was occasionally able to accompany my father as he viewed the desecration and then took steps to restore order. I can remember storms that lifted our sailboats off of their lifts and hurled them onto the piers, pounding the piers into fragments of broken beams and disassembled platforms. Other storms capsized our boats at their moorings, and the wave action generated by the wind drove the masts into the bottom of the lake so far that they could not be extricated. When I was allowed to accompany my father on these damage surveys, I was impressed with the implication of nature's power, but even with destruction all around, the house always seemed untouched. My confidence in the safety of my house was reinforced.

As a family we discussed the weather often, not just because of sailing, but because my parents shared my sense of awe at the power of the weather. My mother often described a long ago experience in which she had faced a tornado at Camp Eyrie in upper New York State. Mostly, she talked about the hues of the day, starting with the yellowing of a clear sky that then metamorphosed to black and then became a vivid green just before the unseen funnel passed nearby. There was something in the telling that made me believe that she may have read this description someplace rather than having been there, but she told her story colorfully enough to pique my imagination. After listening to her tale, I craved to experience a tornado, close up and in the flesh. It is an adventure which has been denied me but one for which I must still admit a hankering. I want to be nearby, close enough to see the funnel, but I have learned from the storm damage I have seen that even that solid old house would not provide the safety that I attributed to it if it were in the path of a funnel.

CHAPTER **IV**

Tough Love at Country Day

In the old days at Country Day School they knew how to raise adolescents. They did it with a rod, one that they did not spare.

The essence of Country Day was personified by its "old-school" English headmaster, A. Gledden Santer, who, if not raised on the playing fields of Eton, certainly seemed to have been. With Mr. Santer in charge, the faculty clearly reflected his values and his sense of discipline. There was no coddling, no gilding the lily; you were what your grades said you were and what your coach saw in your performance. This was not unmindful discipline, it was a well thought out scheme of education, and it did persuade many of us to do the best that we could on the athletic field, in the classroom, and in developing the whole person. And another value was instilled in us—that of school spirit—the love of the institution and history of the school and loyalty to our classmates.

Of course, this stern approach to education affected each of us differently. The athletes and the excellent students whose performances were revered by the faculty were the most likely to accept it. As I look back with sixty-five-some years of reflection with the experience of attending late-life reunions, I realize now that some of my classmates found the Country Day environment unfriendly and even hostile. In a modest way the following memoirs reflect the attitudes and perspectives that were so important to both those who loved and those who took umbrage at the school.

The Royal Order of Mujiji

During the early fall of 1948, my classmates and I acclimatized to our new environment of the upper school. We studied harder than we ever had; and as was the custom, assuredly, it was more than a custom, everyone played football. We did talk in hushed tones about the coming eighth-grade initiation. All we knew was that we were going to get hassled by the freshmen and at some point get paddled and receive an electric shock.

Then suddenly it was Halloween. It was just another day at school except that, at least for me, on this day, the mysterious expectations for the coming evening supplanted productive thought.

As sundown arrived, my classmates and I presented ourselves uneasily at the ominously darkened lower school, where we were to attend a preliminary dinner. Upon arrival, we were ushered into the gym and told to sit silently in the fading daylight, thinking about school spirit, a subject that was still totally foreign to us. After about a half hour of nervous fidgeting, we were led by pairs of silent freshmen, one by one, to the dining room.

As I was marched slowly downstairs and through the length of the basement hall, the enveloping quiet of the candlelit hallway was shattered by the far-off sound of funereal organ music, followed shortly by a peal of maniacal laughter, these disconcerting sounds emanating from somewhere above. When I arrived at the dining room, the consolation of daylight was only a memory. The atmosphere was heavy with foreboding, the tension of the occasion made palpable by the serious demeanor of the faculty, who loomed ominously at the dining room entrance observing our arrivals.

To my relief, we were seated with our classmates at tables of eight. The freshmen, who sat apart at the end of the room, were out of our hair, at least for the moment. While it appeared that we were to be allowed to talk normally among ourselves, providing a window of relief from the tension that gripped us, nevertheless, our conversation soon became stilted. There arose a pervasive sense of unease. Without any apparent cue, the room soon became totally quiet and remained so for the rest of the meal. Even though the dinner was our favorite among the usually subpar school fare, I had no appetite, and I noticed that my classmates only picked at their food. No one touched the dessert.

It seemed an eternity before dinner was over; in the meantime, the invasive silence screamed for relief. At last, deliverance was announced by the sound of the scraping of a single chair on the concrete floor. From his vantage point in the center of the room, Mr. Santer rose reluctantly and eyed us sadly for a moment, the sadness evidently related to something we had done. Then he kicked off the program with a tale of his introduction to a secret society to which we were about to be exposed. He had been initiated into this society, The Royal Order of Mujiji, while traveling in India back in the early twenties. He introduced us to the idea of Mujiji as a real person, a human being at least, but one of a higher order than us. When Mr. Santer had met Mujiji, the man was a young prince who had some years earlier founded this society to improve loyalty and spirituality among young men. Mr. Santer had had the good fortune of experiencing the presence of this Great Spirit at his own initiation into this society and intimated that, while unlikely, it was possible that Mujiji would be present with us on this important occasion. When he had completed this discourse, Mr. Santer raised the subject of school spirit at Country Day School, with the caveat that this mystical quality was the key to our possible but uncertain admission to this society. He went on to let us know that we were on trial and our prospects were in our own hands. He observed that rumor of our raucous behavior at tonight's dinner with our loud voices, laughter, and general lack of respect and awareness of the solemnity of this occasion had reached and somewhat offended the all-knowing Mujiji. As Gullible Gus, a name appropriately assigned to me by my mother, I was accepting, agape, and anxious about my place in this drama. Even as I knew my classmates and I had not made much noise, I wished that I had been more subdued in my earlier dinner table behavior.

There followed dramatic presentations by members of the faculty, stories of their initiations into this secret society. Mr. Raymaker, Mr. Hughes, and Mr. Laird all shared persuasive stories about their introductions to Mujiji. Each had had an unnerving experience, the three of them covering together a wide spectrum of pain and terror associated with their initiations. But it was Mr. Waterman, the strange and wonderful math teacher, who executed the coup de grâce. In his disjointed style, Mr. Waterman told a rambling tale of a persecutory initiation, gradually succumbing to his emotions, and finally falling into dramatic but believable sobs and uncontrolled weeping. After several emotion-wrapped apologies for his inability to communicate the horrors he had undergone, Mr. Waterman was no longer able to continue and was helped, sobbing audibly, from the room. It was a masterful performance, and it was all credible to me. That was the end of dinner.

Again, we were ushered back, one by one, to the lower school gym, this time a little more roughly than on our prior transit of these same halls. Then there was an hour interlude of nonphysical harassment in the now totally darkened gym, this clandestine hazing aimed at reinforcing our sense of apprehension about our immediate future. Then vehicles waiting outside of the lower school conveyed us in pairs to the upper school, apparently dropping us just outside the south entrance to the little gym. There the freshman waited on a grassy knoll for their last shot at us, a time for the anticipated and somewhat unsupervised hazing. Unknown to me and surely a dimension of the adult control over this event, there was a need to go through a fixed and carefully timed procedure to get us into our seats for the final part of the evening's program, that program still being a mystery about which no rumor had reached us. I got batted around a bit, but it wasn't very long before I was picked up, still blindfolded, and placed roughly on what seemed to be a low bench. Then I was pushed forward onto a steeply angled slide, and all of a sudden, I was hurtling down a chute toward a fate that I had known was waiting for me. As I arrived at the bottom of the chute, I was seized by strong hands, those of faculty members, in this case, Mr. Hughes and Mr. Oviatt. They put me on my feet, spun me around a few times, and then Mr. Hughes said, "Bend down and touch the sacred book of Mujiji!"

I bent, and my hand was guided to the book which gave me a startling jolt. As I registered the pain of the shock, I received the predicted, but as of that moment unanticipated, blow to my buttocks. Then before I could react to this assault, my blindfold was whipped off, and I received a blinding flash in my eyes. Then, unseeing and completely disoriented, I was being ushered or, more accurately, dragged to a seat. It all happened so quickly that I am not sure that I ever registered the long dreaded infliction of pain I just had incurred.

So there I was, sitting in a folding chair, knowing somehow that I was in the "little gym," not seeing anything around me because of spotlights directed at me as well as the optical memory of the flash I had just undergone. I had gotten through the hazing and the predicted pain, and I thought, erroneously: *Phew, the worst is over. It wasn't so bad, after all!*

I sat for a few minutes more, hearing behind me the sounds of my remaining classmates being treated to the indignities I had just endured. Then there was total silence.

It was not very long before a judge's podium materialized out of the darkness in front of me, gradually becoming visible with a systematic intensification of the lighting. Mr. Church was seated behind the podium clad in judicial robes and apparently, the master of events to come. Then as the lighting extended my range of vision, the scene in front of me grew to incorporate from the shadows to Mr. Church's left, a strange little figure, standing motionless on a raised platform, appearing as to be a ceramic doll. In retrospect, it might have been the Travelocity gnome. Then the doll moved slightly and became recognizable as a live human form. He appeared to be a fully grown but very short man, perhaps only forty inches high, wearing Indian garb, replete with a turban, which was studded with a giant ruby. What was extraordinary about this figure was that the head and extremities appeared to be those of a normal adult male while the body was incredibly foreshortened, not unlike a dwarf, but then, we were not acquainted with dwarfs. This personage certainly seemed out of the ordinary to me, but at that moment, did not seem to be beyond my capacity to believe. As this apparition came fully into focus, there were audible gasps from my classmates. Even as I was Gullible Gus, my own suspension of disbelief apparently was shared, at least for the moment, by most of my classmates. As the sounds of surprise gave way to ominous silence, Mr. Church began to introduce us to this strange being, intoning in a ceremonial voice:

"Oh, Class of 1953, I present to you the great Mujiji, the founder of this great and highly secret order, The Royal Order of Mujiji. It is he who will decide whether your class is worthy of admission to this society. You should be aware that it is a rare and great honor to have Mujiji himself attend such a ceremony. It is, however, not an unmixed blessing that he is here. While he is here partly because he loves our school, he is here as well because he is concerned about the ability of this class, you young men, to carry on the historical traditions of his great order and of your school."

Mr. Church continued briefly with this introduction, letting us know with every word that our fate was in our hands and that there was doubt about our worthiness. Then it was time for us to hear from the great Mujiji himself. From his elevated station he spoke about tradition and school spirit as it had existed for many years in his Royal Order and how these values had become the key values at Milwaukee Country Day School. When Mujiji had completed his short talk, Mr. Church asked if there was any impediment to his accepting this new class into his society. Mujiji responded that he had heard rumors of lack of school spirit among these acolytes as well as immaturity of conduct. He felt that he could not be adequately satisfied with their behavior and attitudes without further evaluation. Mr. Church proposed that he would examine the leading troublemakers to see if this class was salvageable. With Mujiji's approval, Mr. Church proceeded to do so.

When I heard that the troublemakers were to be on trial, I trembled for myself, as did many members of my class. Based on threats from the freshmen, I felt certain that the coming interrogation is what they had promised me. But one by one, six of my classmates were called and made to respond to the accusations against them. The accused all stood up bravely to their inquisition, and as the last one was called and finally released back to his seat, I began to breathe more easily. When this sixth culprit sat down, Mujiji asked, "Is that all?"

It looked for a moment as if this inquisition was over and I had escaped without suffering the embarrassment endured by my delinquent friends. Then Mr. Church pronounced solemnly that there was just one more miscreant, the most egregious offender of the class. I knew immediately that this one would be me and that they had been saving me for last. So I was not surprised when my name was called. I dutifully took my place in the dock, blessed by a daze of unreality that overwhelmed my senses. Then I suffered the accusations of bad sportsmanship, pride, vanity, unkindness, and other personal censures, responding to each as well as I could. My embarrassing problem in dealing with these accusations was that there was an element of truth to each allegation. Dutifully I acknowledged that these charges might contain some elements of truth. Then mercifully, my moment in the spotlight was over, and I was back in my seat. The rest of the ceremony was lost on me, but I remember my classmates responding to Mujiji's final question, chanting together that the school spirit was alive in us. Then we were admitted to the Royal Order of Mujiji, and the lights went on, disclosing the entire student body that had been hidden in the darkness behind the spotlights.

Four years later, as a prefect, I got to participate in this unchanging ceremony as a principal in the Mujiji drama. My part in the performance was to operate the lights that created the dramatic environment and kept the acolytes in the dark. Two of my compatriots, together, played the role of Mujiji himself, one of them standing behind providing the hands while the other in front putting his hands in a pair of shoes, in which Mujiji moved around his platform. The latter performed the other dramatic functions of Mujiji with his face and voice. Together, they made a persuasive dwarf that might have fooled me again if I had not been stationed behind them. From my elevated station, I could see and understand the careful planning that had made the entire production so persuasive.

For me, the Mujiji experience represented a wake-up call, one that demanded that I begin to act, at age twelve, like a maturing young man rather than as the obnoxious child that I had become. It was an important rite of passage. While the Mujiji ceremony may not have been as important to many graduates of the old Country Day School as it was to me, nevertheless, it represented a long tradition, one that I think is remembered fondly for the most part. Even if it did not do anything for school spirit or for correcting the path of errant youth in the likes of me, it unquestionably served the important function of keeping a bunch of early teens off the streets on Hallows E'en. Nevertheless, for a number of reasons, Mujiji would not work today, the most important of those being that they just don't grow 'em as gullible as they used to.

Foot in Mouth Disease

Tom Hughes was my first faculty friend. He introduced me to advanced mathematics, advanced at least for high school, he brought me briefly to Jesus Christ, and he was my coach in hockey and football. What was most important to me, he treated me like an adult. I had a bunch of interesting experiences with Tom. Nevertheless, as we shall see, Tom did not suffer from an excess of diplomatic skills.

Perhaps the most memorable time with Tom had its beginning at football camp my junior year where Tom was an assistant coach. It was my first crack at varsity football, having just metamorphosed from a one hundred thirty-pound weakling to a one hundred seventy-five-pound muscled athlete. Tom worked with me in the trenches, opposing me often man-to-man, me with full football padding—he with only ancient sweat clothes. His black sweatpants had not frequently seen the inside of a washing machine and were tattered and frayed from years of sweat and abrasion. They offered occasional exposure of his bare butt through randomly located holes and through slippage of the pants down a midriff that had begun to reveal a deficiency of hips. His hooded and pocketed sweatshirt faintly bore the name of his alma mater, indicating its provenance, one that I cannot recall. With Tom being in his late thirties at the time, this garb bore all the stigmata of twenty years of intensive use. On his head he wore an old leather helmet that looked like a ski cap and provided his sparse but still curly locks and what lay beneath with about as much protection as a ski cap would have. Unprotected as he was, he was nonetheless a good scrapper and a tough competitor. Try as I might, I had difficulty learning to block him effectively and only rarely could get past him when that was required. Nevertheless, he honed my skills with his intense personal attention. By the end of camp, I thought I might even have earned a starting position. But when the roster was put out, I was relegated to second string left end, not a totally disappointing result for me, considering where I had been at the beginning of camp.

This era was quite a time for football at Country Day. We had just completed our fifth undefeated season and had run up a winning streak of fifty-one games. The season opener was to be played against Whitefish Bay High, a school some twenty times our size. They deigned to play us only because of our record, which they were certain they would break. By all rights, they had the upper hand. There was no question that they had better player selection than did we; but we had had, and we were sure of this fact, better coaching and preparation than theirs. Ken Laird and his staff had trained us in blocking and tackling at a time when most high school coaches had not yet come to realize that these were the skills that made a winning team. The game looked to be close with us as only a minor underdog.

It was a night game under the lights at Whitefish Bay's impressive stadium, capacity several thousand; and the stands were packed with a crowd that was fully alive. The night was perfect for football: clear and cool with the first hint of fall in the air. The anticipation and excitement of the occasion were palpable, both sides believing that much self-esteem and bragging rights resided in the outcome. The aesthetics too were captivating. The great overhead lights illuminated a playing area completely enclosed by concrete stadium sections and bleachers. It was a scene for me that challenged the excitement of Camp Randall at the start of a Big Nine game. Our opponents even had cheerleaders, and they were some of the most beautiful girls I had seen. The athletic, but what's more important, well-endowed, bodies of these icons eclipsed those of the more familiar Downer girls, whom we had seen mostly in their plain black jumpers. Everyone I knew was at the game, and they all seemed to be caught up in the drama of the situation. This was David versus Goliath, and I was on the side of the Lord. It was awe-inspiring to be part of such an electric scene.

From the opening whistle of the game, my recollections of the night are little more than a blur, what with the snapping reverberations of forceful contact, lights so bright that they seemed to illuminate every individual blade of grass, and the cheering, deafening for both teams, all interacting to inundate the senses.

I did not get into the game in the first half at all and was disappointed at my exclusion. When we went to the dressing room at halftime, we had a six-to-nothing advantage. In a way I was sort of glad not to have played. To me, as a newcomer to the team, the responsibility to the men who had built our winning streak seemed overwhelming. Nevertheless, as we came back onto the field after Ken Laird's inspiring halftime pep talk, I was beginning to believe that I could help. Then Whitefish Bay scored early in the third quarter, made their extra point, and we were behind by a point. After that, it was a seesaw struggle during which we did not get close to our opponents' goal line nor they to ours. The third quarter ended, and I still had not been called. I began to worry that I would not get to play at all. The game continued in the same vein, a seesaw until the middle of the final quarter, when we had, for the first time in the second half, gained good field position—just across the fifty. Then suddenly, I heard, "Gallun, get ready to go in at right end after the next play."

I was ready, or at least I thought so. I went into the game, a holy warrior going to battle, determined to perform my role, more fearful of giving a bad performance than of anything else. I was going to do good for my team and my coach. On my first play, our quarterback, Fred Miller Jr., heir to the brewery bearing his name, called play #80, a pitchout to the fullback, my classmate Bob Gebhardt, who would fake a run to the right, as in a sweep, then as the defense was drawn in to defend against the run, throw downfield to one of the two ends, the primary and deeper receiver being the right end, in this case . . . me. On this play, both ends should have cut to the right, the direction of the play.

The only problem here was the way I remembered my assignment, that being from my usual and, until this time, only position, that of left end. On #80, the left end was to go downfield fifteen yards and cut from the left side to the center of the field. To me, that route was emblazoned on my frontal cortex. Not recognizing that I was now playing right end, I was thinking, "down fifteen and cut to the center." I did so, and as I made my cut left toward the center, Gebhardt threw the ball, expecting me to meet his perfectly thrown pass near the sideline. Unfortunately, I was not there to receive it. The pass was intercepted. Whitefish Bay, capitalizing on this mistake, played conservatively and held the ball until the clock ran out. I was taken out of the game immediately and did not play again that night.

As we got on the bus to go back to Country Day, the scene was subdued but emotional. Some of the veterans were crying. Some were holding each other as they wept softly. I remember feeling really inadequate in not being able to share their emotion. I was not part of this scene; and as my teammates comforted one another, no one talked to me. I felt alone and depressed at my inability to initiate any human contact. Not yet fully understanding the magnitude of my error, it had not yet dawned on me that I might be blamed for this terrible loss. Then I felt a hand on my shoulder.

It was my friend, Tom Hughes, and he said softly but firmly, "I don't want to say that you cost us the game, but you sure took away the opportunity to win it."

Man, did Tom have a way with words!

The Ritual of the Bath

After our defeat at the hands of Whitefish Bay, we went through a whole season and a half without a loss. There was one close call during this period and finally an ending to this winning streak, both of which encounters were with St. Louis Country Day. But it was not until our senior year contest with this emerging powerhouse, that we really took a bath.

Speaking of baths, it was a bath that was the highlight of our junior year trip to St. Louis, not one during the game but the night before. It was Bill Carpenter, then a lithe scatback, who discovered a lady preparing for her bath in the apartment just across and, fortuitously, down one level. That perspective gave us a complete view of her bathroom and concealed us from her view as well. As the lady innocently drew her bath, our classmates, having gotten word of this voyeuristic opportunity, began to gather. I was one of the first to arrive because I was in the next room. I had not seen since I had reached the age of puberty, a fully or even partially naked female body.

By the time the object of our interest finally put her nude foot in the tub and shrugged off her bathrobe, the room had filled with the juniors on the trip, seven in all, and there was just enough room around the window for us all to see. But then the seniors started to arrive, and a shoving match ensued, a struggle that was resolved by our captain, Fred Miller, who determined that we would file past the window, five of us at a time, each group of five taking exactly one minute to ogle before moving on. Fortunately, the lady was in for a long bath and was into careful cleansing, cleansing that led to occasional outbursts of cheering and applause. None the wiser about this acclaim, our subject continued her performance for the better part of a half hour. When she completed her finale and donned her robe, our team was exhausted but exhilarated. We were ready for the game!

The game was an anticlimax. We eked out a victory over a clearly superior team, scoring all three of our touchdowns on the same deceptive long pass play. The play, #81, profited from the fact that from our split "T" formation on every run to the right side of the line, the left halfback faked persuasively that he was going out for a pass on the left flat. When the opposing linebacker got tired of chasing him to the sideline and downfield, our halfback would report this news to the quarterback, and #81 would be called. The play practically always worked at least once in a game. This time, it worked three times, each time for a long gainer touchdown, while nothing else did.

St. Louis dominated the game with a tough defense and an effective offense, but somehow, we held them to only three touchdowns. They missed one extra point to give us our one-point victory. Still, to a sex-starved group of young men, this result paled next to the previous night's experience.

Just a year later, an as yet undefeated Milwaukee Country Day team met St. Louis on Ken Laird Field in Milwaukee. This time, we took the bath.

St. Louis, with their then famed running back, Athen Mertis Junior, ran five touchdowns and five extra points. Their single wing attack, running almost always to the right, ran right over me, I being the defensive left end, and did so for all ten of these scores. I, awed by their powerful backfield, was unable even to take any of the blockers down with me as they rolled past and swept on to the next defender. With his blocking phalanx still intact, Mertis ran over Bill Carpenter as well, doing so every time they scored except when they reached the end zone before they got to Bill.

This one was a bitter defeat for us but more so for the faculty. Even as we players knew that a better team had badly mauled us, the faculty seemed to believe that they had been betrayed. At assembly the following Monday, there was a speech by the venerated German teacher, Herman Fick, who had seen "the mantle of school spirit from the proud head of academia," that mantle not yet completely lost but nonetheless barely salvageable. That afternoon at football practice, we were exposed to "suicide tackling" where the biggest linemen ran one by one at all the rest of us, who were instructed to tackle them head-on. A missed tackle sent you back to the head of the line. You did it until you got it right, then went to the back of the line to wait for your next opportunity to maim yourself.

We learned something from this whole episode that the world was to learn ten years later from Vince Lombardi, "Winning is the only thing."

The Lord of the Ring

Bobby Gebhardt was a special friend at Country Day. He was undoubtedly the best athlete in my class. As a freshman, he made both the varsity football and hockey teams. These early successes put him ahead of the rest of us, but what was most interesting about Bobby, even in high school, was that he was his own man. If he heard the music of the expectations of others, he paid it little heed while he danced to the tune in his heart. He vacated for me his leadership position in hockey when, as a sophomore, he gave up this sport in which he excelled. He did it to become a skier, planning and expecting to become world class.

Bobby did not quite make it all the way to the Olympics, but he did come close, becoming a top-level racer at Dartmouth and a winner at many intercollegiate meets. Not bad for a boy from Wisconsin, where the biggest hills had a vertical drop of only

300 feet, in the days before there was easy travel to the few major ski areas. When I was in college, I heard about a national intercollegiate ski meet at Mt. Washington, where, in the downhill, Bobby was able to blow all the competition away by skiing down the climbing track. The climbing track was iced over, whereas the direct downhill route was covered in slush, a significantly slower albeit a safer route. Bobby was always doing his own thing.

Despite all his success in athletics, my most vivid recollection of Bobby took place in a physics lab. We were studying electromagnetism under the tutelage of Mr. Church. On the day in question, Mr. Church was demonstrating the repelling strength of an electromagnet powered by an alternating current. After explaining how the alternating pulses of the current created a repelling force on the ring surrounding the polar magnet that would push it upward, Mr. Church challenged the class to hold the ring in place for five seconds, not mentioning the fact that the electricity would generate heat. Feeling confidence in my strength, I was first to respond, closely followed by Bobby, who held the same confidence.

I, having been the quickest, was given the first chance. As Mr. Church turned on the current, I found the force not too great and I thought, *This is a piece of cake.*

Nevertheless, in an instant, the ring, heated by the impelled current coursing through it, got hot, quickly *too* hot to bear, and motivated by instantaneous pain, I hastily withdrew my hand. The ring, propelled by the magnetic force, flew up and banged hard against the ceiling. I, somewhat embarrassed by my failure, said nothing about the heat; I just rubbed my somewhat painful hand and moved away from the lab table.

Bobby stepped forward with a barely perceptible but smug smile on his face. Mr. Church, having turned off the magnet, replaced the ring around the magnet, asking, "Do think you're stronger than Gallun?"

Not responding, Bobby just leaned hard on the ring. Mr. Church reluctantly turned on the current. After a second or so, a trace of pain was detectable on Bobby's face. As another second passed, there emerged the smell of burning flesh. Another second, the third at the most, then Mr. Church said, "That's it, five seconds."

Bobby let the ring go, it again hitting the ceiling. Bobby turned away dispassionately and put his hand under the closest faucet; then he walked out of the room.

The next day, Bobby was wearing a bandage around his hand. He wore that bandage for the better part of a month.

I wonder if Mr. Church used that same challenge on the class of '54.

The Runner

As I have written my memoirs, Judith is surprised at the infinite detail that I can muster for unimportant events, events unimportant at least to her. There is, however, a selectivity in memory which brings total recall to occurrences that, no matter how trivial in the scheme of things, did seem important to me at the time, things like a tactic executed in a sailboat race, a clever comment dropped in an unimportant conversation, or even the details of a high school running race.

It was the early spring of my junior year at Country Day, and my sport was track. Mine was a lazy man's life, each day just throwing the discus for a half hour or so, then lying around in the rays of the spring sun while the rest of the team trained. For me, the discus toss was a piece of cake. It wasn't my strength that made it so; it was that I had a natural throw that sent the discus out flat and steady, and, supported by the air currents created by its forward speed, the disc would just sail on and on, particularly if a headwind augmented its relative airspeed. Other throwers had much greater strength than I, most of them were also shot-putters, but their throws were rarely flat, and their discus often fluttered in flight; thus, the wind slowed rather than supported the disc. In contrast, my throws would actually *sail,* first to one side, then to the other as the supporting air extended my toss. Because he was my good friend, Harry Flagg, who served as our team's manager and who, as part of his job, was responsible for setting up the area for the discus throw, I was usually able, at least for home meets, to have the discus toss aimed into the wind. That advantage gave me an useful edge, and with it I was destined to win many meets over the next two years, even as my relative strength was de minimis.

Nevertheless, I felt some discontent with my limited role. As I watched the runners training for their events, I became aware of an urge drawing me toward the exhilaration of the race. As a child, I had enjoyed the aesthetics of running; the wind in my face, the joy of floating above the earth with the ground passing silently under my feet, the freedom from restraints of any kind, the power of the second wind, and, yes, when it was there, the tug of competition. I had lost this attraction as a freshman and sophomore, while I was trying to become a hurdler, a running activity that had provided none of these benefits and had not conformed well to the limitations of my body, particularly my hamstring and groin. But over a period of a couple of afternoons, lying in the fresh grass of spring in the warmth of an April sun, I found my persona drawn inexorably to the magnet of the distance race.

As I watched the distance runners make their circuits of the track, I imagined that I might be able to parlay my high level of conditioning, a vestige of the recently completed hockey season as well as a generous genetic allotment of speed, into a capability that would make me a real player on our team. I gave some thought to running the mile, but that distance seemed to me a bit great, even with my naiveté about the pain of distance running; so I settled on the half mile, a compromise that came easily to me.

These thoughts dogged my consciousness for the better part of a week. I did not share my idea with my coach, Mr. Oviatt, until Saturday, after we had traveled to Saint John's Military Academy in Delafield. I confronted him with my plan as we were leaving the bus at St. John's track site.

"What? You're joking, or are you out of your mind?"

I tried to interject, but he went on, "No way; your job is to throw the discus."

"The discus will be over before the half mile starts so it won't interfere with my performance in the discus."

"But you haven't trained for this event, and it's a long race."

"I'm in good shape from hockey, and I think I have a lot of endurance. Please, let me give it a try. If I can't do it, I will stop."

"Yass!"

"Does that mean, OK?"

"It means y'ass; anyway, I won't stop you. But use your head."

With this hurdle behind me, I went off to throw the discus. I don't remember how I did in the discus that day. That result has been obscured by my half mile and the half century that intervenes.

The race was scheduled for 3:30, and I was there and ready to go at 3:15. Everyone was doing their stretches and prerace warm-ups while I pretended to do mine, not having much experience in the prerace procedure. Just before the witching moment arrived, our number one half-miler, Ian Sinclair, came over, patted me on the back, and wished me good luck—whatever good luck is in a running race. Finally, at the appointed time, we headed for the starting line, and the starting procedure commenced.

"Runners, to your marks!"

The other runners kicked the cinders from their spikes and ceremoniously maneuvered their way into the starting blocks, a ritual that was embarrassingly unfamiliar to me. Despite my lack of technique, I was ready when the next command was delivered.

"Get set!"

On this instruction, all the contestants—including me—raised our asses in the air and stared fixedly ahead, preparing for the initial sprint to see who would get to the first turn first.

Then the gun discharged, and we were off and running, about ten of us. I, having chosen wisely not to compete for the lead and not wanting to be on the outside around the turn, fell into the last position but then ran easily with the pack, letting the leaders set the pace. We ran pretty much in the order gained at the first turn during the entire first lap, a quarter of a mile. Running easily and more comfortably than I had imagined, I enjoyed the unusual early spring weather and even noticed the burgeoning foliage in the trees surrounding the track. There was no pain or even minor discomfort associated with this running; the entire experience of this part of the race was pure pleasure. I just glided along with the group, effortlessly, while thinking optimistically about my finish. The forces that propelled me were my love of competition and emerging confidence that I could win this race. I had formulated a strategy of just keeping up and making my move at the final corner—if I had anything left—a condition that even I had known was subject to a modicum of doubt. Nevertheless, as the race progressed, and my own endurance persisted, my confidence grew. We ran in the same formation for the first lap and well into the second.

As the still tight group entered the final backstretch of the second and final lap, I was still in the last place but only a dozen yards behind the leader, a St. Johns runner, with Ian right behind him. It seemed to me that no one was running very fast. I thought it was time for me to get near the front. I turned on the gas, just a little, because I needed to save my strength for the final kick, but I found myself easily passing the second echelon. Suddenly, I was in the company of the leaders. They did not respond to my move, and I detected no change in my rate of depletion of energy, so I just kept up this faster pace and moved smartly into first place as we reached the end of the backstretch. Rounding the final curves of the track, I just kept going and had opened a lead of about ten yards as I came into the homestretch.

"Boyoboy, this is good, and I haven't even started my kick yet!"

With the finish less than a hundred yards away, and the distance dwindling fast, I moved into high gear—and then it happened. It was as if someone hit me in the groin with an iron pipe! Without warning, the wind went out of me, and I was gasping for breath. It was like drowning; I just couldn't breathe, and suddenly, my legs wouldn't work. I couldn't make them respond to my urgent commands. Somehow, I was able to stay on my feet and was still in the lead with twenty yards to go, but my fate was already sealed as the runners streamed past me as the finish line loomed. Even with the shutdown of my systems, I did finish, falling into the arms of my coach and our team manager. It was fifteen minutes being dragged around before I could breathe at all, and the better part of an hour before I was able to breathe normally and stand unassisted. The race had been just a little too long.

At the next meet and for the remainder of my Country Day time, I did run the quarter mile, competing well and enjoying the competition, but never again challenged the leaders.

Judith wonders today why any high school sports event would be etched in my memory. What does she know?

CHAPTER V

Learning from the Beavers

The year 1935 was a good year to be born —that is, at least if you were born in the United States. It is true that Americans born in that year inherited an unusually good opportunity for improving their living standard, a chance to participate in the great technological changes that lay ahead, a still largely unexplored or at least still undeveloped frontier and negligible risk of military conscription. Life in the thirties was not yet fully comfortable, but the world was laying a base for a prosperous and safe adulthood for us Depression babies.

Even with the Depression lingering on, life was good for my family. People needed shoes, shoe manufacturers needed leather, and the tanning business prospered. So, we Galluns lived comfortably; actually, we lived quite well. Milwaukee, being a highly industrial city, certainly suffered some the effects of the economic malaise, but it possessed a somewhat diversified economy, one that insulated it from the worst ravages of the Depression, and the war brought its economy roaring back to life in the forties.

As the war ended, Milwaukee was one of the top manufacturing cities in the United States, and even factory workers here were doing pretty well. There was no "inner city" yet, just neighborhoods that boasted their distinctive ethnicities. Entertainment was in the local bars and beer gardens, at the movie houses, on the radio, and in the parks. No one yet dreamed of television. Transportation was still primitive with the train the main method of intercity travel. My parents traveled to the West annually, doing so with an old Packard on back roads (because there were no front roads). The West was wild, largely undeveloped, and the plains had recovered from the Dust Bowl of the thirties. What was most important to my generation was that this was a country that had room for everyone, and there were going to be opportunities for investment and speculation as far as the eye could see.

Just seventy-five years later, we have seen a sea change in the way we live. The frontier has disappeared, urban blight and decaying infrastructure have ravaged many of our cities, transportation systems which blossomed in the fifties and sixties have become second rate, and we are overwhelmed by a growing population in a now-limited living space. Is this experience a road map for the future, or are the changes we have experienced a harbinger of a better future? Is the human family learning to cope as well as do beavers?

WITH MY SISTER, Carol, I first visited the beaver ponds below Snowmass Lake when I was seventeen years old. Two years later while in college, I spent a few days camping there with Bill Merizon, a college friend with whom I spent the summer at my family's ranch on Brush Creek. That was the summer of 1955. It would be a long time before I would see these ponds again. During the intervening years, the beavers would change the face of their world.

As it happened, my next visit was in the late summer of 1995 when I hiked with my wife, Judy, and our two dogs, Stella and Max, from Maroon Lake over Sullivan Pass and from the pass down past the ponds and continuing to the Snowmass Valley, for us, a four-day trek. On the way down from the pass, we had planned to spend two nights at the ponds to supplement our bare-bones larder with the descendants of the easily caught trout of my earlier visits. We were traveling light because of the distance and difficulty of the trip as well as the virtual certainty that we would be able to catch our dinner.

As we approached the beaver ponds from heights above them, I was shocked by what I saw. Despite the passage of forty years, I thought my recollection of this place was fresh and vivid. What I recalled were three large ponds, each a deep blue hue proclaiming significant depth. The ponds had stood at staggered levels with the water from each running over a dam into the next, or, in the case of the lowest, back into the river. Nevertheless, what lay before me was a valley so transformed that it bore no similarity to what I had known.

On my first visit, I had come with my sister, Carol, on horseback from my family's ranch, traveling upstream. Our route had taken us up a good trail to the headwaters of Brush Creek and over the Brush Creek-Snowmass Divide, so far, an easy ride. At the divide, we entered the wilderness and descended a narrow and occasionally steep path down to the Snowmass Creek, a mile below. The final segment went for about ten miles up a boulder-strewn trail alongside the creek, finally reaching the beaver ponds as the creek opened into a lush valley. Because of the grades and the irregular footing, the horses shuffled at a snail's pace along this stretch. The entire fifteen-mile trek had taken almost seven hours, an arduous trip for one not used to riding. The ponds stood at the confluence of two creeks, one emanating from Snowmass Lake, a mile or so to the south and a steep thousand feet higher, the other from the then more or less permanent snowfield at Sullivan Pass.

As Carol and I had ridden up the trail, we saw evidence along the way of beaver attempts to tame the creek. I was impressed with their ambition as the creek ran steep and fast in a narrow channel, with a strong flow even in late summer. One could imagine the power of this stream when it was engorged with the spring runoff. It was easy to understand why the beavers had not been able to create a habitat hospitable to them along this steeper stretch of river.

On this first visit I was young enough to remember well my enchantment as a child with the spring snowmelt running down the street in front of our house in Whitefish Bay. Until I was almost ten, I had welcomed the early thaws for the playground they made of the street. I would dam the flowing street water with snow dug f
\om the piles left by the plows and create a series of lakes that sometimes extended across the entire street. Of course passing cars would make a mess of my grandest projects, but those cars would pay for their damage with a soaking from the slush and dirty water they splashed up from the street. Generally, however, my dam building was confined to one side of the street, and the passing cars would, in their own self-interest, drive on the other side, leaving my project untouched. It was my fascination with the water flow and hydraulics that made me appreciate the taming of rivers, no matter if by man or by the beaver.

Immediately upon arriving at the Snowmass beaver ponds on this first visit with Carol, I was able to empathize with the labor of the beavers, understanding their engineering vision and the daunting scope of their work, with the nearest copse of trees some fifty yards from the stream. Looking at the dimensions of the building materials they used, often fully grown aspen trees and Colorado spruce as well as good-sized to smaller branches of both, it was almost painful to imagine the struggle required of these small mammals in securing these materials, transporting them, and positioning them in the midst of what, judging from the height of the dams, was once a raging torrent. My streams had been smaller and my materials easier to obtain.

Carol and I had come to fish in these ponds and in Snowmass Lake above, but first, we needed to set up camp. We did so on a small promontory that overlooked all three ponds, each of which supported a small but unseen beaver community. While there was no evidence of the beavers other than the products of their construction projects, Carol and I both noticed the ripples created by the trout feeding on the insects that flitted across the surface. From the size of these disturbances, it was clear that there were fish of size lurking in the darkened depths. We hastened to get out our fly rods, and because the water was deep, we fished from the banks, rather than wading. We were, at the time, inexperienced fly fishermen, but with a little practice we were able to place the flies atop the most disturbed water where it seemed that the fish were feeding. We were amazed that with two flies on a line, we would not infrequently catch two good-sized trout on one cast; we almost always caught at least one. We threw the smaller back; but, this concession notwithstanding, we caught our consumption capacity in a matter of minutes. It was actually disappointing to find that we could catch fish so easily. What we had thought would be a fishing trip had become a ride with a picnic.

The next day Carol and I climbed on foot up to Snowmass Lake to find some more challenging fishing, leaving our horses tethered and our encampment intact. Along the way, we encountered several impressive waterfalls in the creek next to our path. The path was steep and occasionally steep enough so that we had to employ hand holds as we ascended. The mile or so climb took us the better part of an hour. When we finally broke into the open at the level of the lake, we were welcomed by the spire of Snowmass Mountain, which loomed above us, rising vertically from the other side of the half-mile wide lake, soaring another three thousand feet to the peak, snowcapped even in late summer. A narrow stream, much of it a waterfall, cascaded down the almost vertical escarpment and was so awe-inspiring as to overwhelm the senses. We gasped as we paused, but paused only for a moment; then, having taken note of this unique vista, we assembled our fly rods and began to fish.

Our results were de minimis; if there were fish here, they were not interested in our offerings. The beaver ponds seemed to have created better habitat for fish than did this pristine lake—at least a much better environment for fishermen. Having spent the better part of a day here and seeing no evidence of marine life, we wondered at the differences in these connected bodies of water. My later more educated view about the productivity of those three ponds is that the mile or so of intervening stream below Snowmass Lake, as well as the stream we had followed down from Sullivan Pass, swept a significant amount of insect and other food into the ponds. The stream and waterfall from the peak fed Snowmass Lake, but this stream, being high and unvegetated, surely did not support insect life.

Almost exactly forty years later, Judith and I approached the ponds, this time from upstream. From our elevated position as they first came into sight, we had a broad view of the entire valley. The vista was changed so much it was almost shocking; not that it had deteriorated; it was just so different. Where there had been a wide valley of grassy fields, the span of green broken by three dark blue ponds, there were now more than a hundred ponds, all apparently created by beavers, and no meadow at all. In contrast to the deep blue ponds of yesteryear, the ponds were apparently quite shallow with sandy bottoms because rather than the deep blue of a former time, these ponds reflected in the afternoon sun the amber glow of shallowly covered sand.

Judith and I stood agape for a few minutes while I exclaimed to her on the changes that had occurred in the intervening years. Then we set up our camp on a high knoll that gave us some view of perhaps ten of the ponds. With our chores done, we needed to catch dinner, so I pulled out the fishing gear, confidently expecting to get our culinary rewards. We waded a half dozen of the now shallow ponds, saw lots of very small trout, but were unable to entice any of these diminutive fish to take to our flies. Two hours later, we were sipping wine while our emergency ration of spam warmed over a campfire.

Oh, how the world had changed. I ask myself the same questions you, my reader, might ask. Then I ask another that you probably haven't thought of, "Is this good for the beavers?"

The answer is unclear to me. On the surface, the beaver colony had thrived. But the ponds were shallow, so did they allow for safe entry to the beaver houses during the winter when the ice was thick? What did such an expanded beaver population portend in terms of the food supply during the four seasons? Or did the beavers just build a pond and use it until it silted in and became too shallow, then move to a new pond, allowing the abandoned ponds to eventually revert to an even more fertile meadow than had existed previously? Is this transformation the equivalent of urban decay, or is it renewal? The scientists tell us that the sum of all matter relative to energy is fixed, neither expanding nor contracting, merely reforming. Are the changes in the beaver's habitat, like all of life's changes, a mere detour, a side trip of little consequence that diverts us as we yield to the forces of nature and eternity?

These questions are not unanswerable, but whatever answer you have, you can find someone who will have a different point of view. The answers that I have come up with as I have moved through my life have been subject to amendment or rejection more often than they have survived intact.

CHAPTER VI

Overboard

Sailing gave me many dramatic exposures to weather. While the storms were usually the most exciting of these experiences, heavy wind under a sky of blue was blessed with its own mystique. An inland race in my late teen years stands to me as an event that exposed me seriously to a risk of death at the hands of Mother Nature. More importantly, it was a memorable race not only for me but also a milestone in the history of inland racing.

THE INLAND LAKES Yachting Association held its 1955 annual regatta in Neenah, Wisconsin, on Lake Winnebago, a large body of water often made treacherous by its shallowness. With an average depth of less than eight feet and an overall length of thirty-five miles, the lake could and often did build an unusually dangerous wave structure. Old-timers claimed that the waves occasionally got so big and so deep that the bottom went dry in the troughs. That claim may be a stretch, but reality would find waves of four or five feet with thirty feet between the crests. That meant that in a twenty-one-foot sailboat going downwind, a sailor might be surfing down one wave only to stick the nose of the boat into the next wave at the bottom. This experience often led to broaching, which would place the boat across the wind, often resulting in capsizing. For a young woman, the combination of this lake with a class C-Scow represented something a little worse than night terrors. Of course, there was always the possibility of the entire five-day regatta being sailed in light winds.

Not having a boat of my own, I was crewing with my sister Carol in this regatta. Because of the paucity of female skippers in the entire ILYA "C" class, the difficulties of sailing these boats in heavy winds, and the reputation of Lake Winnebago, there would be only three "girls" in a fleet of about eighty boats. They were my sister Carol, who was quite muscular and athletic; my older sister Barby, who possessed the same physical attributes as Carol and was an outstanding helmsman as well; and Jane

Wiswell, who possessed all of these useful attributes in spades. In addition to these women, there would be seventy-five or so male skippers.

Just before the regatta, my sisters and I had been reading a sailing book written by Stanley Ogilvy, who had been a repetitive U.S. Star champion. In this book, he wrote about making your boat go faster, a subject that greatly interested my sisters and me. One of the ideas to which apparently no one in the Inland had yet been exposed was that of running the rear travelers from which the mainsail was trimmed all the way to the edge of the boat. At the time, everyone had travelers that reached only halfway to the edge. Ogilvy argued—no, he stated unequivocally—that if you can get your trim point further out on the deck, you will, in heavier winds, increase the forward moment of force which propels you while decreasing the sidewise moment which causes the boat to heel. Both of these vectors would help to improve your boat speed.

We understood this argument easily and even wondered why we hadn't thought of it before. The modifications to achieve Ogilvy's advantage were fairly simple. I got out my tools and made the adjustments on both of my sisters' boats, lengthening the tracks and providing a control wire from the car that rode on the track, through the deck and forward to a point where the skipper could make adjustments for responding to a change in wind velocity. We were ready to compete.

The first race was on Monday morning, and it looked like a day for long travelers. It was one of those days that had kept the ladies away. At 9:00 a.m., the wind was already over twenty knots and rising. With these conditions, Carol and I took on a third crew to provide additional ballast. As the fleet gathered for a ten o'clock start, the lake was solid whitecaps almost up to the first mark. The wind looked a little lighter at the first mark because at that location there was some protection from a point that jutted in an easterly direction out into the lake.

The course was a triangle to the right, a course that would take us to the east and far out into the lake after the first windward leg. Even with winds approaching gale force, the competition to gain position on the starting line was fierce. Several serious collisions and capsizings occured in the confusion in the congested starting area.

During the preparatory period, we lurked in the area below the line and looked for a gap in the phalanx of boats to windward of us. With less than a minute to go, we found our hole and stepped into it, preventing the boats to windward from passing in front of us. At the gun, we jumped off to a good start in the clear wind to windward and space to leeward, and within minutes, we were emerging from the fleet. Judging from the speed of our emergence, it was apparent that we were unusually fast. The stability we gained from our long tracks seemed to give us a measurable advantage under the conditions of this day.

As we drew away from the great mass of boats, we noticed that only two boats were staying with us. One was Barby, who seemed to be a little ahead of us, and the other was Jane Wiswell. Imagine three women leading in an Inland championship race and doing so in a big wind, a truly unbelievable turn of events in this male-dominated sport!

Nevertheless, even with the stability gained from the long travelers, this first leg was a continuous fight with the wind and the waves. Our third crew member and I were over the side standing on the bilge boards ("riding the boards") for the entire distance. The turbulent sea poured over the bow and broke against the splashboards attached to the front deck into an airborne deluge which cascaded over all of us. Because the wind was blowing cold out of the north, all three of us were chilled to the bone by the time we were halfway to the mark. While the waves were interrupted by the splashboards, they were in no way defeated, and as we approached the buoy marking the end of the leg, there was a whole lot of water sloshing around in the boat, beginning to weigh us down and making the boat less stable. At this time, before the invention of the automatic bailer, it was going to be a big job for the third crew to bail the boat on the off-wind legs.

Carol and I reached the first mark in second place, right behind Barby, with Jane a half-dozen boat lengths behind us. The fleet was massed well behind Jane, back another twenty boat lengths or so.

At the mark, just as we had thought, the wind was lighter because of the protection of the point, but the waves were big nonetheless, running long and deep. Carol was concerned about the possibility of a nosedive, particularly in light of the water accumulated in the bilge, so she ordered me to sit on the back deck to keep the bow up. This precaution worked well for a while, and we even had a moment to look back to rejoice at the large crush of boats looming two hundred yards behind us. That distance did look like a big lead, but we were on a reach, the fastest point of sailing. At reaching speed on a C, a two hundred-yard lead can be obliterated in about thirty seconds.

We had enjoyed this spectacle for only an instant when we suddenly emerged from the protection of the peninsula. When the full force of the wind on the open lake struck our sails, the boat surged forward with the acceleration of a plane catapulted from an aircraft carrier. Hanging on to nothing but the mainsheet, I found myself jettisoned from the back of the boat and into the water, fortunately still grasping that mainsheet. Because the mainsheet is the line that controls the trim of the mainsail, Carol could not ease the sail while I was attached to it. Alarmed by the risk of capsizing under these circumstances, she shrieked for me to let go. Aware of the fleet bearing down on us at twenty knots or so, almost eighty strong, all possessing sharp bilge boards, this danger augmented by visibility and control problems arising from the wind and waves, I didn't feel too bad about the possibility of capsizing. I was concerned for my life, and a capsized boat offered more protection than the open water. There was no way I was going to let go! Carol struggled with the tiller, trying to head down to reduce the force of the wind upon the sails. After a few anxious moments of difficult steering, she got the boat squared away well enough so that our third crew could help me into the boat. I was back aboard and even with our setback, we had lost only a little ground. And to my immense satisfaction, I was still alive!

It was just minutes after this unnerving experience that we reached the next mark and faced a gibe, always a major danger in a "C." In this maneuver, the boat is steered directly downwind, the sail is brought to the center of the boat, the boat is turned slightly beyond downwind, and the sail is allowed to fill out on the new tack. In a wind like this day's, if the skipper makes a steering error or pushes the sail across too soon, the sail might catch the wind quickly and snap forward against the restraining mainsheet, providing an irresistible turning force to the boat. The resulting turn could force the boat broadside to the wind, causing the boat to capsize. Recognizing this risk as well as the fact that we still held a significant load of bilge water, Carol decided to play it safe and "come about" into the wind rather than attempting a gibe, even though coming about is a somewhat risky maneuver in itself. In doing so, she lost too much speed, went broadside to the wind after tacking, and we capsized anyway.

That was the end of the day for Carol and me. Still shaken by my earlier ordeal, I was just glad to be alive. Carol, not understanding my trauma, felt dejected about losing the great place in the race. Barby, unaware of Carol's and my problems, went on to win the race and proceeded to finish fourth in the regatta. Jane Wiswell came in second in that day's race and went on to establish a lifelong record of successful racing. All three of these women continued to have racing success sailing against the men in the Inland. They were, in the end, the big winners for competing in a man's world because in national woman's competition, sailing against women, women who had raced mostly only against other women, they found themselves starting at the top. In subsequent years, each of them, as skippers, finished in one of the top three positions in the North American Woman's Sailing Championships.

The race described here has been long remembered by most of the men who raced that day. The greatest American sailor of our lifetime, Buddy Melges, was among the spectators. Recently, he remembered many of the details of that day, especially the long travelers. He admitted that he started installing traveler control devices in all the Melges Boat Works boats the very next week. However, what he remembered best was the performance of those three women on that first windward leg!

CHAPTER VII

A Cat Has Nine Lives

My opportunity to learn how to fly came to me slowly. As a sophomore at Williams, I had learned about the Williams flying club from a friend, Ted Talmadge, whom I had sailed against in cub boats at Oconomowoc Lake a few years earlier. Ted belonged to the Williams flying club and mentioned to me that the club owned a Cessna 140, which could be rented by members for fifteen dollars an hour. We talked about flying and went together to the North Adams airport, which consisted of a single concrete runway lying at the base of Mt. Greylock. On seeing this primitive airport environment, I was instantly entranced with the idea of learning to fly and could not wait to get into this exciting new world.

WHILE THE COST of flying was within my reach, it seemed like a good idea to see if my parents might be willing to pay this increment of tuition—big mistake! I went to my father with my proposal. To my amazement, he reacted immediately and negatively. Not only was he not going to pay for it but he, acting way outside of his usual laid-back manner, forbade me in his strongest language, to take up flying, even with my own money. So much for that; if the confrontation had been with my mother, I might have defied her edict; but it was my father, and I always trusted him to have a sympathetic interest in my welfare. As my reader will apprehend, my father had a better understanding than I of the risks associated with flying, or at least initially, it seemed that he did. And he still had a strong financial hold on me, one that I fully comprehended.

So I put flying behind me and thought I would forget this dream for a few years. Besides, hockey season was upon me, and hockey had begun to take up all of my spare time. It also turned out that hockey was to become a key to gaining my parents' support for learning how to fly. The route to gaining this approval may be a little devious, but it is definitely part of this story.

As a sophomore, I had had the team's captain, Bobby Bethune, as my left wing, and that put me on the first line. As the season wore on, I, with Bobby, became the front part of the penalty-killing team and that gave me more defensive-play time than one usually experiences as a center. In a hard fought game against Dartmouth, during two of their power plays, I made unusually good defensive plays, both of which resulted in my upending the attacking Dartmouth lineman. Upending wasn't my usual shtick, but it felt pretty good and the home crowd, all fifty of them, roared their approval.

Unbeknown to me, one of the fifty was the football coach. He visited me in the locker room after the game. He got to the point quickly: he had seen me lay a couple of guys low, and he was certain that he had a position for me on the football team. That was very flattering to me. I possessed an ego that was very responsive to this kind of attention, so I agreed to think about this idea.

As I contemplated his invitation, the downside of my playing football should have been clear: I wasn't great at the game even in high school. Although I enjoyed playing in games, I never liked practice much. In addition, football took a lot of time, and academically, I was already deep in the sophomore slump. To make the correct decision even more persuasive, there was no break between the football and hockey seasons. On the other hand, I was flattered at the invitation. A serious balancing exercise leaned heavily to the negative. Nevertheless, my decision-making process was a little flawed. So I accepted the coach's invitation.

That there was a little more downside began to dawn on me during the next summer. Not that they would interfere in this decision, but my parents were opposed because they thought one dangerous sport in college was enough. They believed that hockey represented that sport in my case; and while they were wrong about the risks in hockey, they had a point in that I had broken my collarbone in a freshman game. More important to me, I would have to go back to school for football practice before the end of the sailing season. Finally, during the summer, it seemed like an incredible task to learn an offense that was quite elaborate and foreign to me as well.

I was having these second thoughts when my father came with a proposition. His deal was that if I gave up the football idea, he would allow—and even pay for—my flying lessons! He thought he was looking out for my well-being, but his priorities were badly ordered. As I would eventually learn, flying held much more serious risks than did football. Nevertheless, his proposal was a winner for me on several fronts, and I readily accepted his offer.

So I gave up the football idea and finished out the sailing season. Then I went back to Williams and started flying lessons right away, doing so with the local instructor, Marty Engel. Marty was a good guy and seemed to know a lot about small airplanes as well as general aviation, which is the universe of noncommercial flying. At my first lesson, we covered all of the basic principles of flying in Marty's office. At the second, he put me in the Cessna "140," and quickly, we were up in the air. Pretty soon, he put me in control, and I was attempting to fly the plane with the simple instruction: "Just keep it straight and level."

It was immediately apparent to me that flying was more difficult than I had thought. There is a lot to control in the three dimensions in which an airplane operates. I am sure that my state of anxiety that day paralleled the experience of many, if not most, neophytes. When I exited the plane after fighting for "straight and level" for half an hour, I was soaking wet, exhausted, and somewhat chastened. Flying was going to be more difficult than I thought.

Even so, I came back for my next lesson a few days later, and as I did so, I was nervous about what I was facing. Marty took the plane up, and as soon as we got to altitude, he turned the controls over to me. To my amazement, my reflex system had adapted to the requirements for straight and level flying. Flying turned out to be much like riding a bicycle; management of the plane had become instinctive. On this second time at the "stick," I was able to control the aircraft effortlessly. With straight and level flying under control, it was a short time until I had learned basic maneuvers, turning, banking, precipitating a stall, and recovering from it. During the next hour, we got to taking off and landing.

The instructor's manual suggested soloing after eight hours; I soloed after four. Forty hours of flying time were required to get a license. I got my license in the spring with exactly forty hours under my belt. To me flying was, in my son Alby's favorite expression of nonchalance, "a piece of cake." What I had missed is that while the skill of controlling an airplane is intuitively acquired through muscle memory or the like, there are a plethora of dangers surrounding any flight plan. Controlling the plane is not a significant issue in the hierarchy of perils associated with flying. The ultimate risk is the failure of a pilot to be aware of dangers to which one might be exposed on any flight.In my forty hours my instructor told me about most of them but as "they" say "experience is the best teacher."

So this is where I started to use up my nine lives. It began as I took my Williams friends for rides, starting with Charles (Yogi) Berry. Yogi was my first willing passenger; he liked to fly a lot except for spins and stalls. Even at the risk of facing these maneuvers, which were part of my practicing regimen, he was a regular companion aloft. He did learn quickly, however, that, when I switched on the carburetor heat to keep the engine from icing up when I cut the power, something bad was going to happen, like the plane was about to drop precipitously, leaving his stomach in his throat. Yogi kept his eyes on my hands, and when he saw me reach for the carburetor heat, he would cry out "No, R.A., no!" His complaints fell on unsympathetic if not yet deaf ears; I was up there to practice maneuvers.

I did not use up any of my nine lives with Yogi, although to hear his side of the story, he may have given up a few of his own or, at a minimum, used up some of the expected mileage on his heart. No, my first exposure to real danger, and mind you, if one is moderately cautious, one should never be so exposed to real danger in private flying, occurred on a trip to New York City with Bill Mauritz. "Maui," as we called him, had become a close friend after returning from a leave of absence at the beginning of our sophomore year. He and I frequently traveled to Smith College, where we regularly dated women whom we were destined to marry. Despite our commitment to our Smithies, Maui and I decided on a stag weekend in the big city. Part of our decision to do so was that a New York trip was made convenient by my ability to fly us there, thus avoiding the drive. I had identified an airport there at Flushing Meadows, which was close to the city just across the bridge to Long Island. The airport was little used and could be reached without impinging on the major city airports and their designated airspaces. It had no control tower, so I would not have to struggle with radio communication, a skill that I had not assimilated.

The trip down to New York was uneventful. It was a beautiful day, and we had no difficulty finding the airport. That there was no competition for airspace around the city might seem surprising today, but in 1955, there was not a lot of commercial flying, much less significant private flying. Bill and I landed, tied the plane down, paid a small landing fee at the airport office, and called a cab that took us into the city. We had a nice evening in the city, stayed downtown overnight, and returned to Flushing about noon the next day.

For early spring, the day was unusually hot and humid, conditions that I noticed only because I was sweating profusely, but I did not consider the implication of these conditions on flying. I had learned in my flight training that heat makes the air expand and become less dense as it does so. Similarly, high humidity, which results from the air holding an excessive amount of water vapor, compounds the problem by additionally reducing the density of the atmosphere. The lightness of the air on a day like this one appreciably reduces the lift provided by the wings and requires that one must go faster to attain takeoff speed and to maintain lift while in flight. These same conditions make the propeller less efficient because it gains less purchase against the less weighty air. The combination of less lift and poor propeller efficiency can make taking off hazardous, particularly with planes that are overloaded or underpowered.

Not being concerned with these considerations, Maui and I got into the plane and nonchalantly went through the preflight checklist and then taxied to the end of the runway. By this time, we were both soaking wet and eager to get the plane moving to create a cooling breeze through the open air ventilation system of the plane. As we accelerated down the runway, my first recognition that there might be a problem was that the wheels seemed to be glued to the ground. My experience told me that I should reach takeoff speed in a couple of hundred yards. That was not the case on this day.

We were almost at the end of the half-mile long runway and beyond the point of no return before I got the plane into the air. When it did finally get airborne, the plane was sluggish, and I was unable to make it climb. We hovered about ten feet off the ground, seeming able to gain neither speed nor altitude. We were aimed right at a red barn at the end of the field. The barn was set in front of a line of trees. Being aware that you don't want to turn a plane at speeds just above stalling velocity, I flew directly at the barn, leaning on the throttle, keeping the nose down and even squandering a few precious feet of altitude, hoping, thereby, to gain a modicum of airspeed. All of my senses sharpened as I recognized that I was not in control of the situation. I tried to lift the plane with my willpower, but it just would not climb. Despite the urge to pull the nose up, I held the plane steady; then, having gained a scintilla of speed, I pulled the nose up at the last possible moment. The plane rose reluctantly, just enough that we cleared the barn, doing so with a couple of feet to spare!

I'll bet Maui never forgot that I saved his life that day. Little did he know that I had another save in store for him on this same flight . . .

There had been no fueling facility at Flushing Meadows, perhaps a good break because a few gallons of fuel could have been just the weight difference that would have put us into the barn. Nonetheless, fuel in both tanks was short as we approached northwest Massachusetts an hour later. Recognizing the possibility of running out of gas, I flew high and tried to keep in view potential emergency landing sites. Even in the fairly continuous forest of that region, there were enough clearings and fields so that we could probably have set down safely from any point on the trip, but a forced landing has multiple risks. In any case, we made it back without testing my alternate strategy. The next day, Marty Engel reprimanded me, observing that there was no fuel in either tank when he checked the plane. I wasn't counting them yet, but I had just used up two of my lives on one trip.

During the next week, I flew alone to visit Kathy Zentner at Smith College. It was a beautiful spring day as I left North Adams for the short hop over the mountains to Northhampton. The trip was uneventful and unthreatening. Kathy met me at the airfield; and as an eternal blemish on her discernment, she agreed to go up with me for a flying adventure. After an hour or so of cruising the Connecticut valley, we began our approach to the Northampton airstrip, coming in from the east toward the setting sun. As we approached the field, Kathy saw directly in front of us some unmarked power lines that had been obscured from me by the brightness of the late-afternoon sun, and she shouted a warning. I pulled the nose up and missed the wires by a mere ten feet. In retrospect, not excusing my negligence, it seems amazing to me that those wires were there so close to the landing strip and unmarked, but they were. A lucky save, this cat's third life, thus narrowly maintaining a promise of life for Kathy's and my future descendants. Think of that, you descendants!

I spent the evening with Kathy and the night at a rooming house, setting out the next morning to fly back to Williamstown to get to classes in the early afternoon. The weather, however, had turned and the clear skies that had followed me the previous day had been replaced by the clouds accompanying a blustering cold front.

I took off into the teeth of a strong north wind, banked to the left, and headed west. As I approached the range of the Berkshires near North Adams, I could see plainly that there was no direct route through the mountains under a rapidly darkening cloud layer. I was only mildly concerned about this weather, being more perturbed about the need to get back to classes, which I could not afford to miss. Then I remembered that there was a pass through this range between Greenfield and North Adams, so I retraced my route back to Northampton, then followed the Connecticut River to Greenfield and turned west to follow Route 2 toward North Adams.

As I shadowed the highway, the valley surrounding it began to constrict and became increasingly serpentine, appreciably reducing my latitude for navigating. Out of the blue, or more precisely, the gray, there was a wall of trees in front of me with barely enough room to turn around. The road guiding me evanesced into the forest and fog. I made a tight turn and regained level flight, but the valley had diminished to nothing, nothing, at least, at my altitude. Beginning to recognize the danger of my situation, I wanted to retrace the course I had taken up the valley, but I had become disoriented; in any case, my entry path had disappeared. I surrendered altitude to stay below the sinking cloud cover, and to my surprise—and, yes, shock—it appeared suddenly that there was no way out of the shrinking airspace. Search as I would, there did not seem to be anywhere to go. I looked around for an emergency landing site but found nothing that looked promising, there being just dense forest with a narrow and winding road running through it. Just as the panic of fatal realization began to set in, I spotted a small uncultivated field almost below me but a bit off to my left. I was too high and had no room to circle, so I headed right toward it, gave up my altitude by "slipping" the plane sideways and made a good landing using practically none of the length of the short field that was available to me. That landing was the coup of the day.

After I was on the ground, the weather continued to deteriorate badly, and within fifteen minutes, fog, rain, and sleet had completed obscured visibility. I realized then that I had been inordinately lucky to have gotten out of this one alive. In retrospect, I would say that I showed good flying skills in getting the plane on the ground but incredibly faulty judgment in every other respect. It was somewhat later that I finally came to understand that most general aviation fatalities are caused by the combination of bad judgment and unforeseen weather. This cat had just used up his fourth life next to Route 2 just short of North Adams.

I ended this experience by hitchhiking back to Williamstown, returning the next day to fly out and over the pass in better weather.

All four of these potential disasters occurred within a period of the two weeks after I had gained my "Private Pilot, Single Engine, Land" license. Surprisingly, I did not experience any other life-threatening adventures while flying at Williams. I did continue to fly regularly at college but did so close to home and in good weather. Perhaps I had learned that small plane flying is okay as a sport but not acceptable as a method of transportation, particularly if you have any schedule urgency. Yet, in truth I had not learned any lessons at all.

I graduated the next June and took that summer off, still hoping that I might get into medical school. Then in the fall, not being ready to go to work and having no idea what to do next, I stumbled on the idea of attending the University of Wisconsin Graduate School of Chemistry. This decision was a way to keep my options open and to stay out of the draft. So it was off to Madison, still with parental support. There, I roomed with EJ Brumder, EJ, a cousin and a longtime friend. While we both were attracted to the Madison party scene, we were concerned enough with our academics that we never got into university life. The most exciting thing we did that autumn was to play bridge with Kathy Zentner's grandmother, that being an activity that did not go unnoticed by the Zentner family, who were soon to become my in-laws. But I still had the flying bug, and I took an occasional flight from the Middleton Airport in a rented plane. One day in the fall I reserved a plane and planned to fly to Evanston to spend the night with my friend Maui and his new wife, Betty. EJ decided to come with me, viewing the trip as the adventure it was to become, and we set off in the late afternoon, planning to land at a small airport in Evanston.

It was a nice afternoon, but by the time we had checked out, taken off, and flown the 150 miles to Evanston, the daylight was fading, and we could not locate the airfield of my flight plan. We circled for a while and couldn't find any appropriate airstrip north of Chicago. As the sun sank below the horizon, the murky atmosphere darkened perceptibly. Not knowing how I was going to get back on the ground, I began to feel a growing anxiety. Then out of the gloom, a lighted airfield appeared about a mile to the west. I headed for it, got into the landing pattern, and eventually turned onto what seemed to me to be the final approach. At this point, I was not used to using a radio, but I received a normal visual signal, a light from the airstrip's control tower. What I would have preferred as a signal was a green light permitting me to land; what I got was a red light that intended to deny me this permission. At this point, it was getting pretty dark, and having no night flying experience, I made a quick decision to ignore the tower's instruction and continued my approach. The signal became more insistent, now flashing urgently in red, ordering me in no uncertain terms not to land. My internal commandant overrode this order and full in the face of the tower's authority, I got my wheels on the ground. As I did so, a large gauge wire net suspended by heavy cables loomed out of the shadows immediately in front of me, crossing the entire runway. I recognized immediately that I was looking at a jet arresting cable and an attached safety net. Quick action was required. A goose to the throttle lifted me over the cable, and I set the plane down on the other side. I had no idea where we had landed, but I understood that I was probably in trouble; so I braked to a stop and shut down my engine to the burgeoning wail of approaching sirens.

In moments, the cavalry arrived as a platoon of a half-dozen Jeeps, all with blazing bubble gum machines strapped atop their roll bars. They surrounded us and their spokesman, who turned out to be the commander in charge, started a dialogue over a megaphone with the rather incongruous, under the circumstances of my having already done so, directive: "You can't land here!"

I was so glad to be safely on the ground, and I knew that I wasn't about to leave, so I reposted impertinently but logically, "I already have," adding, "Where are we anyway?"

We had a brief exchange wherein I learned that I had landed at the Glenview Naval Air Station, and the major learned that EJ and I would not be flying that night. During this conversation, it was decided that our parole or confinement for the evening would be decided by the base commander into whose presence we were to be conducted forthwith. We followed a Jeep, which bore an appropriate sign reading, "FOLLOW ME," to a place where we were instructed to park. Ten minutes later, we had tied down the plane, and we were shrouded in near total darkness, a product of the quick nightfall one experiences in late autumn. I was thankful to be standing on good old terra firma. Then we were taken to the base commander, who, right off, seemed to be sympathetic with our plight. In a half hour, we were out of the base in a cab on our way to Bill Mauritz's apartment.

This adventure seemed like a lark at the time but could have had grave consequences. Again, it was judgment, not aviation skills, that was the problem. It was this cat's fifth life.

Not long after this event, I became engaged to Kathy, and my flying career was over, partly out of financial necessity, but partly because I came to realize that to fly safely, one has to invest more time and care than I was willing to expend.

But this is not the end of the story. Soon after my Evanston adventure, the word came from Williams College that the Williams Flying Club plane had crashed into Mount Greylock killing both Ted Talmadge and Marty Engle. This devastating news underlined the risks of flying small planes. This tragedy, with the instructor in the plane, should have kept me from amateur flying for a lifetime, but I was destined to use up at least one more of my lives.

It was about 1980 when Priscilla Chester arrived at Pine Lake in her Cessna 180, a four-seater that was outfitted with pontoons. She kept her plane on Oconomowoc

Lake and had flown over to visit my sister-in-law, Judy Stark. Judy's husband, Bill, had just arranged for a ride when I came by and was invited along. An aerial look at the lake country was appealing, and it had been many years since my earlier brushes with fate.

What I did not know is that the Cessna 180 was somewhat underpowered for carrying the extra weight of pontoons. What never occurred to me once again was that it was a hot and humid summer day with the associated risks. Further, while Pricilla was a moderately built woman, Bill and I were not small men. We were looking at a rerun of Flushing Meadows.

There was a light west wind, and we started our takeoff run east of the island and into the wind. That gave us a greater than a half mile of water before we got to the tree line. Still, the plane, even under full power, accelerated slowly as the water seemed to be tugging at the pontoons. Gradually, the pontoons climbed in the water and finally were planing on the surface, but the airplane was not yet flying. Even to my recently unutilized senses, it felt sluggish and not yet airworthy. At this point, we were halfway to the trees and traveling about 80 miles an hour. The shore and tree line were coming up fast as we began to attain flight. Even as we cleared the small waves, it appeared that we were not gaining either speed or altitude. Just as I had done in Flushing Meadows twenty-five years earlier, Priscilla kept the nose down and fought for speed. I was starting to sweat and not because it was a hot day. I glanced at Bill and saw that he was gritting his teeth. Priscilla was grimly pushing at the throttle as we came to shore, and then she pulled back warily on the stick. The plane responded by clawing its way reluctantly to a level just above the tree line. Priscilla eased the stick forward and leveled the plane, heading toward Okauchee Lake, which lay less than a mile in front of us. During the half minute or so that it took us to get there, I could feel the plane laboring and could tell that Priscilla could gain neither speed nor altitude as we hovered less than ten feet above the forest top for the entire distance. When we reached the lake, Priscilla nosed down slightly, dropping forty feet or so. That was enough to get us up to a speed barely sufficient for safe flying. We breathed a collective sigh, and Priscilla knew without being told that we had had enough.

This last brush with death, my sixth, was the worst one of all. We had been in serious jeopardy for the entire flight from the moment we left the water until we got to Okauchee Lake. A minor deviation in the wind or our direction would have put us into the oak forest. It is rare to survive a crash into the upper branches of an eighty-foot tree.

This excursion, brief as it was, was an epilogue to my private flying career. Never again did I venture into a small plane. Nevertheless, for Priscilla, this was only a milestone. She dropped Bill and me off at Stark's Pier, apologized for the scare and accepted our gratitude for not killing us. Then she headed for the lee shore and turned to begin her takeoff run for her return to Oconomowoc Lake. As she approached takeoff speed, she dipped a wing, which caught a wave, a misstep that catapulted the plane into a rolling somersault. With each bounce on the water, part of the plane came off of the fuselage: both wings, a pontoon, and the tail. It was a frightening wreck, but Pricilla, still strapped in her seat, survived unhurt. We rescued Priscilla and then picked up the largely intact pieces. They lay in a pile at the Stark's for a few weeks. The plane was eventually reassembled, and Pricilla flew again.

In retrospect, it is sort of amusing that my father, a very rational man, was willing to trade, on my behalf, the risks of football for the perils of flying. He knew something of the risks of football, having been the captain of the team at Riverside High School, and he knew intuitively that there were serious hazards in flying. What he didn't understand was the gravity of the danger in flying and how fragile was life in the face of only marginally defective decisions. It took this cat only six of his allotted nine lives to learn this lesson. Aren't we cats lucky to be given so many opportunities?

CHAPTER VIII

A Bridge to the Future

Even as I became engaged to Kathy Zentner, I had no idea what I was going to do for a career. I had given up my graduate school chemistry program at the University of Wisconsin and with it, my thoughts of medical school. I had committed to spending six months of my engagement period to military service, not because I wanted to serve but to avoid the draft. This interlude gave me space to contemplate the future and, indeed, time for self-evaluation. It was a time for formulating a life plan, one that would provide me with the flexibility to find my way through the hazards of an unknown future, a future for which I seemed to have no useful competence.

The eight weeks of basic training at Fort Leonard Wood were physically demanding, but a greater challenge was learning how to live with a social strata to which I had had no prior exposure. Nevertheless, even relative to this trial, there were still more difficult circumstances ahead. After completing basic training, all of us new soldiers were divided into two classes: the less intelligent, who could not be trusted with the potential hazards of military conflict, were sent to clerk-typist or intelligence school; the others, like me, who were deemed smart enough to be able to take care of themselves under fire, were sent to advanced infantry school. I was ordered to Fort Jackson, South Carolina, where I would be living intimately with a much less civilized cadre than I had experienced at Leonard Wood.

I ARRIVED AT Fort Jackson a week before I had been ordered to report, hoping to convert this week of leave to a later furlough in order to serve as an attendant at my friend Harry Drake's marriage to Ann Blommer. During the week of space that this period provided, there being no program for me. I was left to my own devices—provided that I could avoid the traps established to impress unassigned soldiers into unpleasant activities like KP, guard duty, cleaning weapons, or "policing" the company area. For the uninitiated, that means picking up cigarette butts and other such debris.

Succeeding for the most part in avoiding these traps, I spent most duty hours at the library where I found a shelf of business- and finance-oriented books that might give me a start on a business career. There wasn't much diversion on base, so study became my way of life for most of the nights at Fort Jackson.

During the next twelve weeks, even as I was becoming a machine gunner, I did find the time to digest that entire shelf, in part because I had also become a truck and Jeep driver and was frequently allowed by the officer in charge of my vehicle to read while on duty. Of course, the officer in charge of my vehicle and of me might, and often did, have other plans for me—like washing the Jeep or standing at ease or attention while he performed his duty. By the time I was discharged, even with an occasional zealous officer, I had invested myself on a business trajectory and had started to build an inventory of business parlance and knowledge.

After returning to Milwaukee, I prepared for Kathy's and my wedding, which was to take place six weeks hence. During this hiatus, there was no time to invest in business study; I did, however, select an initial job direction and, with an eye toward a finance career, had initial interviews with Merrill, Lynch, Pierce, Fenner, and Beane, they being the most prestigious broker in town. Because their leader was a close friend of my father-in-law-to-be, this interview went exceedingly well, and they tentatively offered me a job. The only caveat, described as a formality, was that I would have to visit their New York office for a final interview. I deferred this visit until after the honeymoon and proceeded confidently into my marriage.

When the time came for that interview, the encounter did not go as advertised. It was what is called an "adverse" interview, in my case, one held in a small room with me on an uncomfortable chair facing two apparently hostile interrogators, who took turns firing tough questions at me. It was my first real interview, and I was quite ill at ease and for sure, a bit clumsy. My discomfiture was reaching its denouement when I was asked a most perplexing question: "What is your greatest weakness?"

I hesitated, thinking that the query was really none of their business. Finally, after a painful silence, I finally mustered an answer that seemed appropriate to me, "Well, that's for me to know and for you to find out."

The interview ended soon thereafter. When I returned to Milwaukee, I learned that my interview had not been a success. So I got a job with a less persnickety broker, Paine Weber, Jackson, and Curtis.

I had an okay experience at Paine Weber and learned about the stock market, but I did not enjoy selling stocks to friends, an approach that I was encouraged to follow. So I proceeded with my financial education, taking a couple of accounting courses at Marquette. One friend that I had turned into a minor client was Dick Kramlich, and he, having graduated from Harvard Business School, seemed to be on a fast track. HBS looked to me like a shortcut to success, so I began to prepare myself for gaining admission to this fabled institution.

When, a year and a half before I hoped to matriculate, I got the Harvard admission package and started to evaluate my prospects for admission, it occurred to me that, with my record, getting in would not be easy. I had graduated about the middle of my class at Williams; HBS (as it is called by the people who know) clearly preferred the cream of the crop. Although it was true that Williams was quite selective and a top-ranked college, my middling performance did little to recommend me. The application form was quite challenging, asking about twenty questions relating to an applicant's life experience: situations in which he performed leadership roles and his influence on the outcome of each situation. These situations could be drawn from any life experiences, like academics, sports, volunteer work, or the like. Even so, my immediate reaction was that I did not have a lot of these. This stuff looked as intimidating to me as the "greatest weakness" question at Merrill Lynch!

But it was almost two years after my Merrill experience, and I had learned a thing or two and had had a few valuable experiences along the way. Rather than answering the questions directly, I wrote up all the significant experiences I could think of, stretching to the limit my leadership role in each of them. Only when I had completed about twenty-five such essays did I try to match the answers up with the questions. With a little more stretching and some rescripting, the application took shape; with a little imaginative thinking, it was not difficult to make my essays suit the questions. I thought my application made me look competitive, at least more than I knew I was.

But there were still three impediments lying between me and my admission to HBS: my Williams record, the prospective interview, and the GMAT (Graduate Management Admission Test). The Williams record was what it was, and I could do nothing about it; I wasn't too sure about my interviewing skills, but I thought that maybe I had taken something away from my Merrill Lynch experience. In any case, the interview could wait. As to testing, I had always tested well, acing the quantitative sections of tests while doing okay on the verbal. I learned that the GMAT was equally divided between these areas and additionally that the verbal was almost half-based on vocabulary, the rest on reading comprehension and logic. The only part for which I could improve appeared to be vocabulary. So, for the year that was left to me before I would take the test, I worked to develop my vocabulary, using every vocabulary improvement book that I could find. There were plenty of these, starting with *Thirty Days to a More Powerful Vocabulary, Six Weeks to Word Power,* and the like. During the next twelve months, I always had a copy of one of these pocketbooks with me, and I engaged my friends with the word games these books offered.

That spring, Kathy and I took a ski trip to Aspen with our friends Yogi and Kathy Berry and John and Gayzey Taylor. I had at least three vocabulary books to share, so nobody ever went up a lift without a vocabulary exercise or test to attempt with his or her chair-partner. That is, except for the then recently unemployed Yogi, who needed to hand out résumés in order to arrange for a job interview on his ride up the mountain. I think he found a job with the Smithsonian Institution while riding the Bell Mountain chair.

By the time I took the GMAT, my vocabulary was greatly expanded, and as it happened, I knew every word on the test without taking any time to agonize over a meaning. Not only did my word skills give me a scoring advantage, but also they rewarded me with lots of time for the logic and reading comprehension section. While those sections were more demanding, time made them much more approachable. Together, these advantages had probably raised my percentile ranking by ten or fifteen points. My verbal score reached the 99th percentile, and when combined with a 96th percentile in the quantitative area, it put me in the 100th percentile overall. The upside of this result was that it relieved me of the need to go to Boston for an interview; the downside was not mine, it was mostly for my intimates: I began to think of myself as a MENSA. Not really but it was so in their minds.

I was admitted in April and prepared to enter the business school in the fall. With this achievement, I had, in a short period, changed the trajectory of my life.

CHAPTER IX

The Patriot

In 1958, there was no war on the horizon, but there was a military draft that lurked as a potential diversion from the main business of life. When I determined to marry Kathy Zentner, I decided to get my service obligation out of the way by joining the National Guard. My intention, like that of many of my contemporaries, was to hold my full- time service to six months rather than the two years that was required of draftees. As we will see, best-laid plans often fail to develop as planned.

GENERAL FRITZ BREIDSTER was a really big man. He not only had impressive size— significant height and ample girth —but he had a big heart as well. He was substantial in his abilities too, and his stature was magnified by his humility. It had taken me years to learn that he had been a starting tackle for the U.S. Military Academy. What is more important, I remember a speech he made to the troops of the 32nd Division in which he recalled the campaign of the 32nd in Burma, where he had served as a major and later as a colonel during the Second World War. He talked about the plight of the ordinary soldier in the Burma theatre—the extreme humidity and heat, conditions magnified exponentially by indigenous insects, deadly snakes, rodents, and disease, usually dysentery. The general allowed that being an officer in Burma made life marginally more tolerable than it was for the enlisted man, but on the march, there were few amenities even for officers, who marched with the men. After a brutal forced march in the jungle, while his unit was taking a brief break, Colonel Breidster took his boots off and was both treating his bleeding feet and contemplating riding in a Jeep, when he overheard a group of enlisted men talking about surrendering to the conditions, as if that were possible. One of them said to the group, "If that fat old lard ass can make this march, so can I."

Breidster knew who they were talking about, and he marched on.

What I did not yet know was that this remarkable person was going to have an extraordinary influence on the course of my life.

I had gone to high school with General Breidster's son, Billy. Billy and I had played football and track together and had competed for academic honors. General and Mrs. Breidster were frequently in attendance at our interscholastic sporting events, and I developed a comfortable relationship with them.

After I returned from college in the late fifties, I needed to deal with my draft status; and not wanting to risk two years as a conscript, I decided to join the National Guard, which required only six months of active duty training followed by six years of reserve duty. The National Guard unit in Wisconsin was the 32nd Division, and its commanding general was General Breidster. With his help, I was able to get into the division headquarters company in the operation section (G-3) commanded by a Colonel Roth. While aware that I had used influence to get this sinecure, Roth seemed to have no problem with my connection to the general.

During the next few years, I worked as a stockbroker and went to weekly National Guard drills at the Richard Street Armory. My annual two-week vacation was taken up by summer camp at Camp McCoy. In my spare time there and at home, I worked on skills that would get me into business school. In the spring of 1961 I was admitted to the Harvard Business School class of 1963.

That summer was the summer of the Berlin Wall. From the beginning of this confrontation, there was talk of a military call-up. To make matters worse, the conventional wisdom was that that the 32nd was first on the call-up list because it was "combat ready" and rated at the highest level of preparedness.

It seemed, at least to me, that President Kennedy, who wanted to buttress our military brawn, would call up a less-prepared unit and bring it up to our level of combat readiness. Of course, the assessment that we were combat ready belied my recent experience at Camp McCoy. I had seen from my lofty vantage at headquarters the inadequacy of the division's leadership at all levels. The lack of coordination between adjacent and proximate units during division exercises resulted more than once in our van attacking our rear. Not knowing that the art of war is mostly about managing the confusion that your own side creates, I probably attached too much importance to our frequent snafus. Even with all this insider knowledge of the 32nd's real lack of preparedness, I felt fairly safe, knowing that I was going to Boston in the fall to attend business school. I would not be around if the 32nd were called.

In retrospect, it is hard to believe that the threat of war at this time seemed significant. However, even in Milwaukee, many people, including members of my own family, were building bomb shelters. Some, who had built underground shelters, were even arming themselves to defend against their neighbors who had not prepared so well. It was every man for himself . . . an ugly time indeed.

I wasn't immune to this kind of selfish focus. Going past the risks associated with a possible war with the Soviets over Berlin, and being excessively sanguine about the call-up issue, I had become obsessed with the idea of dodging my responsibility to join a Boston reserve unit while I was at business school. My primary motive here was that the required drills would add an additional burden to what I knew would be a demanding academic load. After a few days of thinking about this problem, I hit upon a scheme: I would not transfer to a Boston reserve unit at all. Instead, I would go to my commander and request "inactive status," which would not only allow me to maintain my membership in the guard while serving my enlistment term but also to be absent from all duty. The downside of this position was that if the 32nd were activated, I might be recalled to active duty with it. This risk didn't seem too great because I was sure they were not going to call the 32nd. And if they did, I could probably get an academic deferment.

"I want inactive status," I lied, without any sense of guilt, "because, if the 32nd is called, I want to go with my unit."

Without any explanation that statement was enough for Colonel Roth. Taken at face value, it was a persuasive argument, credible at least to the colonel, who was filled with patriotism himself and wanted to believe that such loyalty resided in his men. My request was granted posthaste, and the paperwork was completed on the spot. Everyone in the colonel's office shook my hand and wished me well. A few weeks later I left for Boston a patriot, at least in the minds of my brothers in arms at the 32nd.

Kathy and I moved to Boston, and I settled into the grind of business school. Three weeks later, I was picnicking on the banks of the Charles River with my eight-month pregnant wife on a beautiful Indian summer day. We had the radio tuned to a popular music station and were enjoying a rare moment of relaxation and togetherness when the music was interrupted by an important announcement. The president had announced a military call-up. In addition to scattered reserve units, the Texas and Wisconsin National Guards, both in their entirety, were being called, the reason for their selection being that they were both combat ready and could be quickly deployed in the current emergency. Tell me another!

Kathy was in shock. Among other things it was difficult for her to believe that I had made such a bad choice when there had been such consensus that the 32nd would be among the first units called. I told her not to worry; I was sure I could fix my status at the dean's office. I went there directly, and was assured that they were already on top of the issue. A couple of reservists had beaten me in to make the same request. The dean's minions were confident that there would be no problem keeping me out. I went home and reported the good news, and when Kathy's mother, Ruth, called in alarm, I confidently reassured her that I would not have to go. That evening, Kathy and I even had a martini to celebrate my narrow escape, something we never did on school nights.

That night around 10:30, Ruth again phoned in a panic. She and my father-in-law had attended a dinner party at the country club that night, and there had been much talk about the big news of the day, the call-up of Wisconsin's National Guard. Apparently, quite a few families, some of whom we knew, were affected. Many young careers were being interrupted. Ruth, having been reassured by our earlier phone conversation, had felt OK about my status at least until dinner was over. Then, just before the party started to break up, General Breidster rose, clinked his glass, and pronounced, "I would like to toast a young patriot whom many of you know, a young man who wants to go to war with his unit—Dick Gallun."

Ruth babbled on, "Is it true, did you *really* say that? I thought you were out of this!"

Both Kathy and I understood what had to be done. The next day, I went to the dean's office and took my name off the list. I was going to war with my buddies in the 32nd. I had tried to dodge the draft, but now, whether I liked it or not, I was going to be a patriot!

CHAPTER X

Hornburg the Educated Labrador

While I had grown up with dogs, I never had had a real relationship with a dog until Kathy and I decided to make the leap and get a puppy. We had not yet had children, so this dog had a great opportunity to make himself the center of our lives. He proceeded to do so using that tried-and-true canine trick of making his peculiarities the essence of his charm, a trick that has pervaded all of the dogs I have owned since this initial relationship.

HOW MUCH CAN you love a dog? My first dog was Hornburg, a black lab whom Kathy and I chose because he was the first to reach us of a six-week-old litter from which we were selecting our puppy. Hornburg and I did everything together for ten years. We romped, we hunted, we played ball and Frisbee, and we slept together with my young wife under a cashmere blanket, a gift to Hornburg from one of his admirers, of whom there were a bunch.

Loving a dog is a learning experience. I got my first lesson from my cousin Ned Gallun, who informed me that if I really wanted to have a relationship with this dog, I would have to take up hunting. Why, you surely ask? Because that is what Labradors do. So, I took up hunting and then read the book that Ned gave me, *Training Your Retriever*, and from it, I learned that owning a dog is a demanding responsibility, one that goes beyond taking up hunting. It comes to this: the dog starts with a pure heart and will always try to do the right thing; his mistakes are really your mistakes, the result of poor training or your inattention. Well, that is not quite a slam-dunk. As it turned out, Hornburg had one deficiency of his own that stood in the way of my scheme to bond him to me, On the first hunt, one for which I had no expectations, I learned that this affectionate and always well mannered dog was just a teensy-weensy bit gun-shy. In fact, at the first sound of a gun, he put his tail between his legs and fled . . . fled even from me. I got him back; and when we got home, I referred to the book and found that this problem could be overcome but only with patient and painstaking attention.

It was partly because of this problem that I decided that professional training might be a good idea; it would not only help to overcome the gun-shyness but would give him the jump on other hunting skills. I found the ideal trainer in Random Lake, Wisconsin, just north of Milwaukee. Ray Sommers believed in soft discipline: rewards not threats; this last approach, that of tough discipline and even physical punishment, being employed by many trainers at the time. Hornburg dutifully met Ray, and Ray liked what he saw. The gun-shyness would not be a problem. The training would take about six weeks or so; visiting not encouraged until after four weeks—an eternity for me.

At my first visit it was clear that while he had become responsive to commands, Hornburg had not overcome his noise aversion, He knew how to retrieve with a "soft mouth," meaning that he could bring back live game unharmed. It was clear that Ray too had fallen under Hornburg's spell and did not want to give up on making him a hunting dog. Two weeks later, the gun was still a problem, but Ray thought he could fix that in another week or so. He observed that Hornburg loved "his game," meaning that he liked to hunt. To stop now would be too bad for the dog and for his master, as well. I was easily persuaded. So the training period grew to seven weeks, then eight; finally after the ninth, Hornburg came home with an advanced degree in duck hunting.

How much can you love a dog? Maybe enough so that when he returns from nine weeks of training and won't fetch the dummy you tossed for him, you swim out to retrieve it yourself, ignoring the ice-cold water—all this in front of your friends, who are yukking it up over his poor performance, while you are not embarrassed in the least. You just hug Hornburg and assume he will do better next time. Maybe you love him enough so that, when you go to the posh hunt country in Connecticut to hunt quail and your hunting companions' dogs all point professionally at the first covey hidden in the brush—while your dog is frolicking in the long grass—you confidently accept their derision, knowing that what he does, which is definitely not pointing, he does well. And when they all miss their first shots, and the entire covey flies off in all directions, you feel intense pride when a heretofore unseen Hornburg leaps from the tall grass, seizes a low-flying quail out of the sky, somersaults on the way down, lands on his feet, and brings the still alive bird to you.

Hornburg, the well-trained Labrador, had two commands to which he would respond readily. The first was "out of the dining room" which served to notify him that he had to evacuate wherever he was, be that the dining room, the neighbors' flower bed or the duck blind. The second was "mmm-mmm nummies" which meant "come" under all circumstances. Of course, both of these commands were originated by Kathy for specific purposes, but with time, were used by everyone in the family and by our neighbors and friends as well for any purpose whatsoever. Even when sound asleep, Hornburg would come to full alert at the sound of a foreshortened mmm-mmm! Strange but very endearing to those who loved him.

From Hornburg's earliest days, the hunting highlight of the year was a weekend at Leo Price's hunting lodge at Necedah. This large hunting preserve was a land of water interrupted by a few areas of dry land as well as many dikes that had been constructed to control the water level for cranberry growing. The cranberry farm had been abandoned some forty years earlier, and typical north woods vegetation had taken over the dikes and dry areas to create a waterfowl paradise. Some of the dikes had been converted to roads for accessing by auto the duck and goose blinds; others had become paths to wander, looking for partridge or an occasional turkey or perhaps a bridge to a small pond offering a jump shooting opportunity.

Our visits to the Prices' found us in the company of a rather rough group. Leo and his son Glenn were in the steel erection business, and they used the hunting lodge to entertain their customers as well as their friends. Their business guests were often the hands-on managers of their client companies and were always rugged and tough outdoorsmen. More to the point, they all had dogs, always black Labradors, and importantly, these Labradors were all vicious. Consequently, no dogs were allowed in the lodge. Rather, they were chained in a kennel or locked in their cars from where they put up a frightening din. Because he appeared to be and was such a gentle soul, Hornburg was not only allowed into the lodge, but he was treated respectfully not only by my host but by these roughneck hunters as well. Previously, they had never known that Labradors were people too, and that one could have such a gentle soul.

When one day I was assigned to share a blind with a couple of these ironworkers, they deferentially left their own dogs back in their kennels and graciously accepted Hornburg as the retriever for our blind. On this first such excursion, my companions learned much about my dog that was attractive and, even to them, truly adorable; and from that point, and through the years, they came to love this dog. On the hunt, there was only one command that worked to get the excited dog into the blind: "mmm-mmm nummies." The ironworkers fought over who was to give the command. Then, to get him out of the blind, there was just one command that Hornburg understood. Of course, it was: "Out of the dining room!" When obeying this command, Hornburg leapt out of the blind. He would quickly survey the scene, skillfully marking the location of fallen bird. Then, depending on the water temperature, which he would first test with his toe, he would look back for further instructions, hoping for a reprieve if the water were cold, which it invariably was. If no reprieve were forthcoming, he would plunge bravely into the frigid pond and head smartly for his prey. Much well intended laughter accompanied this performance, but when Hornburg returned with his bird, suffering visibly from the cold, his audience became part of the act. The ironworkers would compete to see which one could get out of his heavy hunting shirt fastest to share it with the frozen dog. That first retrieve would be Hornburg's last of the day. He would spend the rest of the morning hunt shivering while huddled in the arms of a rugged outdoorsman.

How much can you love a dog? Maybe enough so that returning from one hunting trip at Glen's, when Glen's car breaks down, necessitating our taking the train, you opt for the mail car with your dog rather than the club car with your hunting companions. Despite the unheated mail car, lit only by a Coleman lantern, you feel enough joy from being with your dog that you hardly notice the coffin and its occupant traveling with you at the other end of the otherwise empty car.

In Hornburg's ninth year our Necedah weekend was unusually warm. Although the temperature was on its way to the low eighties, it was close to zero degrees two hundred miles to the northwest in Minneapolis where a blizzard raged. Before dawn, as we put out our decoys downwind from the little island at the center of the Prices' big pond, the wind was brisk and rising, preparatory for the coming storm. The weather anomaly brought with it an incessant stream of ducks looking for refuge, at least for the day; and as we were soon to learn, these ducks were tired and wanted to get down onto the sanctuary of the protected water, throwing their usual caution to the wind. My companions for the morning hunt, Steve Seidel, Pat Gallagher, and I watched dozens of ducks attempt to land among our decoys while we were still in our skiff, setting the rest of the decoys. It may be a stretch to believe that by the time we got into the blind, still before legal shooting time, the live ducks in the water already outnumbered the decoys, but that was the case.

As the sun poked bright and orange above the distant tree line, it looked like a "butterfly day"; that is, it was clear and already quite warm, the kind of day where the only things flying are butterflies. Nevertheless, the ducks teeming overhead belied this impression, circling anxiously, wanting to get out of the sky. Before we started to hunt, we fired a shot in the air to scare away the ducks skulking among our decoys. The no longer gun-shy Hornburg was excited by the firing and looked at me disgustedly when no bird dropped out of the sky. But Hornburg did not have long to wait. The next flight was immediately upon us, and with six shots we dropped six birds. Hornburg carefully marked the fallen birds and went to work, performing, without instruction, a sextuple retrieve. By the time he had completed this task, laying each bird neatly in a row on the beach, more birds had arrived. We kept shooting; and Hornburg, enjoying the warmer-than-usual water, kept retrieving. He continued this activity for more than an hour without supervision. I can't swear that he got all the birds we killed that day, but we searched the downwind shore after we had sated our appetite for ducks and we found none. In any case, I was the gutter in the cleaning shed later that morning, so I had an accurate count of his retrieves. It was way beyond reasonable.

How much can you love a dog? Maybe you don't know until you lose him. Ten years is a short life, even for a Labrador; but at ten, Hornburg had a stroke, and the vet said, "Put him down."

When I went to the vet's to say good-bye, my four-year-old son, Richie, wanted to come along, and he did. Richie and I said our sad good-byes, and Hornburg, who could not move his body or even lift his head, licked my hand and wagged his tail as if to say I love you. It was so hard to leave him there, but I did—I would not do that today. Then on the way home, Richie said, "Dad, can I ask you a question?"

Quite choked up but expecting a poignant question and an opportunity to seize a teaching moment, I barely responded, having trouble speaking at all. "Yeah, what is it, Richie?"

The request came, "Dad, when Hornburg dies, can I have a parakeet?"

How much can you love a dog? You have to be really involved with him to find out. Some might think you were crazy if you told them how much.

CHAPTER XI

Sleep Well Tonight . . . Your National Guard Is

Being a nonentity in the army is a useful tool for adjusting an inflated opinion of one's self and good preparation for life. I believe that military training was, for me, a humbling and humanizing experience, an important part of my education. Nevertheless, whenever I have made this assertion about my acquired humility, some of my friends and one of my wives have opined that perhaps I would have done well to have had more military training. Perhaps they were right, but imagine me if I had not had it at all.

In retrospect, I have to admit that, as it finally played out, my Fort Lewis jaunt with the Wisconsin National Guard was a walk on the beach. It contrasted sharply with my earlier exposure to the military as a machine gunner at Fort Jackson. That experience was not only much more physically difficult but was particularly uncomfortable because of the association with a truly unfamiliar social class.

During my advanced infantry training at Fort Jackson, I had been exposed to, no, rather, I was immersed in, a hillbilly-redneck environment in which one's manhood was tested daily. I was lured into fights with rednecks in which, if I were winning, a rare occurrence in itself, I, being not much of a fighter, my opponent might pull out a knife. Even so, I never did lose a knife fight because I knew how to conduct myself when the chips were down — surrender!

In contrast, the Wisconsin National Guard was made up of young men that were more like me than they were different. Rather than being a truly difficult time, this military duty was to become a time out from responsibility, a time to be with my wife and child and an opportunity to bond with good friends. However, it didn't look like that in the beginning.

While early on, I did not put much stock in the possibility of a real war starting in Berlin, the fear eventually did get to me. Shortly after I arrived at Fort Lewis, the entire division was rolled out of bed in the middle of the night, instructed to pack our military paraphernalia, and taken to McChord Air Base to embark to points unknown.

The trip to McChord was a muddle of disorder with vehicles clogging the roads, lights flashing, and horns blaring. I was in the back of a deuce and a half for this nocturnal excursion; so, being under the shroud that covered the back of these trucks, I did not have direct sensory exposure to the goings-on. Nevertheless, from the interior of the truck, it seemed like we were already entering a battle zone.

When we reached the tarmac at McChord, we were ordered to get onto transport aircraft, headed, it seemed, for Berlin, a city then surrounded by the Soviets. Berlin should have seemed unlikely as a destination because of its location in the Soviet sector; nevertheless, with its noise and confusion the scene at the air base did seem to indicate something important. For just a moment this assignment had become an alarming prospect. But then, after we were uncomfortably settled on benches in the aircraft, there came the announcement expected by many: "This is just a drill. You may return to your vehicles."

So it goes!

HARRY DRAKE, MY lifelong friend, and I had joined the Wisconsin National Guard shortly after graduating from college, doing so to avoid being drafted. Because of our relationship with the commanding general of the Wisconsin Guard, both of us had been able to inveigle our way into administrative work and thus, avoid some of the grungy parts of military service. My job was with division operations, the unit that drew up the plans for movements and placement of division troops when the division would be engaged in military maneuvers. Harry's was with the finance section, a component of the 32nd Administrative Company.

Then came the Berlin crisis, and we were called to active duty, assigned with the 32nd Division to Fort Lewis in Tacoma, Washington. We were surprised to learn that General Breidster had resigned after the call-up to give his longtime associate, General Dunlap, an opportunity to command the division. But that didn't affect us because there is a vast chasm between the enlisted man and the general officer. We would not have expected to see him up close in any case. We both went to Fort Lewis resolving to keep our heads down and to be noticed as little as possible by any officers, let alone, generals.

Because of the birth of my daughter, Elizabeth, I had been allowed a brief deferment and so arrived in Tacoma the day before Thanksgiving, a month and a half after the division had encamped. Thanks to my late arrival, I had lost my desk job in the division operations office and, upon reporting for duty, was assigned to the headquarters security platoon. Since no one at headquarters seemed much concerned about security, I was able to spend most days unsupervised in the barracks, so I whiled away the time playing cards with my fellow security enforcers. I liked that! In early December, my wife, Kathy, arrived with our new baby, and I was able to join them in a rented apartment in a Tacoma suburb while continuing my pleasant routine in the barracks while on duty.

Meanwhile, Harry had become a section head in the finance group and offered to get me transferred to his section, which processed the division's monthly payroll. Without any encouragement from me but clearly with my best interests at heart, Harry had argued to his superiors that I was a genius with numbers and was needed to improve the performance of his unit. Somehow, they bought his line and invited me to transfer to Finance. Not grasping the merit of this opportunity and valuing too highly my poker game and unsupervised life of ease in the barracks, I demurred. However, when the entire division, sans Finance, went on field training in Yakima during the arctic cold of January, I learned that there was a price to pay for my sinecure. Three weeks of paying the price! Although I was still in the seemingly prestigious environment of division headquarters, I was mostly doing guard duty, which meant walking around in the cold with an unloaded gun asking, "Who goes there?" In Yakima in January, this was *not* good duty.

I did get an occasional breather from guard duty and KP during those weeks. One time, it was making and serving coffee in the division operations tent. While I was performing my menial function, General Dunlop entered the tent and by and by, noticed my stitched on name tag, which said appropriately: "GALLUN." The general stopped and addressed me, saying, "Gallun. You must know Vogel."

It was true that I knew Fred Vogel, whose family was an old line leather family like mine. The general's statement was just that, a statement. Nevertheless, it begged for a response, so I acknowledged in military speak: "Yes, sir!"

The general continued, "Quite a guy that Vogel. I understand that he went to Harvard and speaks five languages. We're going to move him to intelligence."

"Yes, sir!"

He explained, "We don't have enough language skill there."

I confirmed for the general that Vogel was quite a guy, even as I was fairly confident that he didn't speak more than two languages. I was beginning to understand how ordinary people got into the real gravy jobs!

While on guard duty a few days later, still in the deep freeze of Yakima, I was caught "resting," they said "sleeping," and spent a nasty time with the sergeant of the guard, the company's first sergeant, who threatened to court-martial me, with dire penalties in prospect. While this flap made only for an uncomfortable twenty-four hours, it awakened me to the realization that my sinecure was no garden party. When I added this unpleasant noncom to the penetrating cold, the general discomfort of living in a pup tent with sleet, snow, and ice, and the omnipresence of salutable officers, not to mention a plethora of disagreeable noncoms, our three-week bivouac had become a nightmare.

Despite that, the rest of the winter passed uneventfully uneventful except for one day in late January, when I heard the cry, "Look! The mountain's out!" Sure enough, there was Mount Rainier, crystal clear in its definition against a brightening blue sky as the clouds skittered away, dissolved by the unfamiliar sun. The mountain was startlingly close and massive, looming right over us, reaching to fourteen thousand feet from our position at sea level and, as the crow flies, only fifteen miles to the top. Compare that to the Rockies which come off of a base that, when you are near the mountain, ranges from seven to nine thousand feet. This mountain was twice as high as any of the Rockies and an order of magnitude more massive.

What was even more impressive than the size of this enormous mountain was the fact that, because of the persistent cloudiness and winter fog of the northwest, I had not even once seen it in the two months that I had been there. The rainy weather we had experienced during this time would not break until June, a month that introduced four months of almost continuous blue skies.

It was early March when I became aware that I faced another, this time, almost a four-weeklong camping trip with my unit. They called it a bivouac. For this anticipated exercise, the entire division, including all the support units that had been exempted from the Yakima pilgrimage, would travel in a convoy to the Mojave Desert in California in the manner that a division might travel when going to war. This trip, particularly the traveling, two days in each direction in the back of a deuce and a half, would likely exceed the Yakima trip in discomfort and general unpleasantness.

At this point, Harry renewed his pitch that I should join the finance group. Reminding me that I would be leaving my wife and child for three and a half weeks, he argued, implausibly to be sure, that Finance would not have to make this trip. His poorly thought out reasoning was premised on the fact that he knew that his unit commander, Colonel Kaufman, did not want to go and that he had influence "upstairs." Based on the information I had gleaned at headquarters, I figured that not even Harry's colonel had adequate pull to pull this one off, so either way, I was going camping in California. Besides, when I had inquired of the first sergeant about applying for a transfer, he had snarled a nasty "not on your life" at me, reminding me of my close call with a court-martial. I knew he was out to get me, and I didn't want to rock the boat. I let this opportunity slip away.

It was two days before we were scheduled to caravan to California when I got a call from Harry. He had been correct; Finance was not going to the desert with the division! Colonel Kaufman had told the commanding general that he would not be able to get the payroll done out in the field, and General Dunlop had accepted this convenient fabrication, having been persuaded that really bad things happened when soldiers are not paid. Harry said he still thought he could expedite my transfer before the major movement began.

This time, not really believing it possible that this transfer could happen, I agreed despite my anxiety about the first sergeant. The wheels of military bureaucracy began to move inexorably, and to my surprise, the next day, Harry informed me that my transfer orders were being cut. Nevertheless, I was not yet out of the woods.

The next morning, nothing was happening regarding my reassignment, at least at Headquarters Company. The trucks were assembled there, and my bag was already on my truck. Prospects for my escaping this unwanted jaunt looked bleak. My truck was ready to go, but I was hanging back when my favorite first sergeant came by and ordered, "Gallun, get in the truck."

I whined that I was expecting orders transferring me to Finance. He just laughed at me and repeated his command.

As I reluctantly climbed into the truck--at that very moment--a pink thunderbird convertible rolled up, its top down and horn blaring. There in the rear of the car, an enlisted man was sitting on the back deck with his feet on the backseat. He was waving a piece of paper that turned out to be my orders. The driver, Colonel Kaufman himself, seeing my first sergeant, stopped and asked, "Where's Gallun? I have orders for him."

The soldier in back, Harry Drake of course, produced the papers. I, seeing all of this drama, dismounted the truck and awaited instructions. The first sergeant glanced at the orders; then scowling, reluctantly gave the required deference to the colonel. Then he turned and seeing me out of the truck, muttered with undisguised annoyance, "You're a lucky f—ker, Gallun! Get the f—k out of here!" and walked away.

He was wrong. I wasn't really lucky. I just had friends in low places.

I grabbed my duffel bag, got into the colonel's Thunderbird, gaining from Harry a cordial introduction to the colonel, who seemed irrationally thrilled to have me in his unit. That was a good beginning to my new life, which was to consist of a little work, good hours, and a lot of baseball and bridge.

With this transfer, I had become part of a highly educated cadre of low-level enlisted men, mostly Specialist 3s, who dealt exclusively with assembling the division's monthly payroll. But finance was only a part of the 32nd Administrative Company, which carried on all the administrative activities of the division and which, in addition to finance, included military justice, quartermaster, and other rear area activities. The enlisted men of this company had an average education of almost eighteen years, that being the level of a master's degree. In comparison, the officers of the administrative company had an average academic experience of eleven and a half years, placing them not quite out of high school. The power of the officer's commissions kept most of us enlisted men in our place, but there was always an undercurrent of derision aimed at the less facile among the officers' group. The situation was aggravated by the fact that about a third of our highly educated soldiers had completed law school (they were the judge advocate's clerks). As young lawyers, they were articulate, and at least a few were adept at the use of barbed humor. Most of these guys lived in the barracks and viewed sparring with the officers as a source of amusement, not being unwilling to suffer the consequences of their shenanigans. The dissonance that emerged kept alive a running tension between the officers and enlisted men.

The conflict between these groups spilled over into situations that led to punishment of the entire company, usually in the evening, and included even those of us who had gained permission to live off base with their families. Harry and I cherished our off base time and decried the capers that brought on this retaliation. We tried to hide from the company formations (read: orderly lineup with a roll call) that were called frequently in response to this mischief. We did so by avoiding the company area whenever we could, seeing to it that we were busy at the finance office until the end of business hours. In any case, we were occasionally caught in the net and subjected to whatever punishment might be applied. The disciplinary process usually began with a formation at which our unit's behavior was decried, and extra work was handed out to the guilty and, just as often, to the not guilty as well.

But even these unwanted formations, command performances they were, held a few memorable moments. At one of them, one that I could not avoid, a particularly mouthy private, Tom Volpe, a miscreant bartender from Milwaukee, had just returned from duty as the fireman in the kitchen, a notably dirty job. Thinking he was entitled to clean up and not caring much for the consequences of failure to comply, Volpe chose to take a shower despite the announced formation, and he had just gotten back to his personal area when the company was ordered to fall in on the parade ground behind the barracks. Tom ignored the call and was toweling himself off as the rest of us rushed out of the barracks and lined up in a military queue. There were a hundred or so enlisted men in the formation, but it took just minutes for the commanding officer to ascertain that Volpe was not present. It took only a moment longer to determine that he was upstairs in the barrack. In a loud voice magnified by a megaphone, the company commander, Captain Dushold, summoned him saying, "Volpe, get your ass down here this minute or your ass is grass" (typical military threat).

We heard a very military "yassir!" from the barrack, and a long minute later, Volpe appeared on the back balcony, naked except for unlaced boots and a steel pot (headgear) covering his head. Then he slowly climbed down the fire escape ladder and with impossible dignity, took his place in the formation. The assembled company started snickering; then, when snickering brought no response from Captain Dushold, the entire company broke out in laughter. The CO didn't seem to know what to do. After a few minutes the formation was dismissed without any punishments being handed out except that Volpe was called to the day room for individual punishment.

It was a rare victory, especially for Volpe, who, in his inimitable modus operandi, enjoyed all the notoriety he achieved.

What was really important, though, about this group of enlisted men was that they all were competent at what they did. In Finance, the payroll clerks were good with figures and were quick and accurate when putting together the payroll. Our group could complete the expected month's work in two weeks. Colonel Kaufmann had his eye on the ball; his job was to get the payroll out and as long as it was accurate and on time, he was no fan of "make work," a ubiquitous military tradition. When we were done with the month's payroll and it had been checked for accuracy, we were allowed to do as we pleased around the office, including reading, doing crosswords, playing bridge, or playing baseball. Occasionally, we were even allowed to go home early.

Harry Drake exacted a lifetime of homage from me for getting me into this favorable situation.

It was after a couple of months of this good life that, having completed the May payroll early, as usual, there were no duty functions for us to perform, so we were playing bridge. As usual, we were dressed in fatigues, the uniform of almost every day. However, on this day, we were a little less polished. Read: not quite up to military standard, because the officers were not to put in an appearance. They were attending a high-level function at division headquarters. In addition, we had spent the morning playing softball in the mud, and any inspector would have found fault with our failure to adhere to military dress standards. Little did Harry and I, both lowly corporals, know that we were about to spend the early afternoon with the fully decked out brass of the division.

It was shortly after lunch, and we were just into our first hand. I was the dummy, and Harry was playing a properly bid and makeable small slam when a Jeep screeched to a stop on the dirt road that served the finance office. An officer in a full dress drove the Jeep, shoes shined, brass polished, his epaulets sporting railroad tracks . . . the insignia of a captain. Despite his exalted rank, exalted, at least to us, he dismounted the Jeep smartly and ran up the stairs, entering the office to the sound of scraping chairs as the finance clerks, including us bridge players, heard the cry, "Tench hut" and leapt to attention. The captain returned our salutes and barked, "At ease," and we all assumed the "at ease" position.

The captain wasted no time making his mission known, doing so with authority: "Where are Corporals Gallun and Drake?"

With a cold stab of fear in my heart—nothing good ever comes of getting singled out by an officer—nevertheless, I stepped forward and said boldly, "I'm Gallun."

Drake then admitted meekly that he was who he was. Then the captain, without ado or explanation, said, "You two men come with me."

And we followed. As we got to the Jeep, he indicated that we were to get into the back, and we did. There being no seats in the back of this Jeep, Harry and I rode on the wheel wells, bouncing along a washboard road in silence, having no idea where we were going. There was no communication from the captain, probably because the wind in the open Jeep inhibited conversation, but it occurred to me that the captain probably did not want to tell us anything either. Besides Captains rarely deign to converse with enlisted men. In any case the trip made us no wiser. Fortunately, it was a short trip because the finance office was not far from our destination, which turned out to be the big amphitheater near division headquarters.

As we drove up to the main entrance, we saw about forty Jeeps parked nearby and could hear the sound of a band tuning up inside. We dismounted our Jeep and immediately were turned over to another captain, this one being an aquaintence of mine, Captain Robert Hoff, who wore the insignia of the division commander's aide. After we went through the military formalities, Captain Hoff pleasantly invited us inside the building and into the washroom where he suggested that we might like to get cleaned up. While we did so, he explained that the former division commander, General Breidster, was visiting and reviewing the 32nd flag officers and that he had requested to see Harry and me while he was at the base. As there was no other good time for his visit with us, General Dunlop had decided to slip us into the reviewing ceremony. It was a relief that we weren't to be punished, but still, it left us in an uncomfortable environment.

When we had gotten ourselves in marginally decent shape, Captain Hoff led us into the "cage" that served for events like this one but mostly served as an indoor athletic facility. It was a big room with not much in it. On this occasion, there was a podium up front, unoccupied as we entered, a band to the right of the podium, and a group of highly decorated officers, all of the rank of captain and above, even the regimental commanders and all the headquarters' muckety-mucks, they standing in formation in front of the podium. What in the world were we here for? What would we do? The captain did not hesitate; he led us to the far right, about as far away as possible from where the officers were standing, and advised us to stand at ease. It was a bit difficult to contemplate being at ease with the lineup across the room of forty or fifty ribbon-bedecked officers of high rank eying us peons in our dirty fatigues.

We did not have to wait long. In short order, a lieutenant entered and gave a signal, and the band jumped into military music which morphed quickly into "Ruffles and Flourishes" as a group of generals entered, headed by Major General Breidster. As the group arrived at the podium, the music stopped. General Breidster looked around, first at the assembled officers, then to his left at Harry and me. Without hesitation, giving no heed to the officers, he took off in a beeline, heading straight for Harry and me. As he crossed the room, silence hung over the entire assemblage, and I'm sure that, as we were, all of those officers were wondering what was going on.

When the general reached us, he first embraced Harry and greeted him with enthusiasm, then turned and did the same with me. After that, still ignoring the officer group, he conversed casually and intimately with both of us, getting caught up on our family situations and even our reactions to our military service with the Division. This exchange went on for about five minutes, and I began to feel uncomfortable for the officers who had begun to shuffle around and move uneasily. At last, General Breidster said, almost sadly, "I guess I'll have to get on with this ceremony," and he gracefully took his leave.

We were immediately excused from the event and were driven back to our post feeling pride in our relationship with the general and gratitude for his thoughtful attention to us. It was a red-letter day for us, certainly part of what made it that was the sight of all the brass waiting for the attention we were getting from General Breidster. They must have been thinking of those immortal words of the Sundance Kid, *"Who are these guys anyway?"*

My enjoyment of this last episode came surely from excessive pride—pride premised on getting the general's attention while all those swaggering officers cooled their heels. I felt more than a pang of superiority for seeing them all waiting for us to finish our intimate conversation. Maybe I was the one with the vanity. Perhaps I needed more military training to curb my own hubris.

CHAPTER XII

The Pawnbroker

My time with the Krause Milling Company was an experience that rivaled Harvard Business School as an occasion for learning. I dived into the situation with enthusiasm and the confidence that I had a lot to contribute, but with little recognition of the nuances of decision making in the real world. The thing that had appealed to me most about this job was that of working directly for the boss. As it turned out, working for the boss, Willis Sullivan, had both merit and demerit. The good was that Sullivan was a great mentor to me, and I learned a lot about dealing with the nuances. The downside was that I would have been better off cutting my teeth on a line job. And as you shall see, I was only an incidental playing-piece in the strategy of a latter-day Machiavelli.

IN THE SPRING of 1964, I had the world by the tail. I had come to the business school with a background in the securities business, I had excelled in all of my finance classes, I was about to graduate "With Distinction," and I had a half-dozen offers from good companies, several of them investment management companies. Because practically no one did it then, it would have been a good time to go to Wall Street.

Despite the opportunities in finance and because I was hooked on the idea of manufacturing, I had come to Milwaukee for an interview with Cutler Hammer, an interview from which I expected little and got nothing. I was at Mitchell Field returning to Boston when I ran into Charlie Krause, an old schoolmate of mine from the Country Day School. In retrospect, it almost seemed that this meeting was predestined. Charlie was looking for a guy who could start an international business for the Krause Milling Company.

The Krause business was that of grinding (milling) corn and processing the resultant particles into useful materials for food and industrial use. The milling industry was one that succeeded the riverside millers of old, who then, using the power of the river, ground grains into grits and flours mostly for food. Long before 1964, the river, as the source of power, had been replaced by the electric motor. For the larger mills, of which Krause was one, access to good rail service had become critical. As I arrived on the scene, the company was processing more than twenty carloads of corn every day. While its product line was diversified, Krause was highly dependent on the breweries, who used corn grits as a partial substitute for the starch provided by barley malt. Malt, a costlier source of starch and formerly the main ingredient in beer, provided an essential enzyme for the fermentation process, but the much less-expensive corn grits could replace a significant part of the starch formerly provided by malt. In the US and Canada, almost all the breweries, that being not much more than a handful in 1964, had seized on the savings offered by employing corn as an adjunct.

At first blush, the business seemed provincial, almost archaic, and certainly not a horse to ride into the future. In addition, it was family controlled with the current heir-apparent not much older than I. It would be years, if ever, before I held a line position. Clearly, the long term opportunity was limited. The fact that the company was headquartered in Milwaukee held little attraction to me. On the surface, the opportunity did not compare with the others on my plate.

On the other hand, it was a manufacturing business, and I wanted to be a manufacturer. Besides, the international prospect was exciting, and the job would report to the CEO with the title of his assistant. A twofer! The prospect of near term of managing an international business and that of reporting directly to the boss—right out of the box! I delayed my departure and went to Krause's downtown office to have an audience with Willis Sullivan, the president and CEO.

The meeting with Bill Sullivan went well. He seemed to be a no-nonsense guy who was focused on making the most of the business. The company, while small, was quite profitable. During the period prior to his management of the company, Sullivan had cultivated high-level relationships with the Krause family, first by becoming the family lawyer (the route most used to gain control of Milwaukee family businesses during this era) and then making himself the executor of the Krause estate. Following the death of Charlie's father, he tightened his grip on the company by making himself president and then closed the deal by marrying Charlie's mother. Firmly in control of the situation and despite the carping of the deceased Mr. Krause's sisters, who were the majority but not controlling shareholders, he had run the company with a determined and intelligent hand. Talking with him, I was astonished at his industry-specific knowledge but more impressed by the depth of his general business knowledge. For me, a route to real decision-making authority was clear. In many ways, it seemed too good to be true. I have since learned that anything that seems so usually is.

I compared this opportunity with a couple of others that had resulted in firm offers, and the Krause deal, other than their pitiful financial offer, took the day. My decision was based on my preference for manufacturing, the excitement of international business, and the proposed proximity to Willis Sullivan. It was a week later that I accepted their offer.

The night before I began my new job, Charlie and Rozzie Krause invited us to dinner at their house. It was to be a cordial affair aimed at making us comfortable with my new relationship with Charlie, who had become president of the company that very day. To the contrary, it was a somewhat alarming experience, seeing Charlie discipline his children in the mode of Vince Lombardi, treating them all alike, "like dogs"—the children fetching his slippers and responding to many commands with a military "yes, sir." Even Kathy, who is generally more tolerant of deviant behavior than I, commented on the significance to me of Charlie's seemingly dictatorial conduct. I responded to her concerns by pointing out, naively perhaps, that I was working for Mr. Sullivan, not Charlie,

The first day of work was one of introduction to all of Krause's administrative employees and of spending some time with my peers in the second level of management. Several of this cadre warned me of the impending visit of Willis Sullivan Junior, whom they referred to as Goonyer, not only because he was the beneficiary of nepotism but also because he used his familial relationship as a weapon. I was assured that even on this my first day, he would "request" my becoming a member of "Tympanuchus Cupido Pinnatus," the society to save the prairie chicken, of which his father had been president for many years. Every member of the Krause management belonged, and I was assured that there was no way for me to avoid this responsibility.

Goonyer arrived on schedule in the afternoon] but not before I had decided on an independent course. When he opened the conversation with his prairie chicken gambit, I, having prepared myself for this moment, responded that I had limited charitable funds and that, in my opinion, the prairie chicken had been saved. I would not be joining. Goonyer gasped and pronounced gravely, "Dad won't like this!"

I accepted that prophecy, and he left. I never heard a thing about it from "Dad," and I only joined the Prairie Chicken Society on the day that I left the company. My courageous refusal did much to establish my bona fides with the second-level management group.

Of course, I spent some time on that first day with my new boss, Sullivan Senior, as he was called by those Krause employees who didn't call him "Dad." My instincts about him seemed right on the money. From day one, he was willing, if not pleased, to take time with me and to answer my questions about the company and the milling industry. He shared with me confidential financial information and, seemingly without artifice, talked about the strengths and even the weaknesses of the company as they related to our much-bigger competitors. The connection he established with me seemed to have all the potential I had hoped for.

Later in our relationship, he occasionally invited me to watch him address, over the telephone, issues which required his serious attention as well as his dramatic and, sometimes, even nasty posturing. He showed me how he could change his demeanor to suit the situation and gain his desired response, freely using fear and intimidation as his weapons of choice. He thoroughly enjoyed these sessions. Once, when he had completed a particularly unpleasant lambasting, this time to his own patsy, the president of The Corn Miller's Federation, he put down the phone, winked at me, and burst into hearty laughter, exclaiming proudly, "I'll bet he won't do that again!" More important than his theatrics, he played well for me the role of mentor. There was a lot to learn from him.

One day, Sullivan Senior (who had invited me to call him Bill) explained to me the charts that decorated all the walls of his office, charts which recorded the company's net position in corn, both in futures contracts and in grain, all such ownership juxtaposed against commitments to customers. These charts, which he had maintained for almost ten years, also recorded the amount of the net corn position of the company, together with the value of that position. Only one chart of this group showed a serious departure from regularity, and that chart showed that Krause had had a large short position for a brief period, the fall of 1962, when corn prices were climbing precipitously. The accumulated losses ran well off the page.

One of Bill's pivotal innovations a few years prior had been to convince the major customers as well as his competitors that there was a day in the fall where corn prices would be at the bottom because of the press of the grain coming to harvest and onto the market. While this assertion had little merit in reality, it was, nevertheless, persuasive to most of the largest customers and was a good tool for getting under control the brutal competition among corn processors. Customers would book their annual requirements on "booking day" with the six major corn-processing competitors. The desired result was that the corn products bought and sold on this designated day would be removed from the competitive arena for an entire year. This scheme had provided stability in a market that had suffered often from destructive competition, a phenomenom that occurs in industries that possess, as was the case with Krause, a high fixed investment in plant and equipment together with large throughput volumes which earned only modest incremental margins. The "booking day" pricing device could have been, if one holds a conspiratorial view, the linchpin of a price-fixing strategy. More importantly, for my education, the invention and implementation of this procedure represented a powerful demonstration of Senior's capacity to persuade and to lead, not just his company, but the industry as well.

That was all well and good until booking day for 1962 happened to fall on the same day that the Cuban missile crisis came to light. Before this crisis became public knowledge, Krause had sold, as had the five other major millers, many millions of bushels of corn, expecting to cover their "short" right away in the futures markets. They had expected to buy futures at equal or lower prices than those on which they had predicated the sale of their corn-based products. The charts disclosed in vivid relief the disaster that they had visited upon themselves. Responding to my questions, Bill described how he had reacted to this calamity. He recalled that there was no trading in grains for that entire week because the price went up the "daily limit" each morning at the opening. Cash corn, that is physical corn for immediate delivery, was available but only at prices that would have bankrupted the company. So Bill girded his loins and waited. His publicly owned competitors, General Foods and Quaker Oats, did cover their shorts with cash corn at inflated prices, doing so because their losses would not be limited by bankruptcy. Their cost of covering exceeded the net worth of their corn-milling business at the time. They both later exited the business because of what they saw as extraordinary risk. At the end of the week the Cuban situation was resolved, and the following week Krause was able to cover its short position at no loss.

Learning the Business

As I settled into my new job, Bill Sullivan instructed me to create my own eighteen-month training program to familiarize myself with the business, doing so with a great range of freedom, subject only to his approval. At the end of that period I was expected to be able to operate and manage a milling business in a foreign country. What I established for my tutorial was similar to an apprenticeship in each functional area of the business, departmental tenures to range from one to three months. The program had a dimension of consulting in that at the end of my term in each department, I would do an analysis of the functional area with recommendations for changes.

My first department was sales. Initially, that involved traveling with Charlie and with other sales executives. During my month in sales I learned that selling grits to breweries was a lot about playing gin rummy with brewmasters. They were good at what they did, the brewmasters were, that being playing gin rummy. While it seemed that playing for high stakes was mandatory for me as Charlie's fellow traveler, it became apparent eventually that losses were not an allowable expense. I had some expensive lessons at cards as the brewmasters licked their chops and showed no mercy.

On my trips with Charlie, the days were filled with appointments, which were tightly scheduled with high-level employees, those who might influence the buying decision. That was called in-depth selling. The evenings were spent entertaining some of the top executives of the brewery, usually the president and often his wife as well. Between travel, socializing at every level at the brewery and long evenings of eating, drinking and conversation, every day was a long one; and a week of this activity was exhausting. Besides, as I was to learn later in Brazil, Charlie was a thoroughly enervating companion.

Ah, but there was one significant learning experience that I got in the sales area, perhaps this one was even a twofer. I spent much time with a sales executive, Gerry Behrend. Gerry, whose title was manager of inside sales, dealt directly with customers and their delivery problems, doing so with aplomb. In a typical instance, a customer had, through inbound testing, discovered at least one bug in an inbound inspection and called angrily to inform Gerry of this catastrophic deviation from the acceptable. I watched him coolly defuse the offended customer and then divert this bug-infested carload of grits to a railroad siding. Then he called another customer who was in desperate need of grits and teased him with a series of short phone calls, indicating that he was looking for a car scheduled into one of the other breweries, a car that he might steal to solve this customer's problem. He would carry his fiction for hours before finding a car that he could divert, one that might even have a "minor" bug problem. The customer would be licking Gerry's shoes by the time he was sure that he was going to get his grits. He did not really have any objection to a few bugs; after all, you didn't pay extra for the protein. It was this kind of stuff that Gerry did intensively all day long. He knew the corn trade in all of its subtle nuances, but what was more important, he understood the role of theater in his job.

While I was with Gerry, a period that lasted more than a week, he told me that he was looking for another job, the reason being that, when he asked for a raise, he had been told by Charlie that he had reached the maximum earning potential for what he was doing. About two months later Gerry, having found a better job, gave notice. Almost immediately, Charlie realized that replacing Gerry's skill and experience was not going to be easy, so negotiations were proffered. When early offers had no effect, Charlie pulled in a young salesman and put him under Gerry's wing for training during the balance of Gerry's time at Krause. When the time came for Gerry to leave, the trainee still looked inadequate for the complexities of the job, or maybe the job had come to look tougher than Charlie had thought. Suddenly, Gerry decided to stay on. I learned later that his new pay level was almost twice his previous salary. What did I take from this exposure? I had learned a lot about stagecraft in selling, but equally important, I had learned not to expect pay increases without having a strong negotiation position.

During this period, I spent time with the top salesmen in the company, both traveling and making calls with them and occasionally lunching in Milwaukee. The era was one that still tolerated the two-martini lunch. Even so, the company policy manual frowned upon such behavior, saying, and I quote: "Should you consume alcoholic beverages at lunch, you shall report to the office manager upon returning, and he will give you the afternoon off."

Despite this proscription, when in the office the salesmen (other than Charlie) , regularly had a couple of pops at noon. When I was with them, so did I. But we always played according to the rules and reported our indiscretions as required. However, we were never given the afternoon off.

After sales came the traffic department, where I worked for Al Carr. Traffic management was like a complex mathematical problem with big money involved. Traffic was responsible for controlling the transportation cost for both inbound and outbound freight. To minimize railroad charges, one had to match favorably the origins of corn with destinations for product. Well, not the corn itself, the corn being fungible, but the inbound freight bills could be used to reduce the outbound shipping costs. All of this offsetting had to be done in accordance with the latest railroad tariffs that were constructed with only a modicum of logic. I have no doubt that today that one man could perform the traffic role much more efficiently and effectively on a desktop computer than Al did with a four- or five-person department. To complicate the traffic function further, the actual inbound freight bill had to be attached to the shipping documents to get credit for the inbound cost. Al's solution to this complex problem was to categorize inbound bills into about ten files which provided favorable rates for a group of destinations and then to apply bills manually using the traffic clerks' best judgment as to which bill in the file would be appropriate for a particular shipment. You don't want to know any more about this stuff; suffice it to say there was a pile of money to save here with an annual freight bill well into seven figures. At the time, the possibilities interested me greatly; it was like putting together a three-dimensional puzzle.

As we got into winter, Charlie Krause made a deal to buy from Archer Daniels Midland a grain sorghum milling company in St. Joe, Missouri. Al Carr asked me to accompany him on a due diligence trip to St. Joe, to assist him in valuing the inventory of freight bills, they representing a not insignificant part of the purchase price. I was glad to go, but I soon learned that my value on this expedition was not much greater than that of a clerk. I did get to sit in on the management caucuses but had nothing to contribute despite the fact that I was the assistant to the CEO. So you can imagine my delight when I was called out of such a meeting to take a call from Sullivan Senior's secretary, Angela, who informed me that I was urgently needed back in Milwaukee. When I smugly reported this message verbatim to the management group with whom I had been meeting, a message that I thought established my bona fides, I noticed a sneer of amusement pulling at a couple of faces in the room. I briefly wondered what that was about but let it go. When I got to the office in Milwaukee late that afternoon, almost no one was there except for Angela, who told me the news. The mill workers had gone on strike, and the management employees were already at work running the mill. My shift had already begun, and I was to get to the mill office in work clothes, ASAP. The lightbulb went on: I knew what those snickers in St. Joe were all about.

That evening was memorable, the first of many new experiences. I found myself in a boxcar at the business end of a "portable conveyor." This conveyor received hundred-pound bags of cornmeal from a chute from the bagging room that was a level up from the railroad siding. With a mechanical assist, I was able to drive the discharge end of the conveyer through the door of a boxcar and right on into it. The conveyor could adapt to the right angle turns involved in covering this distance and was long enough to reach either end of the car. The last six feet of the conveyor had an elevation adjustment that allowed the operator to launch each bag into its proper position. When the bottom levels of a row were filled, and the elevation control was raised above horizontal, the belt of that part of the conveyor would accelerate so that you could literally shoot the one hundred-pound bags into their resting place, even to the top of the car, which was more than ten feet high. If you knew how to operate the equipment, it was not heavy work because, even as you had to guide the bags manually, still the machinery did most of the heavy lifting.

Of course, there was a lot that could go wrong, and it sure did that night. Bags all over the place and the conveyor shut down while I had to move the errant bags into their place under my own power. Hundred-pound bags of cornmeal are *not* a piece of cake. At the end of the shift, I was exhausted, and I had not quite loaded one rail car.

After my initial ineptitude I quickly got the hang of loading cornmeal bags into freight cars. Within a week I was loading three cars a night; with 1,000 bags in a carload that was 3,000 bags or about six per minute. Having mastered the power equipment, I wasn't even tired at the end of a shift. For much of the strike period I worked the evening shift in the plant, from four until midnight, and the next day put in three or four hours at the office, helping out in the traffic department. When bonus time came at the end of the year, I thought my diligence would be rewarded; but, alas, when my bonus came, it was just the pitiful $1,000 which was a guaranteed component of my initial pay package.

All the administrative employees in the company worked hard in the mill for several months, and together, we brought production up to levels approaching the prestrike output. During this phase the worst duty we had was the periodic cleaning of the mill. Cleaning meant almost military cleanliness requirements because of the potential danger arising from dust on surfaces in the mill. The danger would emerge initially as a small explosion of dust ignited by sparks from any source, most likely an electric motor. This detonation would jar the entire building and release from surfaces throughout the mill any ambient dust into the interior of the building. That dust, together with the flame from the initial blast, could be the source of a secondary and much-larger explosion that could destroy the entire mill and kill most of the people inside. This stuff happens in all kinds of mills, and there have been many such tragedies in the U.S. in my lifetime. As a result cleaning the mill made for a long Saturday, and it was not over until the plant manager, having completed a white glove inspection, was satisfied.

As the strike continued, I spent a few weeks unloading corn from boxcars, another esoteric and mechanically assisted operation. This activity was accomplished by first breaking up, with a mechanized wrecking tool, the two-by-six boards which retained the corn inside the boxcar, then allowing the corn to run out into a pit below the rail car and finally removing the remaining piles of corn at either end of the car with a "power shovel." It was this last operation that was most difficult and time-consuming because to work the shovel, which was just a two-foot square board attached in its center to a cable, one had to climb unassisted to the top of the pile of corn remaining at each end of the car, an ascent of about ten, maybe twelve, feet. This climb was performed with all the frustration of Sisyphus what with the instability of the loose corn which turned the ten foot climb into a major assent. When one finally reached the top, he would insert the shovel into the corn, activate the cable by jerking it, and then "ride" the shovel all the way to the door of the car. A problem of this system was that, if you inserted the shovel at too shallow an angle, the cable would make you and the shovel dive down into and under the pile; and you would just get dragged through the pile of corn without bringing much of it with you. At the other extreme, if you went at too vertical an angle, the shovel would just rotate out of the corn, and you would be pulled down with the shovel on top of the corn, bringing with you no corn at all. You had to get the board in at precisely the correct angle. Once you got the hang of it, it was great fun. Nevertheless, it was dirty and always exhausting work. Imagine being dragged through a pile of dusty corn or then climbing a steep pile of corn—one step forward and two steps back. You could readily understand the Sisyphean agony arising from his pushing his boulder up a hill just to have it roll back so he can push it up again.

In early February, the company began to hire strikebreakers, or "scabs," as they were known colloquially. This beginning gradually marked the end of management's participation at the plant, but it was a while before my replacement was in place.

About this time, I had made a discovery in the traffic department that we were very short of what we had come to call "cancellation billing." Cancellation billing, a designation given by Al Carr, was a category of freight bills that had little or no value for offsetting outbound freight bills. Most of these bills originated in Wisconsin or northern Illinois, which, because of their proximity to the markets in Milwaukee and Chicago, had not much inbound freight cost as a component of their price. The reason we called it cancellation billing was that once a year in the spring, grain processors were obliged to adjust their inventory of freight bills to equal the amount of corn held in inventory. It was certain that there were more freight bills than inventory because of process shrinkage, water loss, and truck shipments out, the total shrinkage probably accumulating during the year to about 10 to 20 percent of the corn held in storage. When the cancellation date came around in the spring, we wanted to have our excess bills represented by valueless billing. What I had discovered is that, due to inattention or oversight, we currently had not much low value billing in the inventory of freight bills, not enough to cover the shrinkage in corn inventory. In fact, this shortage was more than a million bushels. Al took this discovery to the board of directors and proposed that we buy a million bushels from appropriate corn origins, mostly to be from Wisconsin and northern Illinois. The board approved this purchase, recognizing that with purchased corn already inbound to cover processing requirements, there still existed excess storage capacity for a million bushels or so. However, the board wondered how we were going to unload it, given the fact that our day capacity for unloading was already committed. Al suggested a night shift using strikebreakers. But what about supervision, which was not readily available? When this problem came back to the traffic department, I volunteered for the job, thinking that some supervisory activity in the plant would look good on my résumé. About a month after this decision was made, I found myself running a night shift at the grain elevator.

In the interim, I had moved to the grain-buying department and got my feet wet buying corn at the Wisconsin Grain Exchange, under the tutelage of B. L. (Bun) Schwartz, vice president for purchasing, a loyal and extremely well paid employee, who was one day to turn state's evidence against his boss, Charlie. Right away, Bun turned me loose to do the buying of corn that came into Milwaukee, most of which filled the bill as cancellation billing. I bought almost everything available over the next couple of months and was treated like a king at the exchange. Indeed, it seemed like I had become royalty. When I made my daily entrance to the exchange in midmorning, all the local grain dealers would rush to my person and would compete all at once for the privilege of my attention.

Probably because I had become important to him, the Cargill representative snuggled close to me and casually one day suggested that he might show me how to make some money doing grain futures spreads. He was aware that I might have a conflict of interest in trading corn, so he avoided corn in his suggestions. (I learned later that Krause had a prohibition for employees against trading in any commodities.)

Despite this proscription, I did, over the next few months, about ten trades, all of which were counterintuitive; even as these trades made no sense to me, every one of which worked out exactly as predicted. My lesson here was that the real power in the commodity futures markets, at least then, rested with the large merchants, whose interest in the cash markets dwarfed the size of the then futures markets. Since the cash markets were pegged to the futures markets (as in ten cents over the July future), the Cargills of the world would find it profitable to manipulate the futures markets to ensure their profitability in the cash markets. I made a lot more money on spreads during this period than I did from my salary. Following my Cargil advisor's advice, I did not have even one unprofitable trade.

In early April, I was back on the night shift supervising my own crew of five scabs unloading and storing twelve rail cars of corn per night. The studied engineering rate was twelve cars, but we started with three and worked our way up while my charges learned the ropes. In a week or so we were hitting the studied rates, and I thought we could go higher, but the rail siding only allowed for twelve cars. It was apparent that my workers could produce more, and increasingly they were dogging it to avoid other work that I found for them when we finished early. Mainly out of curiosity I wanted to explore their potential for productivity, so I suggested that if we finished early, they could spend the rest of the shift playing cards. Production rose slowly at first, slowly, I think, because they were testing me to see if the deal would hold. When I joined in the card game, they began to trust. Within a couple of weeks, we were regularly completing the unloading in four hours. The studied rate was a joke!

The tour of night shift duty ended in late May, and I went back to full-time purchasing for a while. Then in July, after spending four months or so at purchasing, it was time to go to work for Goonyer in the engineering department. I spent some early time here trying to persuade Goonyer that some of the production standards in the mill, starting with the unloading rates, might be a little loose, and perhaps I could get involved with one of his engineers in a new rate study program. Goonyer showed no interest in this idea; he had other fish to fry, or maybe to catch, he being a real outdoorsman and a fisherman who was frequently absent from the office, particularly on nice days. So I occupied myself looking at studies of labor-saving machinery that had been or were being considered by the company. One particular project caught my eye, and I spent considerable time looking at it. To wit:

There was an eight-story building next to the main mill that housed a facility called a cold roll milling facility. This facility took large corn grits from the main corn mill and put them into hoppers on the top floor of the cold rolling structure. From there, they were dropped into large cookers, where they were cooked in batches for a time, and then dropped into pressing mills, each of which consisted of a very hot roller juxtaposed against a cold roller, hence the cold roll mill. The output from this rolling process was a continuous sheet of corn of an appearance like crude yellow paper.

Next these sheets dropped through a series of cutting mills which reduced the corn sheets which came from the rollers to a fine or coarse flour, depending on the extent of the milling performed. Finally, the flour was airlifted up to the eighth floor for a second drop through the plant. The flour was sifted to precise sizes at several levels coming down through the plant to make a processed cornmeal that had many industrial applications, including importantly: binders used in explosives and foundry sands and for human consumption in both food and drugs, such as breakfast cereals and Alka Seltzer. There was an amazing number of uses for this precooked corn flour, perhaps as many as a hundred. What drew my attention was that the engineering department recognized that one or two extruders could replace this entire complicated process, building and all. The cost of the extruders was insignificant when compared with the cost of the building and outfitting a mill, but more important than the savings on original investment was the elimination of labor and overhead. The report that recommended this approach included the information that all of Krause's competitors had abandoned their cold roll mills in favor of the extruder. Wow! Here was an opportunity to for me to make a *real* contribution.

I spent a few weeks digging into the files and talking to people who would have had something to say about the decision to buy the extruder. No one knew why it had been turned down. That is: no one at all, even including Goonyer, who had championed the idea with his father! So I wrote an extensive report, mostly parroting the prior work. When I proudly presented it to Sullivan Senior, he gave me a dismissive look, but he did offer an explanation, albeit a somewhat implausible one, as to why he rejected this proposal. His reasoning was that the cold roll plant represented a replacement value of several million. If anyone could show him what to do with this valuable asset when the extruder replaced its capacity, Sullivan would consider buying an extruder. Not a thinking man's conclusion! This heresy defied everything I knew about manufacturing. Quite obviously one needs to upgrade one's methods if one can get a favorable return on new investments. Here was an investment opportunity with an extraordinary return. Discarding obsolete equipment is part of the process and does not represent real cost. I argued these points with Bill, but there was no way to win this argument against his well tested and -entrenched position.

After leaving Bill's office, I pondered what I had heard. Sullivan Senior had always shown himself to be a more-than-competent businessman, and I had seen how he had a knack for getting to the bottom of any business decision. But here he was mouthing the words of a neophyte in defending a significant and clearly bad decision. It did not make any sense, and I would not understand the real basis for his decision until after I had left the company. For the time, it was an enigma wrapped in secrecy.

There were still a couple of departments that I had not experienced, as in accounting and administration, but it was deemed time for me to wrap up my training and get on with international business. I began to write up a consulting report on what I saw as major opportunities in the company while Sullivan Senior began to introduce me to his Washington contacts. My consulting report was addressed to Charlie, who was now the chief operating officer. It addressed many of the issues that I mentioned here and made major recommendations about organization. It did not mince words in criticizing some company imperfections. Charlie's only comment at the time was: "You sure have balls."

Years later, he told me that they had adopted a number of my organizational ideas, not because of my report but because they had come to these decisions in the normal course of business. Nevertheless, he did admit that he was more impressed with my recommendations years later than he had been at the time.

Getting into International Business

Early the next year, Sullivan Senior forwarded to me a "Request For Proposal" (RFP) from the State Department, which was looking for companies which were involved in basic food processing and were willing to consider making a foreign investment aimed at improving the nutrition of peoples who were suffering from malnutrition, particularly protein malnutrition. Several million dollars would be made available for market and feasibility studies for the grantees that were to be selected for this program. Even though it was an incredibly timely opportunity, and one that was right on the money in terms of Krause's plans, it seemed like a long shot to me. Nevertheless, Sullivan Senior seemed confident that we could play here, so with his encouragement, I went to work on it forthwith.

After acquainting myself with the RFP and spending some time with my boss discussing a strategy for getting this grant, I began my education on the subject of protein malnutrition. This education was mostly a function of reading scientific journals and treatises that had recently been written because of the Johnson administration's interest in the subject. Sullivan Senior had already read most of this stuff, and he provided me with my assigned reading list. It turned out that he knew personally several of the most prominent authors. Through discussions with him, I came to understand that he saw clearly how Krause could participate.

But first, the science of malnutrition, as I came to understand it: Protein is made up of fifteen essential amino acids. The protein will be used as protein in the human body only to the extent that the most limiting amino acid is present. For example, if you had a perfectly balanced protein except that the tryptophan was short by 25 percent, then only 75 percent of the protein would be nutritionally available as body-building protein to the consumer. As it happens, corn is a fairly well-balanced protein except that it is quite short of lysine and mildly short of a couple of other amino acids. As it turned out, soybeans and milk were mutually complementary additions to corn, and these three, mixed in the proper proportion, delivered an almost perfect protein, thus, maximizing the value of all the protein in the mix. All this information can be explained, as it is here, in a couple of sentences; but given the volume of material recently written on the subject and the theoretical disputes pressed by scientific factions, it took me almost a month to get up to speed.

My final exam on the subject was in Philadelphia, where I visited the company's nutritional consultant, Doctor Sid Cantor. Sid, about sixty-five at the time and the proud possessor of a PhD in chemistry, was shaped a bit like a pear, sported a well-maintained gray mustache and thinning gray hair. He was pleasant enough, but he did wear his academic achievements on his sleeve. Dr. Cantor spent a day with me, fine-tuning my understanding of these simple nutritional concepts, but, what was more important, he clued me in on who were the key players in the nutrition field in Washington. After Sid, it seemed that I was ready to go to Washington to lobby for this grant.

Through Cantor and Sullivan's friends, I was put in contact with mid-level employees at the State Department who worked for Jonathan McCabe, deputy undersecretary of state for development. McCabe appeared to be in charge of the grant program. The people I met initially were deeply involved in that program and seemed to be more knowledgeable about Krause than one would have expected. After a couple of trips to Washington and subsequent to meeting quite a few people at the State Department, I was allowed into the office of McCabe himself, who was highly approachable and seemingly friendly to my cause. I was surprised at the cordiality of my reception at this level of government, recognizing that I was a mid-level executive from a rather small company. I began to believe that I was becoming an effective diplomat. I would learn the truth about my good luck only years later.

In my meeting with McCabe he suggested that he would provide an introduction to Dr. Aaron Altschul. I was aware that Altschul was considered to be the high priest in the administration in the fight against kwashiorkor, the scientific name for protein malnutrition. He, the special assistant to the secretary of agriculture for malnutrition, was highly regarded in nutritional circles. I had been told at State that he carried important weight in the selection process for the research grant that I was chasing. My meeting with him was cordial, and he was very interested in the goals of the Krause Milling Company.

I was again amazed at my ability, as a neophyte, to deal with these high-ranking government officials. In three visits to Washington I had established connections with the intellectual leaders of the "Food for Peace" movement. As I flew back to Milwaukee after meeting Dr. Altschul, I was feeling pretty good about my accomplishments.

During the spring, I made a few more trips to Washington to reinforce these relationships, to lobby with other officials, and generally to build connections into the bureaucracy, as well as to gain insight into what our RFP needed to contain. The Washington bureaucracy was very receptive, reinforcing my belief that I had important diplomatic skills. With the background I had attained through study and these meetings, I was able to draft an adequate RFP by the end of April. We filed it with the Department of State in early May.

Sometime in June Krause was selected along with Quaker Oats as a grantee for this program representing the corn milling industry. Another amazing success! According to the provisions of the grant, Krause we to select a country anywhere in the world in which we could envision ourselves setting up a corn-processing operation. The program would fund essentially all of our due diligence. The grant would fund my salary for the duration of our inquiry, consulting resources as we deemed necessary, market research, product development, travel and living expenses, and the like, up to a million dollars or so. In addition, we would have no responsibility to perform, beyond the submission of a detailed report on our findings. We would be required to share our findings with the government; no funds would be forthcoming until we submitted a required but as yet undefined report.

To my surprise, I was assigned the responsibility of determining where we might choose to establish our business. After the involvement of Sullivan Senior and Dr. Cantor in guiding me through the grant process, I had assumed that there would be heavy involvement of others in determining where we would want to locate. I struggled with the issue for several months without any input from Sullivan, the board, or anyone else at Krause. Not having such direction, I did a fair amount of research on the malnourished countries of the world, including India, Brazil, Mexico, and several African countries. In the end I selected Brazil, ostensibly because it appeared that the Brazilians were beginning to emerge from the third world and would provide favorable commercial markets for other Krause products. Further, it appeared in the available literature that they raised and ate more corn than most other then developing nations. It appeared to me that there was a confluence of interest in this country between Krause's objectives and those of the U.S. government. Perhaps most important, Brazil, as a culture, looked understandable to me, having a Western orientation; and even as important, it looked like a fun place to work, Rio de Janeiro and all that it might represent, for recharging batteries on weekends. My recommendation was accepted without dissent or, as nearly as I could see, without any real discussion. We indicated this decision to the State Department, and they accepted it without comment.

My main agenda for the summer and into the fall was to learn all I could about Brazil, while taking about sixty hours of Berlitz to become at ease with the language. I spent considerable time interviewing consultants who could get me to the right places and people in Brazil. With Bill Sullivan's advice and approval, I hired a Washington lawyer, Haskell Hoffenberg, who had had a long experience in Brazil, having lived there for a dozen years with a Brazilian wife and family. Not only was he well connected in Rio and São Paulo society and business circles, but he seemed to have a creative flair as well, one which I thought would be useful in adapting our business skills to Brazil. Finally, I prepared a due diligence plan for internal use as well as to meet a requirement of our grant. This plan involved identification of the corn-eating population in Brazil, particularly in central and southern Brazil, testing the acceptability of enhanced protein corn products, and determining the markets for traditional Krause corn products in the industrial sector, this last area seeming to be the most important.

My first trip to Brazil took place at the height of the Brazilian summer, in January of 1967, with Mr. Hoffenberg, whom I had come to know as "Hack," in tow. It was planned to be a three-week trip which would provide not only an occasion to learn about the use of corn in the Brazilian diet but, more importantly, the availability in Brazil of markets which we had been serving in the United States, especially markets for brewer's grits, foundry binders, explosives, etc. There were twenty or so products that made up the bulk of Krause's sales, and I believed that some of these would provide meaningful opportunities to sell to industrial users as we were doing in the U.S. markets.

When Hack and I arrived at Galeão Airport in Rio de Janeiro, we deplaned about 300 yards from the terminal and had to walk in 100 degree heat and 98 percent humidity to get to the terminal. By the time I reached the air-conditioned terminal, I was sweating in such profusion that almost my entire suit was soaked through and had turned black from its original dark green color. This introduction to the Brazilian climate was auspicious; I was soon to learn that, as often as not, air-conditioning was absent in the business environment. Transportation, whether by cab or train and sometimes even by airplane, was au natural. Three weeks hence when I got back to Milwaukee, the three summer suits, which I had had dry cleaned five times each, would be in such bad shape from odor and sweat stains that Kathy threw them away immediately.

Hack and I got into a cab and took the forty-minute trip to our Rio hotel, the Leme Palace. This pretty good hotel was set on the Leme Beach, which shares with the Copacabana Beach the first bay west of Guanabara Bay, the large bay that was originally designated as the "River of January." The hotel was appointed in a modern style, constructed of steel, concrete, and glass with details in varnished wood. It was sited across the street from the beach on Avenida Atlantica, which traversed the entire bay, spanning the districts of both Leme and Copacabana, about two miles, its full length festooned with Rio's famed mosaic tile promenade running between the beach and the street. The Leme-Copacabana area was the epicenter of the Brazilian culture and a Mecca for tourism, commerce, as well as a plethora of deviant activities.

When we arrived at the hotel, we learned that because of flooding which had destroyed a hydroelectric installation north of Rio, there would be daily blackouts rotating through the city that in the vicinity of the Leme Palace would start at 8:00 p.m. and run for eight hours every night. In a way, this timing turned out to be a blessing because the air-conditioning, which did exist at the Leme, would be off only during the hours of darkness. Then, more good luck! Our rooms were on the third floor, so the inconvenience of not having elevator service in the evening would not be great.

We spent the first week in Rio meeting with government officials, to whom we had letters of introduction from Washington, meeting Hack's contacts who might become our partners, exploring the favelas (slums) whose inhabitants might become our customers, and looking into businesses in Rio which could become industrial customers. Most importantly, to me at least, I had arranged a meeting with the president of Brazil's leading brewery and expected this meeting to give us an entre into a familiar industry. I was optimistic about this visit because the brewery had been using rice as an adjunct. I believed that the president could be moved by the considerable savings a switch to corn would provide. And the brewery, a large one even by American standards, would make a significant customer for Krause. It seemed to me that this call would be the most important contact of this trip—probably the crucial element of our business plan.

While he was cordial and seemingly interested in my presentation, at the end of our meeting at the brewery it was painfully clear that the president was not interested in changing any component of their popular beer for the savings such a change would contribute. The Schlitz management could have taken a good lesson from this guy when they contemplated continuous brewing fifteen years later. WHat I took away from this experience is that you do not alter your processes to save a few cents on production costs when you are number one in your marketplace!

Forays into other potential users of corn products would prove to be equally unpromising. Both here and later in São Paulo and other cities in the golden triangle, our inquiries would lead us to the conclusion that the industrial base in Brazil in 1967 was just too small to support a corn processing operation in Krause's model.. For example the foundry industry, an important user of Krause's industrial binder products, would prove to be no more important in all of Brazil than was the foundry business just in the state of Wisconsin. While Hack and I made a few worthwhile contacts and established good relations with government officials on this first visit, our major finding was that the commercial opportunities were limited.

In the course of our calling on government officials, Hack and I became friendly with a forty-something highly placed bureaucrat in the Brazilian equivalent of our FDA, and he invited us to join him on the coming Sunday at the beach in front of the famed Copacabana Palace Hotel. He told us to look for his large multicolored umbrella, and he would be there with some "friends." We did so with high expectations and found him with a bevy of bikini-clad beauties, ranging from about age ten to perhaps twenty-one. He introduced us to all of them, and we settled in to see what this scene was all about. It eventually became clear through observation that these young women belonged to him. As he later explained, they joined the entourage at ten or so, and he nurtured them until they were ripe for the plucking at sixteen or seventeen. They generally stuck around until they found a more permanent relationship. Apparently there was neither law nor opprobrium against this practice. In truth, it was quite common and was carried on by easily recognized public and private officials in plain sight. Indeed, in front of the Copacabana Palace, the luxury old hotel that dominated the beach scene, I observed several similar gatherings.

That Sunday evening Sid Cantor arrived, and Hack and I waited for him at the hotel. His plane was due to arrive around four, and we expected him at the hotel around five. We waited for his arrival in the lobby bar, which gave us a full vision of the front desk as well as a vantage for people watching. He finally showed up at seven thirty, looking completely bedraggled and wiped out by the heat, his traveling clothes soaked with sweat as ours had been. We invited him to have a drink with us, but he demurred, pleading exhaustion. Then he had a difficult time at the desk and after an excessive clerical delay, got a room at the top, floor seventeen. We walked with him to the elevator and then, at the very moment we reached it, the lights went out. The last we saw of Sid that night was him going up the stairs carrying a candle while a bellman led the way carrying his bags. Thirty-four flights.

Amazingly, Sid was back strong the next day despite his age and the ravages of the trip and the climb. With him, we spent the next day and a half visiting the intellectual nutritionists in the academic community and government. We saw lots of posturing in the scientific community and from Sid as well. Then we flew to São Paulo where we looked into the local corn-processing facilities in the surrounding area. Where we found them, these *fuba* factories were very primitive; and the selling price of fuba seemed to defy, on the low side, any economics that we could understand. To make things worse for Krause, there were no cleanliness standards for operating these facilities, nor any taxes paid to any level of government. They seemed to operate wholly outside the legal marketplace, a context that/ would not be available to us. In addition, it was difficult to get a handle on how much corn was really moving into the highly populated commercial triangle created by Rio, São Paulo, and Belo Horizonte, the region in which we expected to operate. From the small amount of shelf space allotted to fuba in the wide spectrum of marketplaces we visited, it appeared that corn in the center of Brazil did not represent a significant portion of the diet, certainly nothing close to a nutritionally significant part of the diet, even in the poorest areas.

With these concerns, we used the last day of Dr. Cantor's visit to visit the poverty pockets that surround São Paulo, including the vast *favela* that existed in the large São Paulo city dump. Incredibly, this dump was the home for tens of thousands of fugitives from the poverty in the north of the country. We had believed that because of the transient nature of this favela, it would give us a good sampling of the broader food culture in Brazil. In all of our visits on this first trip, we were unable to identify any support for my projections of corn as a key element in the Brazilian diet.

During our visits to São Paulo, we stayed at the Samambaia Hotel, a modern hotel in the center of the city. At that time, the population of São Paulo was as much as 4,000,000, but the city had a distinctly small-town feeling. In contrast to my later visits after the turn of the century, one could feel perfectly safe on the streets, and the businesses we visited were often within walking distance of our hotel. Even the night life was convenient and accessible on foot. There were few good restaurants at the time, but there were a plethora of nightspots, many serving as a venue for commercial women.

Perhaps the most famous bordello in Brazil then and for many years thereafter was a large hall called La Licorne that was just around the corner from the Samambaia. The architecture of the place was functional, with booths around the outside perimeter of an oval shaped promenade and tables in the open area in the center of this large strolling space. The promenade was trod by some of the most beautiful young women in Brazil. Most of these had come from the poor north, where even a beautiful woman had little hope. They were in São Paulo to do business, but what was more important, they had come to this place to find a husband. The La Licorne was the Mecca for both objectives but only for those who could compete—and the competition was severe. The young women walked slowly around the promenade, usually engrossed in talking to a companion or two, but actively searching for any interest from their audience. The slightest eye contact could be construed as an invitation and when recognized, would result in a deferential approach to the source of the invitation. The women were always available to sit for drinks and conversation and often were persuaded to leave with a patron. Despite its openly notorious function, La Licorne maintained a highly gracious environment and was heavily attended by the São Paulo business community as well as by international businessmen, who often carried on their dealings openly with their associates while the attending women chatted among themselves.

After visiting La Licorne on our first night in São Paulo, Hack took Sid and me to a few of his favorite places in that city. He referred to one of these places with reference to the owner, whom he had titled the "Stone Lady." She imported for resale from all over Brazil, rocks of various types which bore semiprecious and even precious gems. In the process of finding these stones, she had also run across a number of interesting fossils including trilobites and ancient fish from the seas that had covered some of the high plains of Brazil. It was the like of these fossils that played an important part of the evidence that Brazil had been conjoined with Africa a few eons ago. Sid and I each bought both ancient fish and trilobites at about five dollars per fossil.

On another occasion, we went to Hack's art dealer who offered recently executed paintings, but she also carried canvasses that had been executed two or three centuries earlier by Peruvian natives in Cusco under the tutelage of the Spanish priests. These paintings, which were clearly very old, had been rendered in a medieval style. They had been painted on canvas that had been used and reused because the natives had had more time to paint than they had a canvas. We were told that in most cases, the paintings selected for permanent display had been permanently and irreversibly mounted in churches, from which mountings they were torn or cut out by brigands for resale to the outside world. The prices were modest if they were what they were represented to be. Nevertheless, we did not buy any on this first visit.

After Dr. Cantor left, Hack and I spent the next week with much the same agenda that we had followed in Rio with similar results. We visited the São Paulo brewery, getting the red carpet treatment, but going away with nothing. Only one of Krause's major markets seemed to be available to us, that being binder for foundry sands. While foundries were an important business in Brazil, particularly in São Paulo, the size of that entire industry was not greater at the time than that of the foundry industry in Wisconsin alone. By the time we left, I felt certain that we were not going to find enough potential in Brazil to justify an investment.

Upon return to Milwaukee, I reported our findings to Bill Sullivan, not mincing any words as to my feeling that Brazil held little opportunity for Krause, suggesting that at this early stage of our work, we might shift our interest to another country. Bill did not take any issue with my point of view and said that he would discuss my written report, together with my oral comments, with the board of directors. A couple of days later, having met, he said, with the board, he directed me to continue my work in Brazil, allowing that he did understand that Krause would probably not be investing there. He was, however, quite firm in his conviction that I must continue due diligence on all of Krause's business possibilities in Brazil right up to and including a final report to the State Department.

All of this seemed strange to me because I had become convinced that Krause did want to internationalize its business. While it seemed clear that Sullivan understood that Brazil was not going to become a viable option for a Krause investment, there certainly were other countries that might offer better opportunities. The amount we had expended on this project so far was a pittance. Even if we abandoned the program and did not receive any of our grant money, there would be no real consequences. Going through the due diligence plan we had presented it to the State Department promised to take another year to eighteen months. That looked to be an awful waste of time and money, a waste that was not lost on Sullivan Sr. or on Charlie Krause. I could not understand the decision to pursue this unpromising course.

Bonus day came around again on Christmas Eve, which, according to general business wisdom, is always a bad time to give out bonus checks. According to a poll current at that time, 78 percent of corporate merit bonuses were viewed as not only deficient but even as distastefully miserly. An award on Christmas Eve often just helped to ruin Christmas for the recipients. Krause provided no exception to this norm. Here, there was the usual gnashing of teeth, not perhaps among top management, but pervasively at the next level. My high expectations based on all of my successful work had been tempered by my previous experience with Krause compensation. Nevertheless, this year's $1,000 was still a tad disappointing.

During the next year and a half, I traveled to Brazil at least once a month spending about ten to twelve days on each trip. Hack came with me on every other trip or so; and, using a couple of market research firms, we performed market tests on a variety of precooked fortified corn flours, all of which were products of the cold roll mill. Regarding locating the existing corn-eating populations, I remember setting up truck monitoring stations on major highways to track the movement of corn from farms in the north to markets in the south. As with many of our activities this research came to very little. Nevertheless, and I was beginning to think along such lines, the "trucked-corn study" was good fodder for the report I would have to write.

There were some high points amidst the daily business tasks. One of the best was an invitation Hack and I received from one of our prospective local investors, to attend a local football game, this one being between the internationally renowned teams, Flamenco, located in Rio, and Santos, the name of the team and the port city for São Paolo. I was totally ignorant about the rest of the world's "football" and did not appreciate that this rivalry was the biggest one in Brazil and perhaps in the world. The Santos team's star was a guy named Pele, a name that meant nothing to me at the time. The game was played at the Flamenco home stadium in Rio, a stadium that held almost 100,000 people, and it was packed.

The day was hot and sunny as we arrived, hot being an uncomfortable ninety-nine degrees with humidity in the same range. The game progressed eventfully in the first half with a few exciting goals and major contact between the players. Injured players, eventually three of them, were unattended, just being left on the field, one curled up in a fetal position, the others appearing to be unconscious. Not only were there no substitutions but there seemed no ability to get help to the injured, even as serious as those injuries appeared.

Just before the midpoint of the game, the clouds, which had been arriving in battalions for most of the game, suddenly began to unleash their payload, and the rain fell in almost solid sheets, propelled by a rising wind. The umbrellas, of which my associates and I had an insufficient number, all went up, and briefly, there was no ability even to get sight of the game. But a cry went up, starting in the highest and farthest removed seats, rolling forward down the stands, almost to the field. Then starting at the front rows and rolling up the stands, as if by royal edict, all of the umbrellas went down and the game came again into view. The injured still lay on the field, now lying in smallish lakes, which were rapidly accumulating. We all sat in the rain, now chilled to the bone while the Brazilians continued to voice their enthusiasm for their teams. It was a memorable experience, diminished only by the fact that I really never appreciated the fact that I had seen the great Pele in action. I was just not ready for this important experience. Oh yes, after the finale the ambulances drove onto the field to pick up the injured.

On an early return home to the U S of A, I had taken my initial rock collection to the museum in Milwaukee and found some real interest. They wanted to do a display of the fossils that supported the Africa-Brazil theory of continental origin, and they wanted geodes for their collections in the basement. They gave me appraisals of $500 for the fish, $1,000 for the trilobites, and various values for the geodes that bore amethyst, rose quartz, and other crystals. Thereafter, I always visited the stone lady and bought as much stone as I could carry. Sometimes to get around flight weight restrictions, I could successfully check in twice. Meanwhile, I had bought a few Cusco paintings and brought them back for friends, family, and for use as charitable contributions.

At a Krause meeting in Milwaukee, I mentioned my Cuscos to Sid Cantor, and he asked me to buy him one. I made the mistake of agreeing to do so, and when I was next in Hack's São Paulo art store, I perused the Cusco offerings and began to understand that it is difficult to pick out art for someone else. Nevertheless, to fulfill my promise, I finally settled on a fragment of a painting of St. Francis giving his blessing, choosing this item, because it was the cheapest offering in the store at seventy-five dollars. When I offered it to Sid on his next visit to Milwaukee, he demurred, not liking it, conveniently ignoring any responsibility to me. So I was stuck with this probably valueless picture.

As Christmas approached that year, I drew, as his secret Santa, my brother-in-law Bill Stark, meaning that I was to provide him with a gift from an unidentified giver. I, knowing that to save on the expense of canvas, the Cusco Indians frequently painted over the works of earlier painters, felt no guilt painting out all the fingers in the blessing hand other than the index finger, thus changing Sebastian's blessing into the "Bird." It was the perfect gift for my frequently unpleasant brother-in-law. He wasn't offended, nor was he much interested in the gift, but it got an excellent laugh from the rest of the family. Bill's son, Peter, came into possession of and to this day still treasures this relic of the medieval history and more recent internecine strife.

Charlie Krause came to Brazil only once and spent a week with me, mostly in São Paulo, returning to Rio on Friday. I had a week before he arrived to prepare for his visit. I knew him to be a workaholic, so I managed to create a weeklong agenda for him that accounted for every minute of every day from Monday morning through the next weekend, from dawn well into the evening. It was so intense that I thought I had challenged his capacity for drudgery. I, at least, was exhausted by Saturday night. For Sunday I had arranged for a cruise on the yacht of a Rio businessman, a business opportunity as well as a good way to spend a weekend day in Rio. It was an all-day affair. When we got back to the hotel around 6:00 p.m., I thought I had shown Charlie an over-the-top week, particularly regarding potential business contacts and public relations opportunities. That evening, I was ready to take a breather from Charlie, who was scheduled to leave early the next morning. No such luck. He first asked what was on the schedule for the evening. Finding, to his chagrin, nothing, he wanted to have dinner in the hotel and discuss our findings. Of course, we did. When he left the hotel early the next day, I took Monday off and went to the beach.

While I was working on the Brazil project, Krause came out with a new product for the United States of America-Donated Food Program. This product, called CSM (for corn, soy, and milk), was made mostly of corn, more than 90 percent as I remember, with the balance consisting of processed soy and powdered milk. It was destined to become Donated Food #2 and the major food donated to the third world as "A Gift from the People of the United States of America." While Charlie was in Brazil with me, we appeared together in front of various groups where he might speak about the company and its products, particularly CSM. On at least a few occasions, he would demonstrate the adequacy of this highly unpalatable food by offering it to a dubious audience and eating it himself with evident gusto. I observed that few tasting it agreed with Charlie's judgment about its taste.

When I finished up in Brazil a year and a half after my first visit, I had to complete the record of our findings for the State Department so that Krause could get paid. This task took several months, and in that time, I managed to produce a glossy report with transparent overlays and whatever other presentation glitz that I could come up with. The report contained more than a hundred pages, mostly bullshit. It would have no enduring value. The only item of interest to the people at State was on the last page, a statement concluding that our projected rates of financial return were too low to warrant an investment in Brazil. We submitted the report and waited to see if they were going to pay us the $500,000 or so that we had spent. Soon I received from a mole of mine in Jonathan McCabe's office, a sub-rosa draft of an interdepartmental memo from McCabe saying approximately:

"Just as I thought, those assholes can't make enough money in Brazil. They want to get back to their nice 20 percent returns in the USA. As to Gallun's report, it isn't much, and it is of no use to us. I'd give it a C minus at best, but I guess we'll have to pay the sons of bitches anyway."

The receipt of approval to pay us was my last contribution at Krause; but while there did not seem to be a job waiting for me back at the company, I didn't have any other plans, so I hung around waiting for something to happen. When it didn't, I went to Charlie and suggested that I was thinking of leaving the company. He responded empathetically, like:

"Oh, when do you want to leave?"

Maybe I hadn't been as valuable as I thought. I might have guessed that from the fact that I was still being paid the same annual amount, $11,000, at which I had been hired as well as the same miserable bonus every Christmas. What had I been doing for those four years?

Before I left, I became aware that formulated food #2 was being made in the company's cold roll mill, which was soon running at full capacity making CSM. As provided by the government specifications for this product, the only way the cooked corn component could be processed was in precisely such a facility, and Krause was the only corn processor who had retained one. Krause was able to off-load its existing cold rolled production capacity to extruders that were bought concurrently as the CSM volume ratcheted up. The Krause competitors hastened to put together mills that could meet the mandated manufacturing specifications, but it was more than a year before competitive capacity would come on stream. In the meantime, Krause, with normal margins in the considerably less than the 10 percent range, was getting eleven cents a pound for a product that normally would have brought a good deal less than a nickel. The soy and milk components which were purchased from outside processors also cost less than eleven cents per pound as well, so CSM was an inordinately profitable product. The cold roll mill returned its value exponentially. Bill Sullivan had had his way; his mill had the second life that he had been looking for.

Postscript and Conjecture

The next few years were highly profitable for Krause. Nevertheless, competition in CSM was coming; and as it arrived, it was not possible for Krause to match the initial profitability of this product. After the other millers had built competitive facilities, the government specifications had been changed to allow the production of the corn flour component of CSM on an extruder and all the cold roll mills were closed, this time, even Krause's. The competitive environment drove the industry to collude on price, probably with Krause showing the way. They were caught at it by the Department of Justice, who went after the leaders of all the companies involved. All the underlings at Krause and probably at the other corn-processing companies turned state's evidence against their leaders to save their own skins. To my knowledge, the only one in the entire industry who did not turn on his boss was Charlie Krause himself, who, because of the deaths or other escapes of the various codefendants, was the only one standing at sentencing time. He was sentenced to a year and did nine months in the high-rise federal prison in Chicago. He came out a better person; and although he was barred from the corn-milling industry, he went on to a successful business career and an important place in Milwaukee's leadership.

Now to the real Machiavelli . . . Bill Sullivan.

It was clear to me soon after I left the company that I had been hired to be a moving piece for him. In retrospect, I was a little slow coming to the conclusion that I had been used as a pawn in a highly sophisticated scheme. My first clue, that of Sullivan's intransigence on the subject of the replacement of the cold rolling mill, was hard to swallow as an act of such a usually thoughtful business executive, but at the time, there was no way for me to draw any conclusions from it. Except when he had been using theatrics on an unsuspecting associate for dramatic effect, I had never known him to behave illogically. I had seen Bill as the consummate purposeful manipulator, and I should have known that he was misleading me as well as others in the company, probably in cluding the board of directors.

My second clue was my reception and success in Washington. I had been treated inordinately well considering the small size of Krause as well as my relatively junior status, and apparent lack of credentials in international business, nutrition, and government relations. In retrospect, it is clear to me that my way had been paved right up to the receipt of the grant. However, my own ego made it easy for me to believe that I was quickly developing serious networking and negotiating skills.

My eyes might have been opened a bit with the scant attention paid at Krause to selecting an area of interest for our taxpayer-subsidized market study. I had been able to get past that negligence by believing that my presentations to management on selecting Brazil were professional and persuasive. I think at that juncture, I still had honestly believed that I was working on a normal business investigation. But when I returned from Brazil after my first visit, reported that we had little or no opportunity there, got no disagreement from Sullivan or Krause but was told that we were going to continue our study regardless of the facts. Perhaps then, I should have realized that Denmark had a problem with decay.

Even with all of these clues, it was not until I realized that, in accordance with newly minted government specifications, the corn component for CSM could be made only on a cold roll corn mill, that I began to put the pieces of this puzzle into context. Finally, I understood that I had spent four years of my life dancing on the ends of strings manipulated by a master puppeteer.

To lay it all out in simple terms, I think the following is a fair summary of the sequence of events surrounding my association with Krause:

Just prior to my encounter with Charlie at the airport in 1964, Sullivan had made a deal with highly placed people in the Johnson administration that in exchange for his performing a study in a third world country that might lead to a Krause investment in the food industry, he would get to write the specifications for Formulated Food #2. Then he told Charlie to find a dupe who had adequate qualifications to be a front man for this scheme, and Charlie found me. It may have been as simple as that.

On occasion, I have wished I had had someone like Sullivan Senior to run my businesses. In spite of the fact that he had entered as an outsider, this man had the welfare of the Krause Milling Company as a single focus. Neither rain nor heat nor gloom of darkness nor the United States statutes would stay him from the completion of his corporate duties. He was dedicated.

CHAPTER XIII

The Entrepreneur

When I left the Krause milling company, I was thirty-three years old with three small children, and I didn't have the vaguest idea of what I was going to do next. While I had a modest inheritance coming from my father, who had recently died, I needed a job to live in the manner to which I wanted to become accustomed.

Although I was at this time four years out of business school, I was still under the influence of one of my HBS professors, who had convinced me that the "true path" was that of making things. That professor, General George Dariot, had taught a course inappropriately called "Manufacturing." I say inappropriately because the course was really about life. In that regard, he gave us a lot of good rules to follow, like "don't live up to the level of your income," "keep a record of the people you worked with and stay in touch; you may need them later," "always remember when you are going up that going up is much easier than going down" and many others, at least one for every class session. These were good precepts, and I would have done better in all aspects of my life had I not just made a note of them but had actually followed them. I didn't. In fact, I violated all of them many times. Even so, General Doriot convinced me that real men weren't bankers, lawyers, or stockbrokers, and the only really productive people made things that other people use.

In the end, it was a good thing that I started very small in the manufacturing business. I was going to make a lot of mistakes here, and had the business been much bigger, any of these mistakes might have ruined me. But to the contrary, many of my misjudgments provided opportunities as I corrected course to deal with the consequences of bad choices.

BECAUSE OF MY background at Krause, I had a significant interest in the food business. I played with the idea of starting a protein fortification business with Hack Hoffenberg, my former associate from my Krause days; and together we developed a business plan which involved using sauces, gravies, and flavorings to carry essential amino acids into poor quality third world protein staples like cassava, rice, and corn.

After putting together some prototype products, we traveled together to Puerto Rico and the Dominican Republic, areas which were experiencing significant nutrition problems but possessed a money economy and a somewhat modern distribution system. En route, Hack and I met an old business school chum of mine, Mitch Milleus, who had become an investment banker. On the plane, while we were catching up on our careers, he read our business plan. Seeming to like what he saw, he suggested that he might take us public. I demurred modestly, "We don't have any substance; it's just an idea."

He responded, "But your science is really current, and food companies are hot today. Perhaps that'll not be the case next year."

"Maybe you could just help us raise some money now to help us prove our case."

"Dick, I don't want to help you build your business. I want to build your estate."

The conversation ended with an exchange of contact information and a promise that he would get back to me. He didn't. Hack and I didn't get the business off the ground; and while we stayed in touch, he and I went in different directions.

My next opportunity had more substance and was a good match for my background and experience.

I had become good friends with my next-door neighbor in Milwaukee, Phil Orth. Phil had a business, P.H. Orth Baking Supply Company, a business which had been started by his father some forty years earlier. The company blended and packaged flours and other baking materials for the food and restaurant trades. Phil took me through his antiquated processing plant, where all the material handling was manual, and the equipment appeared to be out of scale with the significant volume of business he was doing. The plant was dirty, not just by Krause standards, but really filthy by any sanitation measurement. Workspaces were cramped, and materials were fed into mixers by hand directly from bags. My Krause experience gave me clear insights into this closely related business. Right away, I could see a straightforward path to improving efficiency by introducing bulk material handling systems and modern mixing equipment. It also was clear to me that the plant should be relocated to a rail siding so that materials could be delivered in rail carloads in bulk rather than on trucks in bags. Wanting to have him understand that I had something to contribute, I made these observations to Phil, ignoring the possibility of offending him with his company's inadequacies. Showing no umbrage, Phil indicated that he had recognized the inefficiency and had planned to automate, but he had been making negligible profits on about twenty million dollars in annual sales. And he was short on funds. It was evident to both of us that a little money would make a big difference in this business.

Phil and I were friends, and one thing led smoothly to another. It wasn't long before we were talking about becoming partners, with me, at least initially, as the junior partner with something less than a 50 percent interest, at a price to be determined. As Phil was twenty years my senior and was a good guy, having a minority position did not bother me. Time would take care of this situation.

At Phil's behest, I had lunch with his lawyer, Bob Harland, his "paid friend" (as Phil sobriquetized Harland to me). Bob was charming, and we got on well together on a wide range of subjects, including personal values, politics, and business philosophy. I understood that I was being interviewed so that Harland could evaluate me as a potential partner. I thought that I handled these issues well—actually, very well—so I was surprised when Phil got back to me, saying that he had decided not to do the deal. It did not take me long to learn that the reason he was backing off was that I possessed more assets than he did. Harland had advised him that if we got into any difficulties, I would be holding the long straw. So this seemingly perfect opportunity failed to take flight.

Subsequently, Phil hired a professional manager, got a bank loan, built an automated plant with rail access, and saw his business grow quickly. He took me through the new plant a year after our discussions, and I could see that he was on his way to having an important business. Twenty-five years later, Phil, after drawing a more-than-good living from this company, sold it for more than $100 million.

It was shortly after the Orth deal fell apart that Jim Cerny entered my life. I met him in a poker game to which he brought his entire net worth, $500, in cash and an old car, an aged and battered Mustang convertible. Late in the evening, he still had the $500 but nothing more. In the agreed upon last hand of the night, a seven-card stud game, I found myself with a full house after six cards, having bet aggressively from the beginning of the hand. Jim, who looked as though he were playing for or already had a straight, opened the round with a strong bet, and I raised the limit. Everyone else folded except for Jim. He contemplated the situation ponderously, his normal behavior as I was to learn over the next forty years, and eventually saw my bet. I was glad that I didn't have to waste my full house on a smallish pot. Then as the ultimate card was dealt, I reviewed my hand to feign interest in my last card. To my surprise and shock, I found that I had misread my cards and even with the seventh card, had only two pairs. I quickly adjusted to the situation, thinking, *I've played the hand so aggressively as a strong hand that a full house is quite credible. Besides, Jim is now down to his last few bucks and will be afraid of my pot limit bet that now can be $400.*

So, I casually threw my bet into the pot and stared confidently into Jim's eyes. It took Jim forever to agonize over all the possibilities, an eternity here being perhaps five, maybe eight, minutes. When he made his proclamation, I could not believe it:

"Gallun, you're bluffing," and he asked to be allowed to use an IOU for the part of the bet that he could not meet. What could I do? His straight beat my two pairs. It was a bad beginning for what was to become a lifelong relationship—bad, at least, for me.

Soon thereafter, Jim and I began to look at companies together. It turned out that he had been at this activity for a while, that of looking for a company to acquire, and he had some potential backers lurking in the shadows. He did possess good business skills, having operated as a consultant in general management and data processing after serving stints with Corning Glass and Touche Ross. He was a thinker, a steady and dependable influence, and was, by nature, a skeptic, all characteristics that might balance my optimism and occasional lack of attention to detail.

Together, we spent considerable time on a car-wash business that was for sale, and it was only after extensive due diligence that we realized that this business was an incipient bankruptcy just waiting for someone to pull the string. Fortunately, after a month or so of digging, we figured that out. The time was not wasted, however, in that we got to know each other well.

Jim and I continued to work together but came up empty of any real opportunity. Then during the fall of 1969, a First Wisconsin banker, Tom Sproat, contacted me with a business for sale. The company, Electriwire Assemblies Company Inc., assembled wire harnesses mostly for the garden tractor business, but it had a dozen or so companies that purchased wire assemblies in other industries. One of these was Briggs and Stratton, whose chairman, Fred Stratton Sr., was a friend of my wife's, so I called him to get a customer's view of the business. He referred me to his VP of manufacturing, Ed Gronaki, whom he described as a manufacturing genius. After a brief conversation, Ed agreed to visit Electriwire with me.

Prior to visiting this company, I reviewed the financials with Jim Cerny. They looked pretty promising to both of us with monthly sales of thirty-five thousand and better than average, say 15 percent, "apparent" profit margins. Jim thought, and I agreed, that this was going to be just too small a business for us to get into together. Jim decided to take a pass.

On my first visit to Electriwire, a fifth-story loft operation, I was taken aback by the crowded and grubby environment. This negative impression was aggravated by windows blackened with an accumulation of soot, this filth accentuated by inadequate interior lighting. The level of automation was minimal, with many ladies applying terminals to wire with hand tools while only a few had machines that fed the terminals automatically. The workers were almost entirely women, many obese, and most looking well beyond their prime. As it turned out, they weren't as old as they looked;, they just had led hard lives. The manufacturing area, as well as the antediluvian office, was accessed by eight flights of stairs or by a primitive freight elevator that was entered through a heavy wooden gate that needed to be lifted to enter or leave, then lowered in order to operate the elevator. Even with that inconvenience, the elevator turned out to be the preferred way to get to work, not just by the out-of-shape ladies but eventually by me as well.

My second visit was aimed at understanding the manufacturing setting. I had an expert in tow. As I pulled down the elevator door behind Gronaki, he ignored the depressing environmental conditions and observed right away that he felt a rhythmic pace reported in the sound of the presses. From this cacophony, he intuitively perceived a favorable work pace, an observation that was surprising to me. That was reassuring to me. I had thought the pace of work to be quite slow. I did wonder how he drew his conclusion since most of the women were applying their terminals by hand.

The two of us made a quick circuit of the work floor without his making any further comment. Then Ed paused thoughtfully at the elevator and suggested that we go to a nearby bar to discuss his impressions. We spent the next four hours or so imbibing martinis, while he filled me full of general business lore interspersed with an occasional observation about what he had seen at Electriwire. He did make a lot out of the work pace, particularly the rythmic sound of the presses, but had nothing else substantial to say. In my own relative innocence of what I should be looking for, I thought we had, together, completed a valuable piece of due diligence. By the time we left the tavern, I was at least three sheets to the wind. Ed, who had matched my drinks two to one, seemed to be flying above the weather. I hadn't learned much that I needed to know, but I had gained confidence that there was nothing wrong with the manufacturing operation.

The business did stand up reasonably well to my other due diligence efforts, which were directed at the balance sheet and recent operating results. The company had been profitable while growing nicely, and in the current year, both sales and profits were setting records. But I had missed an important part of due diligence.

Beyond reviewing and evaluating the customer list, which looked pretty good, I paid little attention to future prospects, never asking for a prospect list or a pipeline of new business (neither of which existed). Unrecognized by me because I did not dig into changes in the backlog of orders, the sellers had been milking the order backlog by shipping orders ahead of schedule. I had missed a truly significant issue that a more careful due diligence might have revealed.

By the time we closed the transaction on the 1st of January 1970, the pace of shipments had begun to slow. In fact, with December shipments totaling almost forty-five thousand, the order book for January showed less than twenty-five thousand in the backlog. February was worse.

It wasn't just the draining of the order book by the owners. The economy had started to descend into the doldrums of the seventies, and the garden tractor business, which represented almost half of the company's sales, went into a deep slide. To make matters worse, Huebsch Manufacturing, a laundry equipment company and the biggest non garden-tractor customer, discovered that Electriwire had been charging them more than twice what a competitor would charge. They left in a snit, never to return despite the change in Electriwire's ownership and my supplicating entreaties. Huebsch and a couple of other high-margin customers were the explanation for the extraordinary profit margins, margins that were not to persist. By March, the business, which had shown reliable and continuous profitability right up until the day of the transfer of ownership, was losing money—and not just a little.

An apparent bright spot on my horizon, the brightness later to turn into a mirage and eventually into something much worse, came in the form of Milwaukee Coin Industries (MCI), a manufacturer of amusement games which was owned and managed by Dave Nutting. Nutting was an electronic genius but one who displayed many of the idiosyncrasies of the mad scientist. He was taciturn to a fault and highly secretive; one could only speculate about what he was thinking. Nutting had been applying his genius to the design of electromechanical amusement games and had developed a good reputation in the games industry for designing successful games for arcades. Nevertheless, as I would learn to my chagrin, his brilliance was not an indicator of financial success.

We at Electriwire were mainly manufacturers of wire harnesses. The games that Nutting was making required very large and complicated electrical harnesses, and Dave Nutting, as a buyer, did not seem to be too concerned about price. Although his order size was small in numbers of units, it was large in dollars because of the substantial size of the individual harnesses, and the margins were good. Soon, we had replaced much of our lost revenues with sales to MCI, sales that contributed to a favorable bottom line.

It didn't take too long to find out why Nutting didn't pay much attention to his cost of goods. He did not pay his bills promptly, and, eventually, not at all. In about six months, the MCI accounts receivable had gotten way out of line. Eventually, he offered to settle the outstanding account for equity in his company. I agreed, not only because there was no other way to exact payment but also because I liked those big profitable harnesses and wanted to continue making them. Of course, it would be only a matter of time before he would be in trouble again.

Meanwhile, the harness business had grown in other areas, particularly in the kitchen equipment area, with new customers like Broan Manufacturing, West Bend Aluminum, and a young Madison refrigerator manufacturer, Sub-Zero Corp. As well as wire assemblies, some of these customers required unique power cords. Responding to this demand, we tooled up to enter the marketplace for specialty power cords. Doerr Manufacturing became a significant customer.

With the growth of sales and an increasing diversity of customers, inventory management was becoming a problem. Revenues had risen to little over a million dollars by 1973, but even at this modest volume, we had to buy and plan for the use and replenishment of more than a thousand different purchased items. The existing manual inventory control system was getting quickly out of control. Inventory investment already was too high and growing faster than the business. Even with only minimal understanding of the then fairly new tool called data processing, I knew that we needed a computer.

Jim Cerny and I had stayed in touch, and he agreed to come as a consultant to address our growing need for a "manufacturing system," a computer program for controlling all the functions of a manufacturing business between purchasing and shipping. It took more than a year to develop this program, and the installation was not completed until 1975. It was a well-designed system that would serve us for the next twenty-five years. During the time it took to create this system, Jim made himself useful around the business, most importantly in sales and production. Soon, it became evident to me that he had become a critical asset in the business, so Jim became a permanent employee. Shortly thereafter, he became my partner.

With Jim aboard, the pace of new business opportunities accelerated. W. W. Grainger, a nationwide distributor of industrial supplies, bought Doerr Electric, who had become one of our most important customers. After the Grainger acquisition, we worked hard to maintain our Doerr business, and in the process got close to Grainger's purchasing agent for electrical products. From him we got a growing share of the Grainger power cord business, and he suggested that we might have to add capacity as he steered more Grainger business to us.

Jim and I took this suggestion seriously, seriously enough so that we decided to establish a second manufacturing operation. We just could not handle the incoming Grainger orders out of the Milwaukee plant, and it seemed to us that we had established a viable and mutually useful relationship with this significant company. So we bought an old shoe factory in Waupun and modified and equipped it with money from the smallest industrial revenue bond issue ever issued in Wisconsin, just $150,000. In six months, we were in business!

While we were setting up this factory, our sales to Grainger grew rapidly. Our expansion looked like a masterstroke until one day, just after our new plant came on stream, all of our Grainger orders were cancelled. Calling Grainger in a panic, I learned that our purchasing agent had been fired, accused of colluding with suppliers. What's more, we were deemed to be one of the crooked suppliers. With a lot of time and effort, we finally persuaded Grainger that we were not involved in the fraudulent scheme, and they agreed to honor the orders in-house. But our romance with this company was over. They quickly eased us out of the major business on which we had counted on to fill our new plant.

With Grainger's decision, we experienced a large shortfall of demand for our cords, one that left us way short of break even in Waupun. We had a lot of idle plant space and machinery and underutilized supervision and administrative personnel as well. Nevertheless, this misfortune gave us a powerful motivation to find new customers. We searched for customers who used power cords of all types and sold aggressively; and we did so with determination. We found a lot of electrically based companies right in Wisconsin. With our low cost facility and inexpensive labor, we were competitive. Within a year, we were able to bring in enough sales to make the cord business profitable in its own right.

One of the new customers we developed was Hill-Rom, a large manufacturer of hospital beds, particularly electrically adjusted hospital beds. We made the cord that brought power to the bed, and it was a big deal because it had to meet special requirements for hospital safety. This hospital-grade cord would have a significant impact on our long-term strategy and ultimate success. But as with many of the situations in which I have found myself, Hill-Rom seemed at first a mixed blessing. While it got us into the hospital cord business, it happened early on that one of our adjustable bed cords being used in a hospital setting got enmeshed in the mechanism for raising the head end of the bed. As one patient adjusted his bed, the mechanism shredded the cord, shorting and starting a fire that engulfed and killed the patient. Of course, we were horrified by this tragedy. Moreover, when we were named in the resultant suit, we were worried for some time that we would have liability in this accident, even as it was not our fault, and in addition, we were protected by insurance. Our concern was that it would affect our insurance rates, perhaps jeopardizing the entire cord part of our business. In the end, we were let out of the suit but not without considerable agony of worry.

Out of the frying pan and back into the fire . . . It was less than a year after the Hill-Rom incident that MCI fell apart, this time for good. That failure introduced another mixed bag. While MCI was still an important loss, not only for its revenue but also for my investment in it, I did have some recourse in the collateral that I had negotiated.

During the foregoing period, Growth Capital, a Small Business Investment Company (Growth herein), and I had loaned MCI money for working capital, these loans secured by all the equity in a subsidiary company, Red Baron Amusements. Red Baron had established and was operating a chain of arcades, mostly in the commercial malls that had sprung up around the country. The company had contracted for, in a little more than two years, thirty-six such facilities, twenty-six completed and operating before MCI went bankrupt, with another ten locations under contract or in an early stage of build out.

When MCI went down, Growth and I came into possession of Red Baron.

While marginally profitable, Red Baron was suffering from the cash flow stress of its own because of its aggressive expansion in a fast-maturing marketplace, that of game rooms in the malls, where just two years earlier, they had not existed at all. The primary pressure on Growth and me grew out of the burden of completing the unfinished stores. The cost of constructing and outfitting a center ranged from $100,000 to $200,000, depending upon size, so we were looking at a cash need of a million and a half or so. Growth and I worked together initially to finish the first two of the ten undeveloped centers; and while the cash flow from operations remained positive, it fell way short of covering the cost of building out and equipping even those centers. Growth failed to see any favorable potential here and wanted to escape its share of the expected cash shortfall, so they offered to sell their interest at twenty-five cents on the dollar of financial net worth. I took their deal, which cost me $125,000, a risk-laden decision, but one that I would not regret.

The next step was to raise some money to cover the cost of development. Through Dan Winter, who had been Nutting's consigliere at MCI and had stayed on to run Red Baron, I was able to sell a couple of our contracts in the less promising malls to "ma and pa" operators, getting a little money in the sale. What was more important, I got rid of the development and equipment costs for those centers. We were able to negotiate a cancellation of one contract. That left about seven to complete, requiring about $1 million. The business was marginally bankable in an easier lending climate than today, even with its highly leveraged balance sheet, so with a loan, a small equity infusion, some funds from sales of the two centers and an improving cash flow, I suddenly had a business that could stand alone. Red Baron had become an asset, one that, after paying off the debt, provided me with significant income.

As winter approached in late 1976, we found ourselves dominating the garden tractor harness business, having finally broken into John Deere, the last of the majors in this industry. We had also achieved a solid relationship with Caterpillar Tractor. With considerable new production requirements, we needed to add capacity.

The Milwaukee location was not suitable for expansion for a variety of reasons, among which were the inconvenience of loft space reached only by elevator, the dirty and unattractive facilities, and the unavailability of reliable, unskilled labor, the best of which were being hired by larger companies attempting to meet EEOC quota requirements. We wanted a new plant to be within an hour and a half from our office in Brookfield, which meant no more than about eighty miles. After exploring the possibilities, we saw that within our geographic requirement, Spring Green offered a good workforce and an attractive industrial park. Additionally, the town was willing to support an issue of industrial revenue bonds. After completing due diligence and purchasing three acres in the industrial park, we began construction of a 40,000 square foot building late in the year. Things moved quickly, and we had production under way by early spring in 1977.

At this point, Jim Cerny had been with the company (by now, renamed EWC Corp.) for only three years, but he had contributed immensely to the progress of the company. Revenues had increased fivefold from the million dollars of sales we had generated prior to his involvement in 1974. Jim and I had worked well together for much of this period, doing so despite the fact that I had never defined clearly any delineation of responsibility between the two of us. We occasionally clashed over decisions, and more often than not these arguments arose over decisions I had made without consulting him. At one low point in 1977, we came close to severing our relationship, and for several days, we talked openly about Jim leaving.

I was aware that, while I controlled the business, Jim was carrying more than his share of the burden of management. Moreover, I had learned by this time that I was not good at confronting the day-to-day demands of this kind of a business, ones that required attention to detail as well as close and sensitive supervision of the second-line managers. Besides, despite the growth that we had experienced, profitability still lagged. There really was not enough potential in our limited marketplace to occupy both of us. It was time for me to find something else to do.

CHAPTER **XIV**

A Mountain Adventure

For me, 1970 was an exceptional year. After a two-year hiatus following the Krause fiasco, I had started a new business and moved with my young family into our new house at Pine Lake. Those changes, as satisfying as they were, are the type of changes that can bring serious stress into one's life, stress that can even cause health problems. Nevertheless, the year's most memorable event and one that, in retrospect, should have been stressful, was a trip that my brother-in-law, Bill Stark, dreamed up. The destination was a ski lodge in the Canadian Rockies, from which one skied on wilderness peaks and glaciers, using helicopters for a vertical ascent. Hans Gmoser had just opened the lodge in the prior year, and, as we were to learn at our great peril, he had not yet worked out all the kinks.

BESIDES BILL AND me, our group consisted of my wife, Kathy; Bill's wife, Judy; and Bill Buchheit, a brain surgeon from Philadelphia with whom we all had had prior personal involvement. We all considered ourselves expert skiers, and each of us men considered ourselves to be a premier skier among our group. Looking at our skills objectively, I would have had to say that I was best. Probably because of the egoism that ruled our consciousness and because of the willingness of women to defer to their husbands, we honestly thought that we were not undertaking any risks that were inappropriate for young parents.

As Kathy and I planned our trip, we did discuss our concerns for the welfare of our children, if something were to happen to us. We had previously established with the Starks a legal agreement for us to serve as guardians of each other's children in the case of the parents dying in a joint accident. To avoid the possibility of a joint catastrophe that would undo this precaution, Kathy suggested that we travel on different routes. The Starks made their reservations first flying west with one stop in Winnipeg. We found that the only other way was to fly east through Toronto on our way to Calgary with another stop as we traveled west—certainly not a direct flight.

Nevertheless, we took this route and found ourselves leaving at 5:45 in the morning. When we arrived eventually in Toronto, we learned that we were to have a plane change in Winnipeg. After an hour layover there, we settled into the second row of our third plane for the day, cursing our devious route, but congratulating ourselves for our thoughtful parenting decision. Then just as the doors were being closed, the Starks arrived directly from their Milwaukee flight and sat down in the first row. So much for our careful planning!

We arrived in Calgary a couple of hours later and took a cab to the hotel where we were to board a chartered bus that would take us to a desolate outpost called Spillimacheen. From there, we would travel by helicopter about 20 miles into the wilderness to the isolated Bugaboo Lodge, our headquarters for the next week.

It was only a week before this trip that Kathy and I had gotten around to seeing *Midnight Cowboy*, a well received movie of the day (three Academy Awards), about a male prostitute (Jon Voigt) and a sickly friend, Ratso (Dustin Hoffman). In the last and most memorable scene of this classic, Ratso expired in the backseat on the right side of a Greyhound bus.

I thought I was the first to enter our chartered bus, but as I was taking a seat in the middle, I noticed a person huddled in the right back corner looking pretty much like Ratso in the final moments of *Midnight Cowboy*, right down to Hoffman's avian face and the five-day stubble. As I contemplated the seeming coincidence of the movie setting with what I was looking at, Kathy joined me. After sneaking a peek, she confirmed my view that indeed it was Ratso or an awfully good facsimile. The staging was accurate right down to the last detail.

The bus filled quickly, and Kathy noted that one fellow passenger getting on looked a lot like E. G. Marshall, who was then starring in our favorite TV drama. When the doors closed, our trip escort took roll alphabetically, and in due course, got to K. Gallun, then R. Gallun, next, D. Hoffman, and shortly thereafter, E. Marshall. We knew then that there was going to be something extraordinary about this trip.

The trip to Spillimacheen took us about three hours, the time made tolerable by the incredible scenery which included panoramic views of the Banff and Lake Louise areas which nestled grandly on the other side of the Bow River. On arrival at Spillimacheen, there was an impressive unloading of bags and equipment from the bus, beginning with large cameras and panoply of moviemaking apparatus, this paraphernalia followed first by several ski bags emblazoned with "U.S. Olympic Team," then one marked "Czechoslovakia National Ski Team." Apparently we were in over our heads.

Even so, the cast of celebrities was still incomplete. On the helicopter ride to the lodge, I sat next to a woman I had met in Aspen fifteen years earlier. She was "Skeeter" Werner, who had skied with prominence on the U.S. woman's team in the fifties and whose brother Buddy had been the premier American skier for many years until his death in a European avalanche in 1964. Skeeter introduced me to her husband, Doak Walker, who was a Heisman Trophy winner from the late forties and an all-time NFL great with the Detroit Lions. It had been said that you could put Doak in a phone booth with three linemen, and he could escape by dancing his way past them. Partly through the aggressive attention of Bill Stark, the Walkers were destined to become our new best friends over the next four days.

We arrived at the Bugaboo Lodge on late Saturday afternoon in time for tea. The entire group of new arrivals met in the great hall of the lodge. There were exactly twenty-seven skiers because that number matched the capacity of the helicopters to handle three groups, each with its own guide. "Hans" Gmoser, the proprietor and a famous mountaineer from Austria, addressed the assembled group. Hans told us that because it was late April, we would be loading the first helicopter before sunrise every day of our stay so that we could get a good start on what promised to be warm days. He told us that with the warmth and the bright sun, the avalanche danger would increase as the day wore on so that we would be finishing our skiing before 1:00 p.m. There would be limited skiing in the afternoon on selected north slopes for those who wanted to get more skiing. The skiing groups would be set up by the guides after the first day in an attempt to put together compatible groups. Then he told us to have a good time at this afternoon tea that, as it turned out, would be a daily event. Tea may have been a misnomer as these afternoon sessions did include anything from hashish to vodka.

During the subsequent festivities, we had the opportunity to meet our fellow travelers, starting with the movie gang who were there to shoot the final scene of *Who Is Harry Kellerman and Why Is He Saying Those Awful Things About Me,* a movie about which you have never heard because it was so bad that it spent practically no time in the theaters. We learned from Dustin Hoffman that the movie was about his character, a psychiatric patient, and his psychiatrist, who was played by E. G. Marshall and their joint failure to address the problems faced by Dustin's character. The last scene was to find the two of them succumbing to the patient's suicide attempt by crashing an airplane, with the airplane scene metamorphosing into their skiing off into a cloud. The Bugaboos turned out to be the best place in the world to get a totally white background for this one climactic scene. What an effort for a single scene in a movie that would set a record for the shortest time in the theaters!

We met many of the others that afternoon and evening, and it was a compatible crowd. Nonetheless, there was a bit of nervousness in the air as no one knew what to expect on the morrow.

Tomorrow came soon enough as the awakening gong rolled everyone out of bed at 4:30 a.m. for a continental breakfast and off to the helipad at 5:15. Our group stuck together, and we were loaded on the first helicopter, arriving at our first peak just as the sun appeared on the horizon. The helicopter hovered a couple of feet above the drop zone, and we were ordered to jump out, carrying our skis and poles. We landed in the soft snow with the helicopter wash obscuring the entire area and blowing cold snow against our exposed flesh and even into and under our clothes. It was a very chilling experience and one that we would relive again and again during the next week.

Quickly, the helicopter departed to pick up the next group. As we put on our skis in the landing zone, we looked around and could see a vast vista of wilderness, densely punctuated with snowcapped peaks, most of which were pyramidal in shape. The sky was brightening to a dazzling blue made more vivid by its contrast to the ubiquitous snow. Suddenly, the sun was rising, brilliant and strong, its rays already warming our bones. Nevertheless, there was no time to savor this exhilarating backdrop; we were urged to get into our skis and clear the mountaintop so that the next group could land.

The first run was an unforgettable experience, skiing on an open slope atop a glacier in light powder for almost a mile before we got down to the tree line. As we descended, we skied again into relative darkness, as the mountain in front of us rose to cover the sun. By the time we were back in the shadows, we were warm from the effort and anxiety of skiing in unfamiliar and somewhat intimidating conditions. The snow that had been light at the top became heavier as we descended, and there were many spectacular falls as the conditions became more difficult. As we waited for the fallen to repair the damages from their falls, i.e., lost goggles, snow down their necks, released skis, etc., the sun rose again and the day became dazzling once more. Then we approached the valley where the helicopter waited, and my heart was filled with satisfaction. I was the only one in our group who had not fallen during this descent. Surely when they assigned the groups tomorrow in accordance with ability, I would be in the top group.

We got two good descents in the morning, and while there were a few terrifying moments, the worst was saved for another day. Lunch, consisting of sandwiches and lemonade, was served from the helicopter at the end of the second run, about eleven o'clock. After lunch we were given the opportunity to take an afternoon run or to return to the lodge.

I was surprised that there were few takers for the afternoon run—only three of us as it happened. Those of us who did soon found ourselves at the top of a convex slope, which is to say a slope becoming steeper as one descended, enough so that you saw almost none of the skiing surface from the top. There was just sky and the bottom of the slope about a half mile away. Our guide advised us not to traverse for fear of precipitating an avalanche—not the last time I would hear that admonition—and he instructed us to wait for his signal that the slope was safe when he reached the bottom. Then he disappeared into the void, not reappearing for a seeming eternity and then only as a distant speck. On seeing him wave his poles, which seemed to be the positive signal, my companions, both Olympians, took off and, with my heart in my throat . . . so did I.

As it happened, I had two important advantages for skiing in powder over the other guests, even the Olympians, and those advantages showed up on this run, the first real deep powder run of the trip. The more important of these was that I was skiing on very soft old Head skis that allowed me to bounce easily to the surface of the snow. Most of the others, particularly the racers, were skiing on much stiffer skis which tended to stay buried and proved to be difficult to turn in the heavier snow we encountered as we descended. The second advantage was that I had had a great deal more experience skiing in powder, experience gained from skiing with and receiving instruction from my sister, Carol, and her husband, Bob Craig. For years, the Craigs, both experienced backcountry mountaineers, had lead me to find the powder on Aspen Mountain, and they dragged me into the wilderness at the end of almost every day of skiing. In 1970, as amazing as it may seem, most skiers, even the best, did not seek out powder.

While I was cold with fear as I started down this steep descent, I quickly learned that the conditions were perfect. The snow was deep enough to control my speed even as I stayed in the fall line, and it was heavy enough to allow me to easily bob to the surface for turning by slightly unweighting my skis. Within seconds, I found a rhythm that allowed me to feel totally in control. It was an exhilarating run, and as I looked back when I reached the guide, I had left a beautiful symmetrical track made up of a profusion of linked esses. Meanwhile, both of my companions found themselves in deep trouble, unable to turn or to use the depth of the snow to break their speed. They had a long trip down, one interspersed with dramatic falls, each of these accentuated by a cloud of snow and followed by an interminable period of cleanup. It was a long afternoon but an immensely satisfying one for me. I could not wait to get back to the lodge to share my success with my group.

That opportunity came soon enough. At tea, the Walkers joined our clique, and we had a conversation about how the ski groups would be composed. I observed that they would probably separate us by skiing ability and that the Olympians would probably be skiing together, they making up seven of a nine-person heli-load. Only when asked did I mention that I had been skiing with two of them, and under the conditions of the day, I was able to outski them. When further pressed by Bill Stark, I opined that I thought I would be selected to ski with the Olympians.

The next day started as the prior one with the gong sounding at 4:30. We were finishing breakfast when Hans stood up to give us our group assignments. The first group included all of the Olympians and a couple of others whom we did not know. The second group was comprised of a miscellany of male skiers, including Bill Stark and Bill Buchheit. The third was made up entirely of women except for one . . . me. I was mortified and in shock. No one else seemed to attach any significance to their assignments, and they just went about the day's business. It was a long day for me, one during which I felt alone and abandoned, truly depressed over the injustice of the apparent assessment of my skiing. I did not talk much to anyone that day, not even to Kathy, who was in my group. I just nursed my psychological wounds and kept to myself. It was not until we returned to the lodge in the afternoon that Bill let the cat out of the bag, admitting that he had set the whole assignment thing up with Hans to pimp me. While relieved, I was somewhat embarrassed by the fact that everyone was in on the con; and while sympathizing with me, they all got a good laugh out of it. The worst of it was that Bill had gotten me where my ego lived. I had to get even.

That afternoon while Bill was out in the sauna, I hatched my plan. Bill had played football at Dartmouth, and while not exactly a star, he had had some prominence at the game. More importantly, he both savored and overrated his success at football. Doak Walker, with whom we had become chummy and who was in school at the same time as Bill, looked like a good foil to lay Bill's ego open. I persuaded Doak to speak up at tea in front of the entire gathering. His assignment was to ask in an offhand manner if Bill were any relation to the Stark who had played football at Dartmouth in the late forties. Knowing Bill, I thought I had a sure thing here. When the time came to set the hook, Doak carried off his lines well, and I caught the quiver of Bill's lips as pride started to gain control over reason. But suddenly, I saw his eyes narrow in recognition; it was almost like the lightbulb over the head of a cartoon character. He knew that it was a setup, and he parried adroitly, "Why, Doak, don't you remember playing against me in the East-West game in Columbus?"

Doak was completely taken aback and in by this rejoinder, and could not muster any response at all. The crowd, who had been in on the joke, even accepted Bill's imaginative riposte as factual. It was a stellar performance and one of Bill's finest moments. Score Bill 2, Dick 0. Game over.

The next day, Tuesday, the skiing groups were reassigned along more agreeable lines. People ended up skiing with the people with whom they came, which made sense. We had a wonderful morning of powder skiing, and by now, everyone was on the right equipment and was learning to handle the deep snow. We got three runs in before lunch, and according to the records, we received 16,000 feet of vertical ascent in the helicopter that day. We had an exact tally every day because we were billed for skiing based on the amount of helicopter service each of us used.

In the afternoon, I took another run, this time with Les Streeter, a member of the '68 American Olympic team, and a woman from the Czechoslovakian team, who spoke no English and, of course, a guide. It was a warm afternoon even at the top, but we skied comfortably down from the peak onto north slopes where the deep snow remained light because it was sheltered from the sun. About halfway down, the slope entered a ravine that took a turn to the left. We followed a narrow declivity through a pair of rock spires and abruptly emerged from a narrow pass, then finding ourselves at the top of a quarter-mile slope that faced directly into the western sun. It was evident from the geography below us that here were no alternative ways down. Our only route was steep and deeply laden with snow made heavy by its exposure to the sun. It was immediately apparent that our guide was uneasy about the obvious danger. He pondered the situation for an interminable moment and then acknowledged that we were in a bad place. After a bit of hemming and hawing, he delivered much the same instruction we had heard on the prior avalanche-endangered slope. But he did so with greater gravity and with particular emphasis on staying in the fall line. Then without hesitation, he headed down the trail, followed closely by the Czech woman. I stood at the top with Les for a few moments, this time really quite afraid. It wasn't just that it was a truly dangerous situation. I was also concerned with the difficulty of skiing conditions created by deep, heavy snow, which made a fall much more likely, knowing that any fall would escalate the risk of an avalanche. While I was contemplating my situation, Les said to me, "This slope looks really unstable. If it starts to go, get below those rocks on the left side."

With that, he was gone. I waited for a moment, then I started down the run, my heart pounding with trepidation. Following Les's advice, I tried to hug the left side of the slope, ready at any moment to dive into the declivity below the rocks, ready to accept the bodily risks that such a dive would entail. I promised myself that if I got out of this one, I would never get into this situation again. I cannot remember that descent, but I made it to the bottom, clumsily assuredly, but without falling and without causing an avalanche. It was like being given another shot at life. Nevertheless, the lesson received with so much trepidation went unlearned.

The trip back to the lodge was made in silence except for the *whack-whack-whack* of the helicopter rotor blades. Even as we trudged together up to the lodge, there was no conversation. We parted at the door with doleful glances, each reflecting the understanding of the situation we had experienced. I went to my room and threw myself on the bed, falling immediately asleep. Shortly, Kathy awoke me, inviting me to join our friends at tea. I filled her in only lightly on my afternoon adventure, avoiding revealing my feelings of dread and danger that I had incurred.

When Kathy and I arrived at tea, the Starks and Buchheit were discussing with the Walkers another close call, this one encountered by Skeeter during the morning. She had been led across a snow cornice that collapsed under her and pitched her 100 feet down the slope. She had been bruised in this misadventure but not seriously injured.

Nevertheless, the Walkers were beginning to doubt the skills of the guides, including Hans, who had been their guide during this incident. Their doubts were reinforced by the recounting of my two afternoon episodes, casting additional doubt on the judgment of the guides. They were particularly appalled by the second experience, which, in accordance with the precept that you don't ski on steep slopes in direct sunlight, was clearly a big mistake in judgment on the part of the guide. As we talked about these events over the next half hour, Doak and Skeeter became increasingly negative about the risks to which we were being exposed. It became increasingly clear that both of them harbored a deep-seated fear of avalanches, a fear that had grown out of her brother's tragedy. They even discussed the idea of giving the trip up and going home.

These thoughts were interrupted by the arrival of Dustin Hoffman fresh from a long and very expensive call on the radiotelephone. While we were summing up our attitudes toward the risks we were facing, Dustin picked up his guitar and announced in melody, rhythm, and rhyme that we should gather around to hear the day's news. As the group assembled on the floor, everyone hungry for a word from the outside world, Dustin plunged smoothly into the day's events, still in a lyrical and musical form. He covered all the trivia of the day and then segued into the important news, finally getting to Vietnam. As he entered this controversial subject, the tempo picked up a bit, the melody became jubilant, and he triumphantly reported that the American troops were leaving Vietnam. With his music, he made us feel as if we were about to celebrate the end of the war. Then abruptly, the mood changed as he moved to a minor key, the beat slowed, the music became somber, and the words told us that the troops were not just departing from Vietnam, they were marching into Cambodia. It was a virtuoso performance, particularly from an outspoken antiwar liberal. The invasion Dustin described marked the beginning of the Parrot's Beak Operation, a critical escalation that introduced a new phase of the war. The entire presentation, obviously extemporaneous, was composed and executed in less than fifteen minutes. For the moment, we forgot about our concerns with the mountaineering inadequacies of our hosts,

Wednesday came as another day in paradise. It had been cold during the night, and snow had fallen heavily over all the peaks upon which we might ski. Our first run presented us with perfect, deep powder conditions. It was still cold as we descended on the second run, and the snow remained light and fluffy. As we neared the bottom of this glacier, we came to a broad and long slope that became steeper as it extended from right to left. Having been skiing in the shadows, we welcomed the transition to light and warmth as this pitch lay in its entirety within reach of the morning sun. We arrived at the top of this incline on the left side, and our guide of the day, Hans Gmoser himself, led us some distance to the right across the ridge topping this slope.

Then he stopped and said assertively, "I am going to make a track down here, and I want you all to keep to the right of my track."

Because I wondered why we would have any restrictions on a slope that looked so benign, I asked why this constraint was necessary. Hans replied amiably that the slope got steeper to the left, and because of its steepness and the warmth of the direct sun, there was a chance of avalanche. We followed instructions and had a good run on a not-very-steep slope. When we got to the bottom, he led us across several crevasses that were spanned by snow bridges, single file, so that, if our bridge across a deep fissure collapsed, only one of us would end up in the crevasse. Nice odds when you are the heaviest guy in the group!

When we got to the other side of the last crevasse, we looked up and saw the next group descending to the left of Hans's track. Hans became agitated and tried via radio to contact this group. He was unsuccessful. As the second group worked its way down through the deep snow, finally making it to the bottom, the third started to arrive at the top and appeared to be going still farther to the left. Hans became even more distressed but again was unable to contact the guide in charge. As the third group started down in the area of the steepest incline, Hans decided to go down to get access to the helicopter's radio.

The radio didn't help because of interference from the mountain walls around us, so Hans had the pilot start the helicopter, something that was never done until all the skiers were down, and we flew to the site where we had last seen the other skiers. When we flew over the proscribed slope, we could see that an avalanche indeed had occurred and many people were digging into the avalanche debris. At last, the radio worked, and Hans, having absorbed the facts, was busy giving instructions. He didn't report much to us except to say that no one was hurt and the only loss was some ski poles that had been left in the path of the avalanche as their owners fled to avoid getting caught in the slide.

When we got back to the lodge, there seemed to be a security lid on any discussion of what had happened. We were pretty much in the dark until the Walkers invited us to their room to fill us in on the day's events. What had happened was that everyone had made it down except for Doak. The others were at the bottom taking pictures as Doak descended and the avalanche started around him. He tried to outski it as the others abandoned their poles to get out of the way of the accelerating slide. The avalanche caught him near the bottom, and he, with some knowledge derived from his brother-in-law's experience, attempted to swim in the deluge of snow. He kept his head above the surging snow as the avalanche crossed the depression at the bottom and roared up the other side of the valley. As the avalanche settled and stopped, he was totally immersed, but his head was only eighteen inches or so under the surface, a depth at which I believe you can breathe. In any case, he made a pocket for his face, doing so with the last mobility he had with his hands as he became totally locked in ice.

What happens in an avalanche is that the friction of the rolling snow creates both melting and supercooling of the snow, which then freezes to the consistency of concrete as the avalanche comes to rest. Even as he was buried as shallowly as he was, it still took forty-five minutes to extricate Doak from the enveloping ice.

As the conversation evolved into a discussion about all the dangers to which we had been subjected in the prior three days, it became clear that Skeeter and Doak were thinking about leaving. When they heard about our interaction with Hans as the day's main event unfolded, they were convinced that our hosts had been putting us at risk. They decided to sleep on the issue and to make a decision in the morning. The next day, they did not show up to ski, and by the time we returned from skiing, they had been evacuated to Spillimacheen. We never saw them again, although we did have, for several years, continued holiday correspondence with them.

The departure of the Walkers defined the end of the great adventures of this trip. There were, nevertheless, some more high and low points. Thursday was a low with breakable crust that was unskiable for me because I broke through every time I tried to turn. Meanwhile, the lighter men and all of the women could ski the shallow corn snow on top of the crust. It was a very long day and, with the likes of me slowing our progress, we got in only one run. Friday took us to the Conrad Glacier, which was represented to us as the longest downhill ski run in the world at nineteen miles. The descent was, I believe about 6,000 feet, so the grade wasn't much. Nevertheless, it was enough to keep us going downhill for more than an hour, while making a turn or two every time the grade steepened for a short distance. Friday night, it was cloudy, and because the sky was obscured, there was no surface freeze on the glaciers. Saturday was, therefore, a bad day for skiing, the conditions being best described as deep slush. The Walkers didn't miss too much with their early departure.

With the perspective of forty years of hindsight, I believe that I was a little cavalier in dealing with my responsibilities of the day. Looking back on this trip, which seemed like a great adventure at the time, I recognize that the risks were staring me in the face from the first day when I stood atop a run, and the guide instructed me to stay in the fall line for fear of starting an avalanche. Our avoidance of flying commercially with the Starks was purely symbolic and had no basis in reality, particularly when compared to the potential disasters we faced every time we jumped into or out of a helicopter. The time was not yet right for helicopter skiing in 1970, at least not so for young parents. We were all just a tad irresponsible.

As if to confirm this critical view, our hosts, Canadian Mountain Holidays, lost several clients and one guide, all to avalanches, over the next few years following our trip. It was several years later that Hans Gmoser began to outfit his guests with beepers for locating those buried under snowslides. Doak Walker, whom Bill Stark frequently parodied for being slow-witted, was the smart one in our Bugaboo coterie.

CHAPTER XV

Life Is a Lot About Luck

I have argued that the luckiest place and time to be born is in the United States in 1935 or 1936. This birth date would put the newborn into adulthood in 1957 or 1958, a time that gave good odds for avoiding dangerous military service, an economy that was poised to give a lifetime of unusual opportunity, and a country that still offered a frontier for easy exploitation. One's possibilities were improved by one's station of birth; it was preferable to be born into favorable circumstances— like into a family that had been running a business successfully for a hundred years. All of these conditions favored me and many of my contemporaneous friends, but even with these advantages, there is one more influence that is required for extraordinary success. That element is personal luck, recognizing that good luck doesn't just happen, it is nurtured by the individual through work, judgement and perseverance. Even if I did not fully exercise those attributes, I was a lucky son-of-a-bitch. As lucky as I was, not all of these ventures treated me gently.

This memoir is a recollection of speculative opportunities that fell into my lap because of my relationships and connections, which is not to say that they were all good deals. What they had in common was that they all looked good to me. Some were great right out of the box. Others started to unwind shortly after I got in. In poker the most unlucky thing that can happen is to be dealt second place hands. The same is true in business: Just like a poker hand, many good ideas are just not good enough to succeed, but they are good enough to suck you in. And I did have a few second place hands. Well, some of them might have been a good deal worse than that.

MY SPECULATIVE INVESTING began soon after I graduated from business school. A friend, Tom Nelson, was offered for $30,000 an opportunity to buy from Shel Lubar, as he was liquidating the Marine Capital Corporation, a package consisting of $30,000 in subordinated notes plus a ten percent stock interest, both in a failing bread company called Catherine Clark's Brownberry Ovens. Tom invited Albert Trostel III and me to share the investment, and, after modest due diligence that ascertained only that we would either get our money back in two years or we would gain control of the company, both prospects that we liked, we made the investment. Two years later the notes had been paid off so our net investment became zero. A year after that, Catherine Clark, about whose management decisions I had complained during this entire period, sold the business to the Peavy Company for six million dollars. The time was in the sixties when six million was real money. So was the $200,000 we each received. This was a great way to get introduced to the world of private investing.

Towards the end of the bread making investment, an old friend of mine from Williams College, Phil Lundquist, invited me to be his representative on the board of an agricultural chemical company, Agro "K," based in Minneapolis for which Phil, a stockbroker, had done the initial financing. The company had a number of seemingly exciting products, including two that were almost ready for the market: a fertilizer that radically improved plant growth and a boat bottom paint that totally repelled barnacles, withan order of magnitude advantage over existing marine paints. Of course both of these products had weaknesses. While the fertilizer seemed to have a significant beneficial impact on soybeans, it did not affect significantly many other commercial agricultural products. Be that as it may, soybeans made for a big time market. As for the bottom paint, it tended to delaminate (sluff off) in sheets after a few months of effectiveness. Regardless of their weaknesses, the Agro K management was optimistic about their ability to cure their deficiencies; and the prospects for both of these products seemed promising

I had no investment in the company, so my only reward was to be a modest directors fee. The downside was that quarterly meetings that would take an entire day. Nevertheless, because I liked the idea of being on boards, I took the job. It did not take me long to learn that this decision was a mistake.

Harry Rajaman, the president and principal stockholder, was an Indian Indian and was not receptive to advice. He used his director meetings as a theatrical opportunity with himself as the only actor. A year into this assignment I had had enough of Harry's self-aggrandizement and was getting ready to resign from the board when it became apparent that test plots of soybeans were showing an amazing augmentation of leafage. Plants were more than twice as large as those in the control plots. After we reviewed this encouraging situation at a late summer board meeting, an outside director offered to sell part of his holdings—seven thousand shares at seven dollars per share. Looking at the impending soybean success, I jumped at the chance and bought this block of stock. A month later it became apparent that, while the soybean plants were impressive, there were no beans in the pods. All the plant energy apparently had been directed to the leaves so the fertilizer as it was fabricated had no value for soybeans. I did wonder what information the selling director had possessed. In any case, I was left with an investment of dubious merit.

With the weight of my new investment, I stuck around for another year, but the meetings were so stultifying and real progress so slow that I finally resigned. Then I negotiated a sale of my stock to Phil for a note from him at a price a quarter of my cost. I took the loss for tax purposes, but never received any payment on the note. It was thirty years later that Harry's son called me and offered to buy my stock at my original cost. Phil, who theoretically owned my shares but had never perfected his ownership, did not object, so I got my money back. I am certain that my reader would have done due diligence on the question of what had motivated this purchase offer, but I did not want to deal with the inscrutable Indian. I was glad to recover my investment. Unexpected as this windfall was, it was manna from heaven just when I needed it.

While the Agro "K" adventure was under way, I met Dick Clark, an investment guy, who was a friend of my brother-in-law, Steve Seidel. He brought us a few deals that Steve and I invested in, starting with Michigan Cottage Cheese, a yogurt processing company. Steve and I together with fourteen other investors put in a total of four-hundred thousand dollars to buy a preferred stock, the only preference being that, if the company were sold at a value less than our converted stock would be worth, we would get our money back before the common holders got a penny. After a short interval, the company got into financial trouble stemming from exploding yogurt containers. We preferred holders were asked to give up our preference so that the company could raise more money. We were told that unless we gave up our preference the company would have to file for bankruptcy. I, like the rest of the preferred shareholders, was ready to accede to the wishes of management, but Steve suggested that I hold out with him against this uncompensated downgrade. I did. The other preferred shareholders gave up their preference, and the company refinanced despite Steve's and my refusal, and a year later, the company, still not out of the woods, sold out to Yoplait of France and became Yoplait USA. Steve and I got our money back, while the other previously preferred shareholders got a third of theirs. Was that a good break or was it the wisdom of listening to good advice?

My high school classmate and good friend, Dick Kramlich was always a source of ideas, most of which could be categorized as opportunities. His mind was a fertile field, a garden of possibilities in the forefront of technology, starting with Scope Inc. Scope was just a stock trading over the counter, but it was a company that had pioneered pattern recognition for military uses. Their technology had been developed for the navy. What it did was to analyze the silhouette of approaching planes, determining, despite a closing speed in excess of one thousand miles per hour, whether the plane was friendly or enemy. Having made this determination at a ninety percent confidence level, the software unlocked the guns. Too bad for you if, as an incoming friendly pilot, you were in the wrong ten percent. The company had developed a few commercial products that eventually came to nothing, but these products gave the stock cache.

Scope earned its place in my heart almost right out of the box. A week after I bought the stock, it started to go up, and within two months it was rising in increments greater than my original purchase price. In the end for me it was a "twenty five banger," and that in a little more than a year. Paying attention to an useful adage of Frank Mayo, an investment mentor of mine from my Paine Weber days: "when you have a satisfactory profit and don't know what to do, sell half and hope you were wrong," I sold half at the absolute top and, not being wrong about that half at least, sold the remaining half after a fifty percent retracement.

Even more than Brownberry Ovens this speculation provided me with a lot of seed money. As for the Scope stock, it was on its way to whence it had come, that being obscurity.

Then there was Carter's Jeans, another Dick Clark opportunity, which arrived in the late seventies. Headquartered in Concord, New Hampshire, it was a good company, having a competitive product, a well made blue jean, in a fast growing market, with revenues a little over two million dollars. For the size of the business it was adequately financed with somewhat thin equity, supplemented by a bank line of credit that served its seasonal needs. Because it was thinly financed, the company needed to borrow heavily during the spring to correspond with the blue jean buying season; but it paid the line off in the early fall. Shortly after I invested, the directors got fancy and bought a company that made winter clothing, doing so to balance their seasonality. Not that my opinion mattered, but this strategy seemed to me like a good plan even as it turned out to be a very bad idea.

I visited the company later that year on the day of the December directors meeting, expecting to meet the principals of the company. When I arrived in Concord, I was told that the directors meeting had been extended because the banker's were present and were "ironing out some problems." Waiting for this endless meeting to end, I finally learned that the bankers were pulling the rug, doing so because, with the offsetting seasonality of the new acquisition, the seasonal line of credit could not be paid off. Sadly that was the end of Carter's jeans. And it was a good lesson about bankers.

Just to remind me of how long it took me to learn from my mistakes, it was about thirty years later that I found another company that had a seemingly bright future but failedm to understand the impetuous needs of their bankers. The company was Wonder World, a specialty small box retailer with a national presence and a good record of operating results. My friend, Bruce Beda had just become a director in late November of 2008 when the company had an opportunity to buy out a major competitor and did so--with their bank's blessing! Bruce mentioned to me how good he thought this acquisition was and how it would improve the excellent prospects he envisioned for the company. I asked Bruce to find me some stock invest, say $50,000 worth, and he did, doing so just before Christmas. Shortly thereafter— a matter of less than three weeks— it turned out that Christmas sales had been slow and the combined inventory loan could not be immediately paid off. The bank called the loan and Wonder World was forced into bankruptcy. My $50,000 was lost in less than a month. It was a replay of Carter's jeans only quicker.

Reserve Oil and Minerals was a uranium mining company with properties in Colorado and New Mexico. It was a public company controlled by a family out of Albuquerque, the Melfis, and was made known to Harry Drake by Dick Kramlich. The story was that the Melfis were sitting on a significant uranium bonanza of which the public was not yet aware. (Inside information was commonplace in those days.) Harry persuaded me to go with him to the company headquarters in New Mexico and to visit the mine, which was located nearby.

In Albuquerque we met the family, the father JJ Melfi and his two sons, Frank and JJ Jr. They had high hopes, great enthusiasm and confidence in a dangerous strategy they had launched in the mode of David vs Goliath. They had obtained a long term lease for the mineral rights on a property that abutted the Picuate uranium mine, the then largest uranium mine in the world. The lease had been previously held by Kennecot Corporation, who, the Melfi's said, had allowed the lease lapse in a move aimed at negotiating a more favorable arrangement. Regretting the outcome of that decision after the lease was assigned to the Melfis, Kennecot was suing to reinstate the old lease. The Melfis were confident in their position, but the value of their company hinged on the outcome of a suit which pitted them against a corporate giant.

After meetings with JJ and with JJ Jr, in Albuquerque, Frank took us out to the mine. As we left the environs of this then small city, the sky was blue and the temperature was in the nineties-- a typical spring afternoon on a dessert landscape that contained only sparse vegetation and showed no signs of any kind of life. The only sign of habitation was an occasional group of primitive shacks that Frank said were occupied by Navajo Indians but there were no indians in sight. It was a forty mile trip across this desolate dessert, a short distance made long by the primitive road.

Suddenly, as we came down a small declivity, there loomed in front of us a vast abyss, a mile across and probably more, its depth almost as great as its span. In the bottom of the pit, looking like ants from our heights, a large number of bulldozers and earthmoving machines labored busily, scraping and loading earth into trucks, apparently determined to make this chasm even deeper. The loaded trucks regularly wove their way up a precarious road that zig zagged up the other side of the defile, meeting and dangerously making their way around the empty returning trucks. The activity was intense and organized.

This extensive enterprise was the Picuate mine. We had known that it was the largest open pit uranium mine in the world but seeing it in operation gave perspective on the scale of the undertaking. But more importantly it gave us perspective on the importance of the Melfi claim. The Picuate property and their excavations ran right to the fence line of the Melfi property. We saw drilling rigs on the property in question and Frank explained that, according to his intelligence, Kennecot had taken core samples that showed a continuation of commercial levels of ore onto this property. It appeared that the Picuate lode ran right on into the presumptive Melfi leasehold. Frank asserted that once they had a positive decision from the court, they would have a sure thing. It seemed so to me.

After this long day of interaction with the Melfis, Harry and I became confident that their lease would stand up in court. Back in Milwaukee we did some reasonable due diligence on the trend of the price of uranium, certainly a concern here, Harry and I formed a partnership, which we appropriately called Resources Limited, each putting in a small sum. Together we borrowed heavily, in a then friendly banking environment, to buy 80,000 shares at about six dollars a share. But even after the Melfis won the suit several years later, our investment lingered at prices half of our cost and did so for several years. The market apparently did not believe that the Melfis could raise the money for and manage the development of the mine. The bank was getting nervous and so had I become.

In the mid seventies, about four years into this deal, Reserve took on Standard Oil of Ohio as a partner and the stock finally popped into the low teens. We were glad to have an opportunity to get out and did so right away, doing so with a nice profit. After our exit, SOHIO took over the development of the mine, and against the advice of the Melfis, tunneled into the Melfi lode rather than using the open pit method. In the process, apparently to save money, they employed pillars that were too widely spaced in an unstable sandy environment. A year later, this mistake became a disaster. The mine collapsed and so did the Reserve Oil stock. It never recovered and the Melfis lost everything. We were lucky to be out. Lucky again!

It was in the early eighties that my TEC group met with an economist who had recognized early the approaching collapse of inflation and interest rates, following the financial malaise of the seventies. He took the entire morning to explain how he had done it. His presentation took three hours and was quite interesting, but more importantly it was persuasive in the simplicity of his logic. Despite his verbosity, I can summarize his talk in three sentences.

It was during his summer vacation with his family that he travelled east to west across the country, observing first on the east coast that oil tankers were anchored off shore at the major ports because there was no room left on land to store the oil. As he moved into the mid-west there was, even before the harvest, grain stored on the ground next to most granaries. Throughout his trip he saw vacancy and for sale signs on apartments and houses wherever he went. With these observations he concluded that the main components of the cost of living index, energy, food and housing would all be under pressure. He saw it as a "sure thing." Soon after he published his conclusions, the inflation broke sharply and deeply. Those who listened to him, including his own Chicago bank, had prospered greatly.

I made sure that I sat next to this oracle at lunch, and in the course of conversation I asked if he had any more sure things. He responded, "Why yes I do, and I'm glad you asked."

He went on to say that the dollar would be weak against the strong currencies of Europe and Asia, the Swiss and German Marks and the Yen. He was certain that the dollar would lose half of its value against these currencies. He explained why, and his reasoning was persuasive. Besides, even to me the dollar had appeared for some time to be overvalued. I had been given the next sure thing!

That afternoon I called my broker and told him begin to accumulate ten spreads between the dollar and the German mark, going long the mark and short the dollar. I had calculated that with about one hundred thousand in margin I would, if the mark went from twenty five cents to fifty cents, make a million dollars.

My only mistake here was that let my broker's fears guide me. I was in and out and never held more than three contracts and that position only briefly. The mark doubled in less than two years. With a great deal of trading I had made twenty five thousand dollars— coincidentally the exact amount I had paid in commissions. Of course I was in charge, and I should have insisted on the execution of the original plan, but fear is often contagious. And then I ask myself "How often do you have a sure thing?"

The answer is clearly "not often", but when you do, you need to pay attention. And when you have a good friend looking out for your interests you should pay close attention! To wit; Harry Drake, returning from a late lunch, less than half hour before the NYSE closed picked up the early edition of the Milwaukee Journal and while walking back to Paine Weber, opened to the business page which on that day bore the headline: *Schlitz agrees to sell to Stroh*. Harry scanned the article and found the sale price to e $25 per share. Harry didn't hurry back to the office, being confident that the incipient sale would be immediately reflected in the price. When Harry got to his desk, he checked the price and to his surprise it was still close to the previous days close, that being $15. By now the market close was less than ten minutes away, but there was time to call me. When I got the call, I was wrapped up in other things and I gave Harry short shrift, just trying to get rid of him. Ten easy points with no risk!

And when the SEC called Harry six months later to find out what had prompted such a timely purchase, I could have said just what Harry did when they called him about the thousand shares he bought at five minutes to three, "I was acting on tape action." Of course a more direct response would have been: "I read it in the newspaper"

There were a few others like these "investments" but the stories are not as good. In any case the penultimate deal was the worst. That was a real estate investment I made with my high school classmate John Walton. Now I was academically first or second in my class for many of my years at Country Day and during the same period John was mostly last, so I might have known better. Nevertheless, when he came to me with a plan for developing residential lots on a thirty acre tract, I was all ears. My investment would be $200,000, covering the cost of the land, John would finance the development, using the land as collateral and we would split the profits. It was straightforward and the pro-forma looked good.

John proceeded to develop the first ten acres into thirty lots, sold the lots quickly, and together we "pocketed" a $200,000 profit of which half was mine. Pocketed may be the wrong word here because, while John's half supported his lifestyle, mine was earmarked for the second phase. Then John had a great idea. "Let's build condos. We can make a lot more money with condos."

When I saw the pro-forma for condos, I saw what he meant. It was a lot more money. Being who I was, that being occasionally careless and superficial, I agreed to the new plan. That was a big mistake, followed by a bunch of additional mistakes made by my partner, which included a sewer that tried to run uphill and other construction blunders, but most importantly it was overspending on amenities like shake roofs in a marketplace that looked for economy. Our construction costs were greater on a square foot basis than our competitors selling prices. Early on, before we were committed to our building specs, I asked John how he made his marketing decisions. His answer should have stopped me in my tracks: "I know what people want."

This project got more and more complicated and could make a story in itself, but the fact is that once we reached the point of no return, there was little opportunity to reverse course: we were deeply indebted to the banks with loans that I had guaranteed. We needed to finish the build out to get our (actually the bank's) money out of the land. I lost two million dollars here, actually much more because I raised money by cashing in early most of my Fiserv options. I'm afraid I made my luck here through blatant carelessness.

But then all of these experiences, especially the losers, gave me the insights and experience to take a significant risk on a company that my son, Rich, was building before the turn of the century. Rich had been working for a company that was developing a system for third party administration of health care insurance. The marketing plan for their regional system collapsed after they had developed a front end, that being the system for enrolling individual employees in their customer's benefits plans. The principle shareholder, Rich's boss, decided to abandon the business, but Rich, who held a small interest at the time, saw value for this system in the then emerging benefits enrollment marketplace. Rich got no help from his former employer, but seeing an opportunity to develop a real business, worked for sweat equity for the next five years. He started with a barely adequate product and no customers, thus no references, a difficult position in a market having competitors with a history. Nevertheless, Rich persisted.

In 2000 when Rich was offering some of his personal stock to raise money to live on, the shares priced at seven dollars a share, I put my toe in the water, not understanding the business, but having faith in Rich's business skills but more so in his commitment. Then I watched him manage the early phases of developing the business, doing so in troubled waters, including 9/11, which almost put him out of business. Rich struggled in a situation that seemed hopeless to me. Nevertheless by 2007 he had worked his way through the survival stage and had a business that was recognizable as a viable competitor in his marketplace. By this time he had sales approaching ten million, but still showed significant losses, largely because, in a rapidly growing "software as a service" (SaaS), company the front end cost of selling and servicing new customers consumes all of the profits and then some. In fact the faster you grow the more you lose. bswift by this time was growing annually at 45% plus and hemorrhaging cash.

That year, 2007, Rich looked for outside capital, using an articulate investment guy to present the company. This consultant identified, at least for me, the characteristics that would inure to the benefit of the owners: first, the stickiness of revenues arising from the difficulty and cost of changing vendors; and second, the extraordinary margins on all future revenues after the second year a customer is on the books. Additionally from my Fiserv experience I understood how SaaS companies build barriers to entry by developing software that addresses their customer's ever changing requirements. By identifying needs and paying for software which addresses problems, the customer actually pays to develop the SaaS company's competitive advantage. As it happens, time in service in these types of companies is an advantage that money cannot buy. I was beginning to understand that Rich was building real value with this mechanism.

I brought together many of my friends, relatives, business associates and acquaintances to consider this investment, but together with the investment guy, we could only interest a few, and hardly any of those were of size. Given a second opportunity several years later, my good friend Willard Walker, after referring the offering to his own company's CFO, pointed out that you should not buy stock in a company that is losing money. Willard offered me a meeting with this adviser, who would share his analysis with me, I demurred; I had become a believer in the business and in Rich and his partner, Ray Seaver.

By this time I had liquidated all of my other investments, borrowed money and invested it all at forty seven dollars a share. That may sound like putting it all on red. To the contrary it was more like putting it all on 22 black. (my lucky number at roulette) There were years of discomfort ahead with cash flow always a nagging problem—not just for bswift but for me personally. Nevertheless, the next sale of stock, this to a private equity firm, was at a price over three hundred dollars. Six months later with the help of our new private equity partners, the company was sold to Aetna at a thousand dollars per share. My oft lurking ship finally had made it to shore.

The payoff from this investment, rewarding as the profit was, was really in the satisfaction of seeing my son manage a growing company in the most difficult of circumstances. He had entered a business space that was occupied by established competitors; and while he understood the business well and had a vision for its future, he nevertheless started with very little money, an also ran product, and no customers in a seemingly maturing market. From this inauspicious beginning, he created the best software in the industry; then he and his partner Ray Seaver turned major attention to perfecting customer service, and finally they focused on organization building. In the process they attracted to bswift the best minds in his competitive arena. Aetna took them out just as they had achieved real dominance in their industry.

I started this memoir with the comment that life is about luck. Surely good luck has played a part in my "investment" "success," but there is a lot to be said about making your luck with hard work, learning to judge risk against opportunity, performing meaningful due diligence, and having the experience that hardens your stomach against fear of loss. But most of all, to paraphrase my oft quoted Chinese curse; " it is good to live in favorable times."

CHAPTER XVI

The Ice Age Cometh

While the weather had been an aesthetic interest from the time of my first memories, it was to become, over my lifetime, an intellectual interest as well. In spite of my fascination with weather phenomena, my introduction to climatology didn't begin until I was well into my thirties. While this introduction was engaging and captivated my absorbent, some might say gullible, mind, my first intellectual encounter with the subject of climate would prove to be somewhat misdirected.

IT WAS SHORTLY after I got involved in Electri-wire that I joined a continuing education and business consulting organization called The Executive Committee, TEC for short. My TEC group, which was comprised of ten or so CEOs of local companies, met eight times a year. The TEC experience had three basic elements: 1) a meeting with one's TEC chairman, at which we identified key problems in the business for possible discussion with the group; 2) a meeting with one's entire TEC group, which consisted of a dozen or so other business leaders; and 3) an interaction with an outside resource on various subjects relating to our businesses and sometimes to our personal lives.

One of my first TEC meetings occurring in June of 1971 featured a speaker, Doctor Iben Browning, who represented himself as a climatologist, although he had no educational background in climatology. Browning was a ponderous man, both in his body configuration and in his speaking style. Not that he was boring, he wasn't that, but with his deep and stentorian voice, he made big, even momentous, statements, like, "The Ice Age has already started, and because of it, your state will be almost depopulated within a generation."

He said things like that, and his authority over his audience demanded that he be believed. He assumed we were there to learn. And he was correct—we were.

Doctor Browning opened up his presentation with a series of questions:

"How long does an ice age last?"

"What is the interval between ice ages?"

"How long has it been since the last ice age?"

My reader probably knows the answer to these questions, but in 1971, no one was paying a great deal of attention to climate issues. The shocking answers, 100,000 years, 10,000 years, and 11,000 years, made listeners, if not believers, of most of us. When you consider these answers, and they are based on solid studies of the geological history of the earth, you can quickly grasp that ice ages are normal, and the interglacial periods are only short interruptions in a frigid eternity. At first, the realization that an ice age is somewhat overdue on a statistical basis is somewhat disturbing. The consideration that makes this reality less threatening than it seems is that the statistical variation for these periods is plus or minus 30,000 years.

His theory, as he explained it to us and as he presented it in his book, was that weather is the primary cause of important human events, documented plausibly in his lecture with charts and historical tables as well as anecdotal details. According to Browning, all the historically important religions, dynasties, and empires were established in periods of bad weather and succeeded because the weather and the related economic conditions only improved thereafter, at least for a time. When the bad weather, caused not by ice ages but by intervening geological or solar phenomena, came hundreds of years later, the successful institutions had established enough authority to weather the storm, so to speak. In the case of religions, if the bad weather came too soon, it was too bad for that particular bunch of gods.

I was persuaded by most of these arguments and amused by others. One narrative that tickled my fancy was his explanation of how different population groups dealt with the adversity that the bad weather wreaked upon them. One such group was the "confessional religionists," his description of Catholics. They blamed God for their problems and were helpless to oppose misfortune, so when the bad times came, they just drank more booze, i.e., the Irish during the potato famine. Browning had an applicable chart showing that the death rate from liver cirrhosis for Catholics, particularly the Irish, rose steeply in bad times. A second group, whom he called the "contritionists" (which turned out to be Protestants), built their religion on atonement for their personal guilt. These people blamed themselves for the problems created by bad weather, so they addressed the issue by committing suicide. His charts reflected this outcome. The third group, tribal aboriginals (his aphorism for blacks), generally blamed other people for their troubles; so their murder rates went up. Perhaps there was a trace of racism here, but the upward curving chart supported his argument well enough to persuade me. Besides, the theory did fit in well with the accepted racial stereotypes of the day.

From the beginning of my relationship with Dr. Browning, I tended to be fully accepting of his theories. Rather than attributing my deference to gullibility, I would contend that he was very convincing, what with quantitative support and well footnoted scientific references as well as his own arcane observations from the natural world. Nevertheless, I retained a modest level of skepticism about many of his assertions and did look for a chink in his armor. While I had no problem accepting as factual that the permanent snow line was advancing across the entire Northern Hemisphere, I was startled at his statement that all the world's glaciers were advancing. *Aha*, I thought, *this time he has overreached.*

I had recently returned from a ski trip in western Canada where we had skied entirely on glaciers. Judging from the recently exposed glacial debris lying downstream of these ice sheets, all of the glaciers in this region appeared to be receding. I thought I had found a flaw in his always certain knowledge. So I raised my hand and asked smugly: "Iben, do you mean *every* glacier in the world?"

Iben seemed to relish this question and took a short time to savor the moment. "Why no. As a matter of fact, there is one place in the world where, because of a shift in the Japanese current, the glaciers are receding. That would be in British Columbia."

That was the moment that he attained the status of Delphi. It wasn't just that he knew what was happening in our world; he even knew the whys and wherefores that stood behind the facts. From that time forward, I would sit at his feet and absorb his wisdom whenever he came to Milwaukee. These visits were not infrequent because, based on his seeming command of esoteric science and his shamanistic power to convince, as well as an ability to manipulate his pronouncements to match business cycles, he was consulting with many Milwaukee companies. Often, when he was here, he would call, and I would take him to breakfast at the University Club. A fair trade: my breakfast for his wisdom.

These meetings went on for the next several years, and the events that occurred over this period provided evidence of a rapidly cooling world. The economic effects of bad weather were unpleasant, with food prices and energy prices increasing at an accelerating pace. International relations were unpleasant, perhaps no worse than they had been since the onset of the cold war, but Dr. Browning was good at making current events fit into his paradigm. I looked forward to these meetings and thought I was making use of the information he shared with me. In retrospect, I'm not sure that he influenced any decisions that I made, but he was a presence in my thinking, one that kept me cautious.

I still remember the last breakfast I had with Iben in early May of 1977. On that occasion, I was especially concerned with the economy, which still wasn't doing very well under the stewardship of Jimmy Carter. Inflation, interest rates, and unemployment were all at or approaching double digits, and the stock market, which had been in the doldrums for most of the seventies, appeared headed for a downturn. My business always suffered painfully in downturns, so I greeted Iben with trepidation. Getting quickly through the pleasantries, I asked him straightaway: "Are we going to have a recession?"

He responded in his normal wry and aloof manner, talking directly down his nose to me: "That's the good news, young man, we're not going to have a recession."

He paused, giving me just enough time to register relief, then added dryly, "The bad news is that we are going to have a depression."

Being a believer in almost all things from the great man's mouth, I was immediately depressed by this prophecy. Nevertheless, I sat down, listened, and learned that Wisconsin was going to get the worst of it. Iben reminded me that Wisconsin was already in a great drought. "Why," he observed aridly, "there has been so little rain in the last nine months that there was no frost in the ground all winter."

Again, he had detailed knowledge about a small part of the world! I was aware of this local phenomenon because I had just built a factory in Spring Green, where the ground had been so dry that we could dig foundation trenches in December without difficulty despite the inordinate cold. Again, he seemed to possess demonstrable evidence with which to support his most dramatic, even bizarre, predictions.

As our discussion progressed, Iben fed me more bad news; the drought that had been in effect since the previous summer was going to continue as part of the early manifestation of the anticipated ice age. Because they were already stressed from the shortage of moisture during the late summer, fall, and winter, the Wisconsin forests would begin to die in the midsummer heat and would be mostly gone by fall. This prediction seemed a little over the top, but the continuation of the drought at some level seemed likely.

Two weeks later on Memorial Day weekend, I was putting in my pier at Pine Lake. The water level was already down about two feet from the prior spring, and as I installed the first section, I saw that the platforms were already three feet above the water. As I contemplated this situation, I realized that any sort of drought would have the pier at a dangerous height. Being a guy who addresses problems, I pulled out the first section, got my chainsaw, took a compromise twenty inches off of each six by six post, and this first section looked much better for the expected conditions. Then I installed the rest of the pier, cutting down the supporting posts as I did so. When I finished, the surface of the pier was about sixteen inches above the water level, and I was ready for the coming drought.

That very night, we had a thunderstorm with a whole lot of rain. That was good news for Wisconsin, but when it rained more or less continuously for the next thirty days, it was clear that I had made a mistake with my pier. By the Fourth of July, the lake had already risen about two feet, and my pier was floating. I had to take it out and nail the pieces I had cut off back onto the shortened posts.

The summer of 1977 turned out to be a wet one throughout the Midwest. The drought was definitely broken, and soon, so was the string of unusually cold years. It was only a matter of a few years when climatologists, many of whom had been predicting an ice age, turned their attention to the likelihood that global warming was the greater threat. That meeting with Iben Browning in May of 1977 turned out to be my last meeting with him; perhaps his Milwaukee clients also vanished with the collapse of the great man's invincibility.

During the next twenty-some-odd years, I paid little attention to long-term climate change, feeling comfortable that there was no impending crisis deriving from the weather. I put my head in the sand and went sailing.

CHAPTER XVII

A Timely Opportunity

Fate has a way of sneaking up on us, and sometimes, the best-laid plans fail for unforeseen happenings, often through no fault of our own. On the other hand, fortuitous developments occasionally bail one out of the plights in which one finds oneself. Luck was a major factor in my life. More often than not, it was not only good luck but good luck just when I needed it. Such an opportunity began to present itself to me in the mid-seventies at a time when I needed a course correction.

It was in late 1976 that some seeds I had planted in the late sixties bore fruit.

After my father died in 1968, I had taken his place on the board of directors of the Classified Insurance Company, a small direct writer of auto casualty and homeowner's insurance. As a direct writer, the company sold its product through advertising and direct mail rather than through agents. The company had a major asset in the endorsement of the Wisconsin Teachers Association.

While Classified was to provide an occupation for me for the next seven years, I did not cover myself with distinction in managing the business. When I took over the leadership here, there were quite a few obvious problems that were subject to straightforward solutions. Fixing the problems were not going to be difficult; the hard part would be in laying a path for the future and in identifying the right opportunities.

AT THE TIME of my father's death, I was looking for something to take into the future, something to build. I had left my job at Krause and had not yet found Electriwire Assemblies Company. I needed a job and a place to hang my hat. That is never a pleasant situation, and indeed, it was an uncomfortable time for me.

Then I came to understand that this little company, Classified Insurance Corporation, was ripe for a takeover at a price that I could afford. Besides, as a director, I already had an inside track. The stock was in the low single digits, with just eight hundred thousand shares outstanding, and I had a small share interest in the company, about 3 percent. With a vague strategy in mind, I gradually increased my ownership position, doing so at prices in the two to three range, reaching a 13 percent stake in 1969. I had made myself the largest shareholder and had done so at low, single-digit prices.

Next, I tried to increase my influence in the boardroom by taking a more active position. My approach was to try to put a little creativity into the company's marketing program. Sales had been flat for several years, so I put together a plan for accelerating growth that recommended changes in our advertising and sales proposition, using ideas that I had picked up at Harvard Business School. Without advising management or the board of my intention, I dropped a ten-page memorandum on the board a couple of days before a scheduled board meeting.

The plan took a couple of subtle shots at the company's leadership—I thought they were not unreasonable criticisms. As careful as I thought I had been, I had not anticipated the political necessities of this kind of a proposal. Most importantly, I had failed to enlist any allies and had not even considered that these board members of my father's generation might not want to consider my ideas. I figured that they would be impressed by my erudite presentation. It should not have been too surprising to me that my proposal was immediately and snidely panned by the president, "Skee" Holton. He had used the time between getting my proposal and the meeting to prepare a scathing disparagement of my ideas, doing so well enough that I was unable to respond effectively. I found the reaction of the board to be surprising. To my chagrin and without any real discussion, they rejected my plan "out of hand." To a man and with little consideration, they voted to table this proposal. I had gotten another lesson in humility.

After this repudiation, I licked my wounds and decided to bide my time and wait for something to happen. I had found another business with which to occupy my attention, so I just stayed on the board and kept my mouth shut.

Time passed, but finally, in early 1972, my patience was rewarded. A look-alike company and similarly sized company, Educator and Executives Insurance Company of Ohio, was acquired by JCPenney for a high price. The effect of this transaction was to balloon the price of Classified from the middle single digits into the low twenties. I was ecstatic about this run, having gained a book profit of more than two million dollars, and I immediately started to sell the stock, rejoicing in my decision to stay with this investment. However, there was something I should have known and learned quickly from our legal counsel: I had become a controlling shareholder, first as a director, but additionally, as a greater-than-10-percent shareholder. Being such, under the law, I was not permitted to sell more than 1 percent in a six month period until I held less than 10 percent and had not been a director in the prior six months.

Seeing what I must do to take advantage of this good luck, I sold the allowable amount right away at the top of the price range, twenty-one dollars a share. At the same time, I resigned from the board, an insignificant move in that I had no influence anyway; and over the next year I sold the allowable 1 percent after each required six-month wait. By mid-1973, with my holding down to 9.9 percent, I was free to sell the rest of my position. Unfortunately, by then, the stock was back under ten. Nevertheless, I kept on selling until the stock hit four, a price still greater than my average original cost. By then my holdings were about 5 percent; but I had all my money back and then some, so I determined to sit back and wait some more.

The waiting lasted until 1977, at which time Classified was having serious financial problems. In the most recent year the company was operating at a loss, and the stock had sunk to less than a dollar per share. There was concern in the financial market that the company might fail.

Knowing that I had been in opposition to the failing management, a dissident group of shareholders approached me to head a slate that would oust the current board and the management as well. They suggested that I be the leader if their slate won. While I was considering this proposal, the then chairman of the Classified board, Andy Spheeris, called, probably having gotten wind of the plans of the dissident group, and asked me to join their proposed slate of directors. He assured me that they would support any changes I proposed, including a change in the operating management. The major concern of the board seemed to be their wish not to be associated with a failing enterprise.

I met briefly with the board and could see that they were at sea, unable to deal with their situation. Nevertheless, they did seem to understand that they needed to replace the president. I sketched briefly my views of what needed to be done, mainly replacing Holton with a professional manager and then introducing good management practices. As sketchy as my presentation was, they accepted my approach and agreed to support my election,

At this time, I was, in point of fact, out of work again because I had turned over the management of Electriwire to Jim Cerny. Even as I had a title and a salary there, I needed something to do. Besides, my lifestyle was running a bit ahead of my income. Andy Spheeris held the job of Classified's chairman of the board. Even as he understood that we had to shake up the management, Andy did not want to do any of the real work that needed to be done, particularly firing and replacing the president, so he agreed to delegate his authority to me right after my election and then to resign his position in my favor within six months. Although the path to a real job was not at all clear here, it was evident that my bread was buttered with this situation. I went along with their offer and was elected to the board at the annual meeting.

Immediately after the annual meeting, like the next week, I met with Holton and discharged him. Holton had not seen this firing coming, and he was particularly angered that it had come from me. He ranted and raved and threatened suit.

Eventually he accepted the fact that I had the authority of the board, and he cleaned out his office and left.

With the putsch completed, the next task was that of hiring a chief operating officer, not a chief executive, as I planned to have that position later on. With the help of a headhunter, I found an old insurance hand, who had risen to the upper ranks of CNA Insurance and was for some reason—never quite clear to me—looking for an opportunity to manage a small insurance company. He was Robert Griffing, who possessed an excellent pedigree and had a broad range of insurance experience. After several satisfactory meetings with him, he accepted the job as president and was on board six weeks after the annual meeting.

As soon as he arrived, Griffing and I began working together at restructuring the company, doing so department by department, and almost everywhere we looked, discovering evidence of poor management practices. As we reviewed the second-level management cadre, we were fortunate to find a rough jewel within the ranks. Our discovery was Jim Cizek, who had been an assistant vice president and possessed a good grasp of the internal workings of the organization. We were surprised to find out that he seemed to know exactly where the sewer was leaking.

We learned right away from Cizek, now a vice president, that the most serious problem was in the claims area, where a generous payment policy had been Holton's strategic imperative. Interestingly, this was not new information to Cizek; he had been complaining to Holton about the claims policy as well as our legal defense team for years. I quickly came to understand the obvious: that being generous with claims is like burning money.

Compounding this problem, Classified's underwriting rules were not adequately enforced but perhaps more importantly, they were occasionally misapplied. An example of a significant underwriting miscalculation had been Classified's taking on the Minnesota police association at discounted prices. While the driving experience of this group was excellent, and driving record is a good proxy for risk, that is not enough information. What the underwriters didn't consider at the time was that policemen don't give tickets to other policemen. Because we put our trust in the driving records provided by the motor vehicle department, we had no idea what was our real risk. The problem might have been anticipated; but if not, it should have become evident through evaluating the results, looking at losses retrospectively. However, Cizek pointed out that financial control was minimal with an inadequate information system.

As we got into the issue of information processing, a vital function for a casualty insurer, Cizek already had a team working on developing a user-directed data processing system. This system would not only accommodate administrative functions but also would allow sales agents to underwrite and to price individual policies over the phone in real time. At this early stage of the development of data processing systems, that being 1977, the idea of a real-time system for management of administrative functions for a casualty insurer was way ahead of the competition and, for the most part, was not deemed practicable. We continued the development of data processing and completed the system within a year. By the early eighties this administrative system would be Classified's most important asset.

Fixing these problems of claims, underwriting, and the information system took the better part of a year, but the progress we made helped me establish my bona fides with the board of directors. Six months into the new regime, I proposed my becoming chairman, Andy stepped aside gracefully, and the board approved the change. I became chairman and shortly made myself chief executive. I again had a real job.

It was improvement in two areas, underwriting and claims, that allowed us to stop the bleeding; and gradually we inched our way into the black. Our new data processing system, which had become a full-blown casualty insurance administration system, paved the way for improvements not only in underwriting but also in accounting, claims, and most importantly, in sales.

But still, direct mail sales lagged, and we needed to address the growth issue. Griffing was aware of a marketplace in which we could rapidly increase our premium income. It was that that of managing general agents (MGAs), agents who controlled books of business addressing specialized risks and who needed an underwriter. He had had experience here, and I was easily convinced that this was a good way for us to accelerate our growth. Over the next year we took on a half-dozen MGAs; and as we had hoped, we had gotten on a growth path.

By the early eighties, I thought we had the business well in hand. Classified was in the black, and with our MGAs, we seemed to have found a way to control our sales volume. With our computer system, we had the ability to manage the cost side of the business. We had sold two data processing systems, and those customers were raving about how well the systems worked for them. Jim Cizek, reflecting what he was hearing from these users, suggested that we consider starting a data center for processing other insurance companies.

We did a superficial and ultimately inadequate study of the marketplace for administrative systems in the insurance business, finding right away that insurance data processing was dominated by Profit Marketing Services (PMS). PMS had a mixed reputation: their product worked well enough but was not popular with users; the company was difficult to deal with, but through brute force they owned the marketplace. There were not many small insurance companies not already in PMS's hands. After a cursory look at this opportunity, we decided not to participate for two reasons: we didn't know the business, and we were afraid of PMS. Besides we were an insurance company, not a DP company. This decision, though reasonable, was likely one of my most serious mistakes. With later experience gained while I was building the insurance service center business at Fiserv, I came to realize what the value of an effective real-time administrative system might have been in 1980. As it happened in the era that followed, new insurance companies were springing up like weeds after a summer rain. PMS went on almost unchallenged to become a multibillion-dollar company.

By 1983, the error of Griffing's and my MGA strategy began to unfold. Several of our agents turned out bad, and that entire segment of our business was barely breaking even. With growing premium income, much of that growth on the backs of MGAs, we were pushing the statutory limits of our capital. Soon we were under pressure from the insurance department to increase our capital. Being mostly unable to raise capital in the terrible stock market of the early eighties, we raised a little money by selling convertible debentures to our shareholders, but that was just a stopgap measure.

Then out of the blue, they having become aware of our state-of-the-art administrative system, Geico and AIG, both major players in the casualty insurance business, appeared. Both companies were interested in acquiring Classified, each willing to talk prices in the low twenties at a time when our stock was stuck at eight. The time seemed right to exit the business. Nevertheless, after preliminary due diligence and seemingly productive discussions, both of them backed away. As they kissed us off, GEICO indicated that the value or our DP system was diminished by the fact that, even though both of these users had agreed not to distribute the system, there were still two versions of it in the marketplace. Then as they pulled the plug on our negotiations, AIG told us that they were allergic to the MGA business because we had surrendered control of our underwriting to these often shady operators. In retrospect, the MGA decision turned out to be another bad decision for which I was the decider. I could forgive myself for selling the DP systems because we did not have any idea of the potential of the system at the time of those sales. Nevertheless, these two experiences took a lot of wind out of my sails; I did realize that I had made some seriously bad decisions here.

Throughout the negotiations with GEICO and AIG, I had experienced continuing pressure from the insurance department. I had deferred dealing with the issue, expecting that the acquisition by one of these companies would resolve the statutory capital problem. With those hopes dashed, I needed another solution. I had one ace up my sleeve—well, maybe not quite an ace, but at least it seemed like a winner.

He was Philo Smith, and he had, during my tenure as chairman, traded our stock in modest amounts but always successfully. During that period, he had courted me occasionally on the phone, indicating that he might invest directly in the company if we needed a capital infusion. Because he had been a small investor, never owning more than 20,000 shares at a time, I did not take him seriously as a source of capital. However, when asked, he was willing to invest $8 million at the then current price of eight dollars a share; and, because he knew the company and me, he could close quickly without conditions.

I knew that the amount proposed would give him close to 50 percent ownership, but naively I did not see control as a risk. He had been a passive investor who managed money directed specifically at insurance companies. He had seemed to respect the progress of the company since I had been in charge. As we discovered in our due diligence, Philo had managed his portfolio with uncommon success, having averaged a 35 percent return on his insurance investments over the previous ten years. Further, he had never been involved in the management of any companies in which he invested. All he purported to want for his investment was stock at the market price and a place on the board.

The transaction went forward at eight dollars a share just before Thanksgiving, 1983. Upon its completion two directors who had opposed the deal sold their holdings to Smith at eight dollars. After these transactions, he did have absolute control.

It was in early January of the next year that I discovered that we were required under the law to seek approval from the state insurance commissioner for the change of control that had occurred. So I, together with Philo, headed to Madison to visit this information upon the commissioner. Not surprisingly given the inflow of capital resulting from the transaction, the commissioner had no problem with this change, and so, after a brief and cordial meeting, Philo and I headed back to Milwaukee.

It was a crisp but sunny winter day, and we had an amiable conversation as we exited Madison and got onto I-94. It was just before we got to the Lake Mills exit that the conversation turned to business. It started casually, but from there it went quickly to ominous.

It began with, "Dick, there are a couple of things I want you to do."

In reality, there were three things he wanted me to do, and I disagreed with all three, feeling that they were not just bad for the company, but they were really bad ideas. The first and most important was that he wanted me to sell the bond portfolio in its entirety. The bond portfolio was scaled according to maturity dates to match the company's cash requirement for paying claims, some of which would not have to be paid for up to seven years. Because the bond market was about to hit a generational low, the portfolio, which had a total market value of about $40 million, showed a current loss of around $10 million. Because we could, in accordance with statutory accounting, carry the bonds at cost, and because we planned to carry the bonds to maturity, the "book" losses did not have real importance unless you sold them. However, upon a sale the losses thus realized would become an impairment to capital, more than offsetting the effect of Philo's entire investment and putting the company again in a capital shortage position. It would be a ten million dollar mistake, more than offsetting his eight million dollar investment. I argued this rather obvious point for about thirty miles along I-90, also disputing the wisdom of his two other "requests." I believed that I was still in charge and that Philo would surely see the wisdom of my arguments. I was quite surprised that he held so strongly to his position.

As we were coming up on Johnson's Creek, I finally addressed the real issue between us in what I thought was a lighthearted vein: "Philo, your problem is that you don't want to be confused by the facts."

That this was a momentous piece of imprudence on my part, especially to a man who was thirty years my senior and in control of my fate, is surely an understatement. It took Philo only a few moments to digest my words and to respond. While he pondered, I noticed the Gobbler Restaurant on my right and was thinking of lightening the conversation by suggesting that we stop for lunch. As I came out of my reverie and just as we reached the Johnson's Creek exit, his response came back hard and cold: "I think I will accept the resignation you offered me when we struck our deal."

Not much to say to that. His response came at me as a total surprise, even as I realized that my statement had been somewhat provocative. And the way he said it! I had no doubt that I had passed the point of no return. Lunch being forgotten, I thought about his demand for a short time, realizing that a good portion of my "liquid" net worth was invested in this company, and besides that I was receiving a significant salary from the company. My comfort level had been severely exceeded, and I felt a stab of panic. I had boneheadedly stepped into a bottomless swamp and had no idea of how to deal with this situation. For an indeterminate but painfully long moment, there was silence in the car. Clearly, there was to be no relenting on his part. Finally, as we approached the Ixonia exit, I asked cautiously, "Will you buy my stock?"

Philo thought about this question for only a moment, this time coming back with, "Yeah, I will." (Long pause) "I'll pay you seven dollars."

This was a truly disappointing price, as he had acquired his position at eight, the stock was trading at eight and a quarter, and he had recently paid eight to two other directors. At the same time, there was a thin market for the stock, trading perhaps 10,000 shares a week, and by this time, I owned more than 100,000 shares as well as $600,000 of the convertible notes. I had grasped the frigidity reflected in his words and realized that I would not get even one more chance from this man. There was no room to negotiate. All these thoughts raged through my mind as I wondered what to do. Nevertheless, I knew that I had to act on the spot. I came back with my response: "Done."

And it did seem that our business was done for the day. We were not yet anywhere near Oconomowoc, and what were we going to talk about while we drove all the way back to our office in Waukesha? I am sure that I don't remember. I do know that it was a long trip, and I was glad when we parted. The entire process, including the terminal silence, had taken less than forty minutes.

Philo lived up to his word and bought my stock. He would have bought my convertible debentures at par, but I liked their 15 percent yield and decided to keep them, believing them to be low risk in light of Smith's commitment. That judgment was wide of the mark, and this decision would haunt me for many years.

Shortly after my dismissal, Philo brought in some cronies who not only carried out the policies that had induced me to fall on my sword, but together they ran the business into the ground. I shortly came to realize that my remaining stake was at risk, and I tried to find a buyer for my debentures. With the handwriting evident to all, there were no buyers at any price, even considering the 15 percent interest rate that was paid reliably every quarter. Because of my significant investment, I stayed in touch with the company and remained on cordial terms with Philo. I was only a little reassured as he kept making up for the growing losses by putting more money into the company. Throughout his ownership, I believe he invested in Classified as much as $30 million, maybe $40 million, and, despite this unfailing support, there was no one willing to buy my notes. I had completely given up hope of ever getting my principal back, when in 1990, out of the nowhere, I got a notice from the company that it was redeeming the convertible notes at par. I was dumbfounded: It was manna from heaven. The company completed the transaction quickly, and I got my $600,000 back, every last penny. Two years later, Classified declared bankruptcy. I am a lucky guy!

The final act in this drama could have been a comedy scene. In 1999, as I was putting together an insurance data service business at Fiserv, I realized that the data processing system developed at Classified Insurance might still have value that could be useful in helping Fiserv's new insurance division to address the auto casualty insurance markets. Even though Classified had gone bankrupt, it was not clear that the business had not survived and with it, the data processing system. With this thought, I tracked down Philo and managed to get him on the telephone. The conversation went something like this:

"Hello, is this Philo Smith?"

"Who wants to know?"

"This is Dick Gallun."

"Dick who?"

"Dick Gallun!"

"I don't know any Dick Galloon."

"Dick Gallun—you know, the guy you fired from Classified back in the eighties."

Long silence, maybe only ten seconds, but long enough to be uncomfortable, then finally, in a low growl, "Whah da ya want?"

I explained my business, and quickly it was immediately apparent that I would get no help from Philo. Without providing a scrap of information, he made haste to get off the phone with not so much as even one friendly word. He was a strange man. I think his behavior was not primarily the result of a bad disposition. I am guessing that his Classified experience had ruined him and he needed no reminders of this embarrassment.

CHAPTER XVIII

Ice Hockey, My Lifetime Sport

As I was putting the final touches on these memoirs, I realized that I had not written about my lifelong love of ice hockey. If I had been asked when I was ten years old, or thirty, or even fifty, what were my most important interests, hockey would have always been in my top three. Sometimes, it would have been there after or before sailing, sometimes after business or politics, and sometimes, maybe often, after girls. Hockey was to become a dominant diversion of mine, one that became more important to me as I grew older.

MY ROMANCE WITH hockey grew rather naturally from my early exposure to skating with my family on Pine Lake. It was perhaps at four or five that I got my first pair of skates. By the time I was seven, I had begun to play in early-season pond hockey games on Mud Lake and later in the year, on Beaver and Pine lakes. Then at ten, I was playing hockey at Country Day School's lower school, joining a pickup game on the school's small and primitive rink, skipping out of mandatory basketball for almost an entire winter season before my absence was noticed. My truancy resulted in disciplinary action—extra study sessions and, of course, mandatory basketball. Nevertheless, I retained my love of the sport and was not dissuaded from sneaking out of basketball for my time on the ice. Eventually, my teachers acknowledged that hockey was a reasonable alternative to other gym activities, and they left me alone.

I got away from the hockey-unfriendly environment of the lower school when I moved to the upper school in eighth grade. I played with the junior varsity, and we had practice every day, but there were still no outside games to play.

With my earlier experience, I was ahead of my classmates and was good enough to make the varsity as a freshman. That was a big step for me because, for the first time, I was in real organized hockey with outside games and a real coach, Mr. Church, who knew how to play the game and had a few tricks to pass on to his charges. One that worked for me, even later at Williams, was to draw the goalie to a feint toward the left side of the cage as I skated around behind it. As the goalie went down to defend the danger on the left, I, in the mode of Mr. Church, would continue around the cage and backhand the puck into the undefended right side. My Williams coach saw me trying to execute this maneuver a few times when it didn't work and he suggested that it would never work against a competent goalie. He stopped giving me that advice when I used it to scored a goal against Amherst in overtime. But I must admit it was a maneuver that worked better in high school than it did in college.

Country Day hockey was not much of a place to learn the game in the early fifties because there was so little local competition. When I was in eighth grade, our best in state and only competitor in the Milwaukee area, Shorewood High School, exited the sport because of budget restraints. I never got to play against Shorewood, but I watched Country Day's last game with them. It was memorable.

Shorewood had a great center, whose name was Krueger, and he scored a hat trick that day while Shorewood overpowered us in a not-too-close game. Krueger possessed a skill of which I was not yet aware, and I was not sure that it was yet in use even in professional hockey in 1949. That skill was the slap shot. Krueger scored his first two goals with it, and the shots were impressive: While skating along the boards just inside the blue line, he suddenly took his stick way back and then slapped it onto the ice right on top of the puck; and as he followed through, the puck went straight and true right into the corner of the cage. Both of his first two goals were in the corners. Our goalie never saw either of them. Then toward the end of the third period, he, controlling the puck, stopped at the red line at midice and took a backswing, one that brought his stick almost over his head. He hesitated for a long moment as if to say, "Watch what I am going to do" and then let fly with his shot.

This one was Krueger's last game—at least at Shorewood. From my vantage point, I later equated his hesitation to Babe Ruth's signal toward the left field bleachers as he presaged his most famous home run. Krueger didn't have to point; we knew where he was aiming. Well, the shot went hard and flat, straight to the cage, the center of the cage, at eye level. That was where our unfortunate goalie, Morton Flora stood, trying to gain sight of the shot as it winged toward him at race car speed. He said afterward that he never saw it coming. It is difficult to believe that Mort was not wearing a mask and maybe he was: but if he was, the pieces of rubber that the surgeon picked out of his shattered nose an hour later were not fragments of a shattered puck as Mort reported, but were pieces of an inadequate rubber mask. Oh yes, when Mort fell on the ice, unconscious, the puck dropped into the cage.

With Shorewood no longer playing hockey, only Country Day and St. Johns Military Academy supported a hockey program in Southern Wisconsin. Our regular schedule would be limited to St. Johns and Lake Forest Academy, we playing each of them four times during the winter season. Not a heady schedule, but it was almost all we knew. The pinnacle of our hockey season was an annual trip to northern Wisconsin to play Wausau and Rheinlander high schools, both very good teams, or at least better than us, their superiority a product of having a half-dozen "up north" teams to play, supplemented by their having a greater number of ice days provided by their subartic climate.

My first northern Wisconsin trip occurred in my sophomore year, and it was an eye-opener for me. For the first time, I was able to grasp the tangible aesthetics of this sport that I had come to love. Arriving at Wausau High School around six o'clock in the evening, I have a vivid memory of my impression of their rink. I had never seen such a perfect sheet of ice. The rinks that I had played upon previously had always been marred by easily chipped surfaces, the product of insufficient temperatures during the ice-making process, large cracks and, even on the best days at Country Day, large yellow-brown circles that emerged from the mud below, rising an inch or two above the playing surface.

In Wausau they even fixed the ice between periods! They had a barrel on a cart, which dripped water onto a rag attached to the cart. The precursor to the Zamboni! But it wasn't just the better ice that made this place so attractive. Overhead lighting, that turned the place into downtown Las Vegas, illuminated the entire area. Not having ever played under any artificial lights, I was used to playing in the kind of daylight that, under the cloudy skies of winter, quickly faded to twilight after midday. It is difficult to imagine how illumination changed the aesthetics of the game for me. In addition to the playing conditions, there were bleachers around the rink that, as we arrived, were already filling with enthusiastic local fans, in numbers way beyond what the players' families might provide. This scene contrasted sharply with our environment at home of few fans, they mostly leaning against the boards or huddling atop the piles of snow cleared from the rink as they shivered in the gloom of winter afternoons. The scene at Wausau was what the hockey environment should be, and, as I was to learn a few years later, was just a little bit better than the hockey scene that I would find at Williams College.

In my sophomore and junior years, we dominated the southern Wisconsin competition, such as it was, and put up a good fight against these northern hockey teams, but we lost in both years to both of these excellent teams, losing in our junior year to each of them by only one goal . . . Such as a state championship was in those days, Rheinlander was recognized as that in both of those years.

I was fortunate in my junior year to team up with two classmates, Bill Carpenter and Jerry Kloppenburg, both of whom were dedicated to developing their individual and team skills, particularly controlling the puck and making and receiving passes. When there was ice, that being not a whole lot of days in the Milwaukee winter, we skated from dawn to dark and even after dark. Skating in the dark was a way to improve stick-handling skills, when one can not see the puck. If there wasn't ice on our rink, a frequent circumstance, we would go to Estabrook Park, where the skating pond was usually kept in good shape.

The line of Carpenter, Kloppenburg, and me, fortified by an excellent goalie, Jim Meyer, led the team to an undefeated season in our senior year, soundly defeating those northern teams that had been our Achilles' heel in the prior years. Other than becoming the de facto state champions, the most memorable event of that hockey season was the Christmas Eve snowfall of 1952, with more than thirty inches of heavy snow in one day. We began to move that snow off the rink on Christmas Day and spent the next eight days clearing the ice. It was backbreaking work as we, shovel by shovel, dug paths to the middle of the rink, carried a thirty-inch-thick shovelful to the edge of the rink, and then lifted it over the boards. As the snow piles mounted, we had to move them away from the boards to make room for the next loads of snow. By nightfall on January third, we had a clean sheet of ice; and as it had stayed cold, the ice looked pretty good. The next day presented us with a huge change of weather: the temperature soared into the high forties, and a persistent rain began. Two days later, the snow we had shoveled was gone, but so was the ice. There was no skating until late January. That was the life of a hockey player in Milwaukee in the fifties. How would I ever gain the skills to play in college?

That March, the Williams College admission director, Fredrick Copeland, visited Country Day. Knowing what I was about, Mr. Copeland gave me the right message to lure me to Williams, talking mostly about hockey. Right out of the box, he promised me a place at Williams in the class of '57 and told me that he had already picked a roommate for me, one who turned out to be the captain of the hockey team at Nobles and Greenough (and destined to be my competitor for the center spot on Williams's freshman team). He went on to tell me that Williams did not have artificial ice yet but was building a new rink next to the gym. While acknowledging that the new rink was not covered, he failed to mention that it was next to the coal pile that served the central college heating system and thus, would be occasionally covered with a film of coal dust. He acknowledged that the Williams hockey team had been zero and twenty in the season just ended but noted that he was recruiting hockey players. With these recruits and the new rink, Williams's hockey would have a bright future. That sounded good enough to me. I was not put off by Williams's pitiful record; in fact, it appealed to me as in, "This is a hockey team that I can make."

As it turned out, Dean Copeland brought into my class fifteen high school captains, mostly from Massachusetts and Connecticut prep schools but a couple from the Midwest. What was surprising to me was that I was competitive with this group, all of whom had been raised on artificial ice and had had extensive game schedules. I think the balancing factor here was that, when we had ice, my Country

Day teammates and I had skated all day and even into the nights. My eastern teammates skated mostly during the hours that they were assigned "ice time."

Freshman year was a major learning experience. Williams had hired as the freshman hockey coach Bill McCormick, a '53 graduate and a star player and captain at Michigan State, a serious team in the Midwest (where Wisconsin was not to even think of a hockey team for another ten years). He knew the game, and he, being just a little older than we were, related well to my new teammates and me. Practices were disciplined and directed much at improving basic skills with an emphasis on speed and conditioning. The improvement of our play during the year was impressive. With a good schedule of the top hockey-playing prep schools and a smattering of college JVs and freshman teams, we ended the year with an undefeated season. We did, however, have one tie; that was with RPI, whose varsity won the NCAA championship that year. Meanwhile, Williams's varsity was 0 and 21, if you include as a loss the one time we were allowed (unofficially) to play them. We were ready to play at the varsity level.

By the end of our freshman season, we had become the darlings of the college, and a movement was started to promote Bill McCormick to become the varsity coach. It was a widely supported action, reasonable because the then varsity coach was ill equipped for his job. As a protest against the slow action of the athletic director, our hockey fans did a peaceful march to the president's house, and the unfortunate varsity coach finally got the picture. He resigned, making the promotion of McCormick an easy move for the athletic director, who, not liking to being pushed around, might otherwise have resisted this protest.

Over the next three years, we played most of the top teams in the east, compiling a pretty good record, somewhat over 500, in all of those years, doing so against many of the players who made up the Olympic team of 1960, the team which led the USA to its first miracle on ice. We beat all of them at least once in those three years except for RPI and Harvard. Those two teams contributed importantly to that Olympic win, and we played them creditably in our senior year, losing to RPI, four to two, and to Harvard, nine to five.

One of the reasons we were able to compete as well as we did was because we were the vanguard of an important change among college hockey teams, a change that was related to the recruiting efforts of Fred Copeland. Because we were long on prep school talent, we had more players than we needed to field two lines. Bill McCormick saw his opportunity and decided right away to go with three lines. Seeing how this change contributed to our success as freshmen, he carried that idea into our varsity years. The extra endurance obtained from shorter trips inured importantly to our benefit in every game we played. It was not until after we graduated that three lines became de rigueur in college hockey.

We had one other advantage over some of our competitors, one that we didn't know about until it appeared. It was in the Middlebury game in our junior year that the wind was blowing from the north, and our ice rink received many swirls of coal dust from the coal pile that lay at the north end of the rink. Our uniforms were blackened by the end of the first period, but, more important, our skates were becoming dull from the carbon abrasion. We sharpened our skates during both of the interperiod intervals and, being able to skate better than this excellent competitor, went on to win the game. We should not have been too proud of that win, but we did beat a better team.

I had one disappointment in hockey at Williams; that was not being elected captain, a position that I had coveted as I had become a leader of the team in scoring and on defense, as well, particularly as a regular defender against the power play. The captaincy was important to me beyond the honor of being elected, and that was that much of my identity at Williams was tied to hockey. I was not the student I should or could have been. In fact, now, with six descendants and two spouses of descendants having attended Williams, I have, with room to spare, the worst Williams's academic record in the family. In any case, in the election at the end of our junior season, I was one of three who tied in the voting. In the runoff, I lost to George Wells and John Holman, both fine defensemen and lifelong friends.

Despite this disappointment, hockey was the best thing for me about Williams College. That sounds like a sad commentary about me at a college that had so much to offer. But in addition to being a thoroughly actualizing activity, hockey taught me a lot about teamwork and discipline, and it introduced me to people who were to become lifelong friends. They were a tight-knit bunch that showed great dedication to the college, returning year after year to support our class's involvement in the school. They came first to play in the alumni hockey games; many came later to observe their own children's athletic events and then to become valued old friends at later reunions. Several stood with me fifty years later in the rain at Weston field watching my grandson catch his first college pass, cheering like banshees when he grabbed the ball and ran over two defensive backs, cheering despite the fact that Williams was ahead 45 to 0, the rain was falling in sheets, and there was no one else in the stadium. Good friends make for poignant moments.

In any case, an important part of my hockey life was about to begin after I left Williams. In the beginning, it was just old men's hockey—first in Lincoln, Massachusetts, where Kathy and I lived for two years and a coterie of ex-college players competed, and then back in Milwaukee on the old Country Day rink, by then having artificial ice. But it was not long before Albs and Richie came along and were willing to be indoctrinated into their dad's sport. Kathy and I raised them on Pine Lake, where, in their early years, I saw to it that they always had a rink in front of their house. Whenever it snowed, I always plowed our rink in the early light before going to work, doing so to see to it that the ice would not be ruined by daytime thawing and then freezing of the surface snow. The rink was useable throughout most of the winter because the winters were colder than they had been in the fifties, and the lake ice held the cold better than did the ground under the old Country Day rink. The boys learned the basic skills, particularly how to give and receive passes, skills that too often took a backseat to individual play.

I made a commitment to Richie at age six to drive him to the Winter Club, then at the Country Day rink, so he could get a start at organized hockey. He was ready to play skillwise, and he already loved the game; but when he suffered a bloody nose at his first practice, he decided against organized play, a decision that lasted seven years. Nevertheless, during those seven years, the three of us, Alby having joined the game at age four, played together regularly on our rink and in addition, got in a fair amount of pond hockey with a growing group of hockey-playing relatives and friends.

On a Thanksgiving weekend, we were playing hockey on Mud Lake with a large group of all ages and sexes. As we began, the ice was only three or four inches thick, but it was black ice, and we quickly became comfortable that it would support us. Black ice is newly frozen ice, and it tends to be very strong. However, after skating for a day and a half in fifty-degree weather, I noticed that the ice was getting rubbery, visibly bending under my weight. I, being the biggest of the skaters, decided that it was time to leave, and I did so. As I neared the shore, one foot went right through the ice. Not to worry, I pulled it out . . . but as I did so, the other foot went through. The next thing I knew, I was underwater and came up gasping for air. I tried to pull myself up onto the ice again and again, but the ice just kept breaking, and I would fall back into the water. It was just a few moments later that I saw my brother-in-law, Bill Stark, crawling toward me with a hockey stick extended to me. He had me grab onto the stick and told me to support myself on the ice but not to try to raise myself, rather let the ice sink under my weight, allowing the water to run onto the ice, then to crawl as he pulled me forward with the hockey stick. It was a slow process, crawling all the way to shore, keeping a moving body of water around me as I moved. The entire operation took about fifteen minutes. I never felt the cold until I got to shore, then all of a sudden, I was shaking violently from hypothermia, and I kept shaking until I had been at home in a hot shower for almost ten minutes. Meanwhile, two or three others went through the ice and had to be rescued as well. Amazingly, it was only a half hour after I went into the drink that the lake was entirely clear of ice.

Later we moved to Fox Point because all of our children needed a larger environment than University Lake School. Thinking clearly, we bought a house that was within easy walking distance of the Winter Club rink, a decision that saved us an infinite amount of transportation time. It yielded real independence for our children but just as important, some freedom for Kathy and me.

Richie, now "Rich," was thirteen, and he joined the Winter Club as a "bantam," the fourteen and under group. Not to my surprise, he fit in right away with this group who had been playing organized hockey since they were six. Alby too was playing competitively right off as a "squirt." Like Rich, he had developed skills equal to or better than many of his contemporaries.

Old men's hockey became much more convenient for me than it had been when we lived at Pine Lake, and hockey replaced skiing as the main weekend activity. The walking thing was great for Kathy and me, and hockey fit right into all of our lives, but then I got tapped for coaching the squirts, Alby's level, a responsibility that had me at the rink at odd hours and at distant game locations more than I would have wished. I did coach for four years, and I had the good fortune of having acolytes with a talent for the game.

After my coaching phase, I was often asked to referee games and had the misfortune too of refereeing one game in which Alby was playing. In this game, Alby was behind Blake Wigdale in the rotation of lines, meaning that Alby went on when Blake came off. At this point in his life and perhaps always, Blake was a pretty chippy player who accumulated a lot of penalties. On this particular day, he played cleanly . . . until time was running out his rotation. Each time he was ready to come off, he committed such an egregious and obvious offense that gave me no choice but to call a penalty. When I blew the whistle to exact a penalty on Blake, the lines would change, Blake would head for the penalty box, and Alby would stay on the bench. I penalized Blake six times that day. I was annoyed by this result, twelve minutes of penalties for Alby in a game where his total ice time would have been about twenty minutes, but more so by Blake's coach, who did not seem to notice this misplacement of consequences.

It was a few years later that Rich was playing hockey at Williams, playing under my old coach, Bill McCormick. It was a pleasure for me to see Rich playing for Bill.

But I must digress before going on with this vignette. When I went to Williams, it was with my friend Harry Drake, who had for some time called me "R A," as had many of my high school classmates. As a result, I became R A to everyone at Williams and am still called R A by my Williams friends. My name was R A.

It was when Rich was a sophomore that he raised a question that delighted me. "Were you called R A at Williams?"

"What prompts that question?"

"Well, Mr. McCormick, when he gets excited, sometimes exclaims 'R A, get out there!' and then looks at me, expecting me to respond."

It's good when your old coach still wants you to play for him thirty years after you did!

CHAPTER XIX

From a Sow's Ear

By the mid-seventies, it had become apparent to both Jim Cerny and me that EWC was not going to become a business on which to ride off into the sunset. Even as Jim had added a professional dimension to the organization, we invariably had fallen short of our profit goals, usually far short. While we had always seemed to be able to find new customers, the competition was increasingly nipping at our heels and compressing margins. As the business grew larger, our customer base became less loyal and had become highly visible targets for our competitors. When we finally opened our eyes, we acknowledged that we were a commodity manufacturer with absolutely no competence that differentiated us from the competition.

Maybe we were in the wrong business. Maybe it was time to find something else to do. Of course, by this time, we had three factories and almost ten million dollars of business. That's hard to walk away from. There had to be some value here.

BY 1981, EWC possessed an expanding harness business with plants both in Milwaukee and in Spring Green and a solid cord business working out of our factory in Waupun. Things were finally starting to look pretty good. The recession of the early eighties was taking its toll particularly on our harness business, but growing business with John Deere had offset much of the downturn. The Deere account had grown from nothing in 1978 to more than two million dollars in 1981. Then suddenly, that business, all of it, was up for quotation. Even though we thought that our loyal and attentive service gave us an edge, we knew that Deere was determined to lower their cost significantly, so we responded with very aggressive pricing. Nevertheless, in the competitive environment of the day, we lost the entire account, undercut by almost 20 percent, to a competitor pricing at our direct costs. Despite our relationship and history of satisfactory service, we were given no chance to requote the business. Well, we wouldn't have improved our quote anyhow.

This loss was dire news. Deere represented more than a third of our Milwaukee production. Jim and I realized right away that we were going to have to rethink our strategy. But first, we were going to have to eliminate a lot of overhead. It was apparent that we did not have enough business to support two plants making harnesses. After agonizing over the pain of what we had to do, we determined that it was the Milwaukee plant that had to go. Our dilemma was that our corporate management and our most experienced labor pool were in Milwaukee. We had additional space both in Spring Green and Milwaukee, but we owned the factory in Spring Green, while we operated Milwaukee in rented space. Besides, we held a lease we could terminate on short notice, eliminating a bunch of costs in addition to the rent.

The Milwaukee plant was history within six months, but not before we learned of our responsibilities under ERISA. Our final concession in each of the four contracts we had negotiated with the Electrical Workers had been to give them a pension contribution of a few nickels an hour. While we had provided what we thought was a defined contribution, the union and ERISA defined it as a "guaranteed benefit," one for which we were responsible. Anyone who thinks the government is always inefficient would be amazed at the speed with which they unearthed and defined this responsibility. In any case, we were out another $150,000 for the thirty-cent per hour contribution to the union pension fund that we were making for about one hundred employees at the time.

Closing the Milwaukee plant was not a strategic decision, but we understood that it was time for us to be strategic and to address, among other things, an exit plan for ourselves. Jim and I realized that we had been operating in a highly competitive marketplace and that our products, which were distinctly low tech, were viewed much as commodities. We had tried to address this dilemma for many years without finding a solution. We had exhaustedly surveyed potential markets for engineered wiring products and found that standardization of connectors in industries having significant wiring needs had largely eliminated the ability to differentiate our services. There seemed to be no significant market where we could add value through engineering or special wiring competence.

However, by 1983, we had developed a significant business in hospital-grade power supply cords, and this product line brought us marginally into the medical device market. We had generated our first medical device customer, Abbott Labs, with our hospital cord; then we had fabricated for them a unique wiring component for their familiar digital oxygen monitoring device. Because of this business, even though it was marginally profitable and not important revenue, we began to see the advantages that the medical devices industry might hold. What we learned was that all medical device manufacturers used unique designs in their connections, designs either of their own or their wiring supplier's invention. And they were often innovating and modifying their designs requiring a continuous redesign of their wiring connections. Here was an opportunity to add value to our manufactured product using engineering and customer service. Consequently, we began to pursue the medical device market aggressively. To our chagrin, we had no success in selling to any of these companies because we had no real experience with medical systems, particularly with EKG systems where much of the medical device business existed. Even with an intensive and costly effort, we were not able to penetrate this market, not at all; so we looked around for a business that we might buy.

Our search led us nowhere. Searching for more than a year, we were unable to locate any wire-fabricating companies that supplied the medical device industry. That is, except for one company on the West Coast who made it clear that they were not for sale. We concluded that most medical device wiring components were fabricated in-house, which, indeed, in many cases they were.

It was in early 1985 that it came to Jim's attention from one of our wire suppliers that a company that manufactured wiring components for the medical device industry was having trouble paying its bills and might even be for sale. At the time, we had not been aware that this company, Colorado Wire, existed; it had never surfaced in any of our searches. We found out that the company, which was located in Broomfield, Colorado, a north suburb of Denver, was indeed on the ropes. We recognized right away that this company could become our portal to the medical device marketplace, so Jim contacted the owner, Charles Ellis. It took awhile to get Ellis to agree to a meeting, much less to admit interest in a sale; but after a month of bantering on the phone with Jim, he finally offered Jim an invitation to visit the company factory in Broomfield.

A week later, Jim and I flew to Denver and took a cab to the factory in Broomfield where we met Ellis and a small entourage of his executives. We suffered through an insufferably long tour that took about three hours, touring a pretty small factory that was much like ours. Then we went to a hotel where Ellis had reserved a conference room. The three of us had lunch together while his other attendants made themselves scarce.

Over soup, Mr. Ellis introduced the subject of a sale and asked how serious our interest was in buying the business. The answer, of course, was "very serious." He bobbed and weaved, trying to get a range of value out of us, and we responded to his queries that we needed more information, mostly the information planned for the afternoon. We tried to get at his sale price, and he said he hadn't given value much consideration because he hadn't really decided to sell. This inane discussion went on through the main course, and then over dessert, Jim gave him our hypothetic view that both his business and ours would be valued at four or five times earnings. He blanched at this, because, as we had guessed, his earnings turned out to be negative.

During the afternoon, we got a pretty good picture of a good business that was being badly run. Looking at the financials, we determined, as we suspected, that the margins on the medical device wiring mechanisms were much better than ours while their management was inadequate. We could see waste in their manufacturing practices, and their inventory was bloated.

As the afternoon progressed, it became apparent that Mr. Ellis was not involved in the day to day management. He liked keeping his hand in the business, but he was not comfortable in this role. He often corrected the factual statements of his managers, and when we were alone, complained about their skills and decisions. It appeared that he had an awkward relationship with his management; and, of course, he blamed the poor results' performance on them. He was anxious for a deal.

What we had learned that afternoon was all we knew about the business, but Jim and I agreed that it was enough to negotiate a letter of intent. Late in the afternoon, Ellis hinted that he too wanted to get to negotiations. We seized the opportunity and suggested that we negotiate a preliminary contract. He readily agreed and asked that we make an offer for the business.

We took a break for Jim and me to discuss a proposal. Jim and I met briefly and agreed that we wanted to get to a price anchored on net asset value or net worth—perhaps as much as 25 percent over asset value. Then we developed a plan to get there, doing so in about thirty minutes.

Returning to the meeting, we proposed a price based on net worth but with discounts on doubtful assets. Giving 100 percent for cash, we proposed discounting receivables by 10 percent, depreciated equipment by 15 percent, and so on. As we expected, when we got to inventory, which was the company's largest asset and which we discounted at 25 percent, Ellis exploded. We talked about this issue for half an hour, finally agreeing to full value for inventory upon professional valuation. By this time, the die was cast that we were going to value the business at book value, but it took another half hour to get there, with us conceding to Ellis's persuasive arguments on each issue. The last concession was to be ours. It followed his plea, "We are so close. Why don't you just pay net asset value, and we can have a deal today?"

That was the deal we wanted! For any business you really want to own, net asset value is a very good price, assuming that the assets are fairly valued and needed in the business. Nevertheless, I knew that buyers who are hot to trot often freeze up in the ice of seller's remorse. If you have a deal you like, get it in writing!

Having no lawyers present probably worked to our advantage. I suggested that I would draft an agreement, keeping it simple. During the break that followed, Jim and I wrote a four-sentence agreement, checked it out on the phone with my attorney, John Hazelwood, for its capacity to bind the parties, and returned to the meeting where we rewrote it incorporating some language from the seller. I got a chance a little later to check the amended product for legal issues, particularly for its ability to bind the parties. It passed muster, and we all signed an agreement, it being conditioned mostly on our satisfaction with the due diligence results. We had a six-sentence agreement.

As the closing date approached, the property had stood up to our due diligence and we were ready to close. But, as we had feared, Ellis was getting cold feet. Suffering from the anticipated seller's remorse, or perhaps looking at a better offer, Ellis went silent and would not return our calls. Late in the final day before closing we threatened suit to hold him to the deal, but even in the face of this ultimatum he remained incommunicado.

As the closing date arrived, we prepared to take over the business despite the antics of the seller. We had no idea whether or not we had a deal. Despite our concerns, we did have several people on the ground in Broomfield that morning, hoping that they would be allowed entry. Jim called the company at 8:00. The phone was answered, "EWC Corporation."

Our people were in place! That was a fine moment.

This purchase was a watershed event for EWC; it was going to change the nature of our business. Nevertheless, there was a lot to do to fix up this operation and to become competitive. As we had touched on in our due diligence, the purchased company did not possess a good reputation in the industry either for service or quality; but with the passage of several years, our attention to these issues began to yield rewards. We began to find satisfaction among our inherited customers, and eventually they became valuable references. In the end, this acquisition did for us what we had sought: It gave us a place in the medical device industry.

Over the next dozen years, we added almost every major device manufacturer in the country, often sharing their business with the company in California that we had identified in our earlier search. Our medical customer list eventually included Abbott Laboratories, Marquette Electronics, Pfizer, Hewlett Packard, Ohio Medical Systems, Space Labs, MMM, Burdick Manufacturing and Siemens. That accounted for just about all of the majors in the industry. Finally, we were growing and at last doing so with reasonable margins. We built a research and administrative headquarters in Waukesha, where we could, through the blessing of CAD/CAM, design connections and supply prototypes within days. We strengthened our engineering department and developed relationships at all levels of these companies. Jim himself spent a lot of time in the executive suites. We were trying to be the best, and we were succeeding.

Still, we had our problems dealing with these large companies. After EWC was their "supplier of the year" for three successive years, Marquette decided to bring their wiring systems in-house. It had been $2.0 million of profitable business and was growing. That was a big loss for us. The bullying of the bigger device companies was costly too. We spent a lot of money and more than a year's intensive effort working around a German supplier's patents in exchange for a promise from Hewlett Packard for their annual requirements for EKG yokes and patient monitoring leads (more than three million annual dollars). When we met their required parameters, they balked and added more tests. After several iterations of new requirements, they finally gave us initial orders. But when their German supplier realized that he had real competition and was losing the business, he fell in line, and Hewlett decided to kiss us off. Even with mud on their face, Hewlett dared us to sue them. Of course, we couldn't; we still had other significant business with them, business that was clearly at risk. Generally, it's tough to go up against the big guys and usually inadvisable as well.

It was a mix of successes and failures that kept us going without the much-bigger success to which Jim and I aspired. By the turn of the century, we had a twelve million-dollar business, by then all medical, and a new customer, Valley Labs, with whom we were starting to produce a half million disposable electrosurgical kits per month on a highly automated production line in Broomfield. With the Valley Labs job running at capacity by June, we were on our way to a sixteen million-dollar year with expected profits of a million-plus.

Unknown to me, Jim's health was failing, and he came to me right after the start-up of the Valley Labs business. At the time, he didn't mention his health problem but suggested that it was time to sell the business. We had discussed an endgame for many years and knew that TYCO, who had, several years earlier, bought our California competitor, was the only genuine ace in our deck. Jim thought we had TYCO well positioned to take us out at a good price at the right time.

During the late nineties, there had been major consolidation in the devices marketplace. Among other combinations, Siemens had bought Burdick, and OSI Systems had acquired Space Labs. Each of these transactions had led the survivor to attempt consolidation of vendors. In both transactions, EWC had maintained its business at existing prices because of our well-nurtured multilevel relationships and a record of service, while TYCO, not having well cultivated in-house allies, was forced to reduce prices to meet our lowball prices for the business that had been theirs. After these confrontations we became confident that TYCO would like to see us gone.

In mid-2000, General Electric acquired Marquette Electronics and put out an RFP for more than $20 million of annual wire requirements, GE's prior internal requirements, plus about $4 million of Marquette's. The bid was to be on an all-or-nothing basis. Jim knew that we couldn't handle that volume, but he was confident that we could punish TYCO and accelerate their attempt to get rid of us. Our business and profitability were at an all-time peak, or more accurately, were projected to be so by the end of the year.

Jim wanted to lowball the business, representing that we would do it all, expecting that GE would never entrust us with such a large order; they would prefer the safe path of dealing with the much-larger company. Indeed, they would be right in this decision; it would be impossible for us to meet the immediate engineering requirements for setting up and tooling the business, not to mention the manufacturing demands that would follow. So we went as low as we dared to go, down to our direct costs, just labor and materials and a trace of overhead, barely keeping our quote within the realm of reason. Our greatest fear was that maybe we would win the contract. If we had, we had no idea what we would do; whatever it was, it would not have been pretty. So we just crossed our fingers and submitted a professionally prepared proposal, one that dotted the i's and crossed the t's. We invested several man-months of engineering and management time preparing the quote. We wanted to look serious.

Well, as we expected, we never got a sniff of any part of the award. TYCO won it all. And as we had hoped, they had been persuaded to meet the prices we had quoted. Two weeks later, we got a call from the president of the TYCO Health Care Division. They wanted to discuss a deal.

Over the next two weeks, the TYCO's division president and Jim talked and bantered about a purchase of EWC. Then in short order, TYCO offered us a price amounting to about eight times our "projected" annual earnings, an extraordinary price for such an ordinary business, about twice as much as we had a right to hope for. Jim and I discussed the offer briefly; he wanted to accept. I persuaded him that we should reject the offer out of hand. Theirs was a first offer, one that evidenced a real desire to get rid of us. Even if they despised our position in rejecting their offer, they would not disappear as a buyer. It was clear that TYCO understood that we were hurting them, and they did not know how else to dispose of us. After considerable debate, Jim agreed to my suggestion. He reported to TYCO that we were not interested in their offer, making as if we were not even vaguely interested.

It was an uncomfortable week as we waited for a reaction. Even as they were apparently dumbfounded by our rejection of their truly generous offer, they came back with a price that reached *eleven* times our "projected" earnings. We considered this offer overnight—rather, we celebrated, crossed our fingers—and reluctantly agreed to it in the morning. We had to suffer through a few weeks of due diligence, but our contract left no easy ways for them to exit the deal. Besides, they had gotten what they wanted. They had eliminated their last competitor.

After the closing Jim discovered the cause of his ill health, an issue that he had not wanted to look at while the responsibility of managing EWC burdened him. He had suffered calcification of the spinal column, the calcification pressing on his spinal cord. Surgery with a long rehabilitation was required. Jim had sensed the seriousness of his illness and had known that he couldn't afford the time away from the job over those last years. He did recover, and we remained close friends until his death in 2008.

Just before he died, Jim made a comment that he meant as a compliment to me but which could be viewed as an indictment. He said that he had appreciated my friendship over the years, but he had been amazed that it continued after we sold the business. His value to me as a business partner was indeed crucial in my life, but my inability to communicate to him the value to me of our personal relationship continues to sadden me to this day. We went through so much together in our partnership, and since his death, I have become increasingly aware that he bore most of the burden of making something of a business that for many of its years showed little potential.

Jim was a better guy to manage my business than would have been Willis Sullivan, the CEO of Krause, during my tenure there. Jim was as dedicated in a business equally as difficult as the corn-processing business, but he figured out how to make the best of a bad situation while remaining in conformance with the U.S. statutes.

CHAPTER XX

A Brush with the Mob

I fell into the ownership of my amusement games business somewhat by accident, through the bankruptcy of Milwaukee Coin Industries, to which I had loaned money secured by the stock of Red Baron Amusements, a business possessing leases in thirty-five malls, twenty having already been built out as arcades. Bally Corp., through its subsidiary, J. Robbins Distributors, was Red Baron's major supplier of games. With sixty or so games per center and a rapid turnover of games required to keep the customers interested, I had become important to Bally.

It was in the middle seventies that I met Bill O'Donnell, Bally's CEO. I spent some pleasant time with him and his beautiful blond wife at amusement games conventions in Las Vegas. The family was as Irish as their name suggested; and while there were rumors of Mafia connections with O'Donnell and with Bally, the O'Donnells seemed like charter members of "the beautiful people." In any case, I had always discounted the rumored Cosa Nostra connection, because, to me, Bally was an honest and gracious business partner.

IT WAS LATE in 1977 when I got a call from Bally concerning Red Baron. The arcade business was booming, and Bally, among others, was trying to get into the business of owning and managing game rooms in shopping malls. As was often the case, I was looking for liquidity, so when Bob Mullane, a Bally vice president, called me and proposed that we meet to discuss Bally's purchase of Red Baron, I jumped at the suggestion. We agreed to meet at Howard Johnson's in Kenosha, a location, right off the expressway, which shared the traveling equally between us.

I arrived at HoJo's promptly at 5:00 p.m., the appointed hour, and liking olives, ordered a vodka martini while I awaited Mullane's arrival. When he strode confidently in at 5:20, even before he introduced himself to me, I was appalled at his appearance. He was the caricature of a Mafioso Don with a large belly, a fixed sneer, and a vivid scar running down the right side of his face. The disfigurement surely was the result of a knife fight. Nevertheless, I quickly learned that he was a congenial guy, possessed of both grace and style. We conversed easily as we waited for the waitress. When she arrived, Bob ordered, and my recollection here is precise, a Tanqueray martini, which was delivered in a glass about half the size of mine. He looked with annoyance at his diminutive drink, but let the moment pass. Then we began to discuss the value of Red Baron's centers, one by one, with an occasional interruption whenever he needed another drink. When his glass ran dry, and without missing a beat in our negotiations, he would commandeer the waitress, ordering, "Get me another and one for my friend."

Each time the waitress would bring a big glass for me and a little one for him. Totally innocent of what was happening here, I tried to keep pace. Then as Mullane was ordering his fourth drink, he complained with a touch of annoyance, "Why are you bringing me these shitty little drinks when you bring my friend such big ones?"

The waitress responded ingenuously, "Why, sir, this is 'double bubble hour.' Your friend got a double because he was ordering the bar liquor. You ordered a premium brand."

Mullane absorbed this information and responded without hesitation: "I'll have a double."

I said, realizing that I had had the equivalent of eight or ten drinks, "Hold mine for a round."

By this time, we had been through the pricing of some dozen centers, and I was amazed that I had no sense of my excessive alcohol consumption. I felt that I had negotiated a favorable price on each property. I think it was the adrenalin generated by the tension of the situation that inoculated me from the usual effects of drinking. During the next hour or so, and at a slower pace of drinking, we were able to get through the remaining centers, and by nine o'clock, we had a deal, to which we both agreed. We signed a letter of intent the next day for an early closing in Chicago.

Two weeks later, when John Hazelwood and I arrived at Bally's conference room to close the deal, we found it filled with lawyers and accountants, all with long faces. Right away, we were informed that because I had acquired Red Baron in a bankruptcy, the proposed transaction did not meet the tax requirements for a "merger of equals." They could not see how to move ahead unless we reduced the price. John and I conferred and then demurred on their proposal, which looked like a setup for additional negotiation. We went home with a bad taste in our mouths and a new understanding of Bally. Maybe they really were bad guys.

It was some years later that Bally attempted to get into the casino business in Las Vegas. The Nevada Gaming Commission denied their first application for a license because of Bill O'Donnell's reported connections with organized crime. That was shocking to me because of my favorable opinion of the O'Donnell family. Even more astonishing was the news that Bob Mullane had been made the president of Bally, and he had been acceptable to the commission. I had not wanted to judge Mullane because I liked him, but his appearance suggested that he might have had a better future as a hit man for *The Sopranos* than Mr. Clean for the Nevada Gaming Commission.

About this time, I got a call from the president of a new Bally subsidiary that operated their chain of amusement centers, the subsidiary being Aladdin's Castle, the new president, Antonio Garbanzini. On the phone, Antonio came across forthwith as a first-class asshole, this image projected mainly through an arrogant and condescending manner and exacerbated by a total lack of grace. Not wasting any time on useless introductory conversation, he jumped right to the point; he was here to buy our remaining centers. Even though I was suffering immediate aversion and remembering my previous dealings with Bally, I was still anxious to get out of this business, so I consented to discuss a deal with him.

During the prior three years, I had gradually reduced the number of Red Baron centers by selling some and closing those that were not profitable. I had left about a dozen centers with annual revenue of almost a million and a half dollars and about $300,000 of annual profit, all personal income to me. As such, this income was taxed at high-tax rates and had limited value to me, so I was interested in cashing out. Even as I felt strong immediate antipathy toward this man, we were able to discuss the proposed deal dispassionately on the phone; and after a couple of such negotiations, we arrived at a mutually agreeable price. Nevertheless, right after we reached agreement, I realized that because of a glitch in my lease with the Dayton Mall, there was no way that I would be able to deliver the center located there.

The game room in the Dayton Mall was far and away my best center, providing almost half of Red Baron's total net income. The Dayton lease contained a provision: "If the lessee asks for a reassignment of the lease, the lessor may grant the request, deny it, or rescind the lease." I was certain that the owners of the Dayton Mall, the DeBartolo family, who owned many other malls and later the San Francisco 49ers, were not going to be willing to assign the lease. I was also sure that, if I asked them to assign, they would opt for the provision that allowed them to cancel the lease because young Eddie DeBartolo was operating arcades in many of their other malls. Moreover, I had been aware from prior communication that he coveted mine in Dayton.

I needed to address this issue right away, not just because Dayton was such a star but because I was aware that my negotiating opposite was easily unsettled. So, the next day I called Garbanzini back, explained the relevant lease provisions, and suggested that under the circumstances, he was the best person to ask for the assignment, since that action would not give the lessor the opportunity to cancel the lease. He understood that simple logic and agreed to take on this task. Then I suggested that we value the Dayton center forthwith, so that if he were unsuccessful in getting the assignment, we would know how much to reduce the price. I was pleased that he agreed quickly and then jumped to the next step, asking me how I would value the center. Having had time to think about that issue and believing that it was worth at least $300,000, but expecting negotiations over the price, I responded without hesitation; "$275,000."

Garbanzini, not realizing that he was not the buyer in the proposed adjustment (he was, in effect, the seller here), shot back flippantly, "That's ridiculous. It's way too much. It ain't worth even $250,000."

Right away, I realized that he was unknowingly negotiating on my behalf and did not understand his place in this transaction. Seeing my opportunity, I had the presence of mind to argue with him, weakly perhaps, but persuasively enough so that he was pleased when I acceded to his assertion and the value was set at $250,000.

Afterward, as I had expected, he failed to get the assignment, and the deal closed with the agreed upon deduction from the purchase price. Liking the last word myself and not liking this guy at all, I wanted him to know what a patsy he had been. I itched to tell him how he had taken himself for a ride. John Hazelwood, who always looked out for more than my financial interests, persuaded me that such a disclosure might not be good for my knees.

It was about three years later, after having netted close to $125,000 per year in Dayton that I thought that this bonanza was going to run out. With the emergence of home video games, the arcade business did not look so bright. Besides, I was paying ordinary income taxes at very high rates, reducing my take-home by 65 percent. I had previously made a couple of overtures to DeBartolo, but he had shown no interest in buying me out of a lease that, as far as he was concerned, expired in only eighteen months. After these unsuccessful probes, I realized that he was unaware that I held a five-year renewal option. So, knowing that misdirection works better than a frontal assault, I wrote to his real estate manager, telling him that we wanted to upgrade the property but would like to renew our lease to include the extension before we did so. DeBartolo's arcade guy was back to me within days, wanting to take me out of the lease. We had little difficulty reaching a price of $300,000.

All of the Bally characters here were Italian except for O'Donnell. How could one tell who among them had mob connections?

CHAPTER XXI

Thinking on One's Feet

An important skill of business leaders is that of thinking on one's feet. Often, a quick but thoughtful response can shift the control of a situation from others into your own hands, changing the momentum of a discussion or your own influence in a group. Sometimes, creative thinking is coming up with a clever repartee, or, better still, it is the off-the-cuff delivery of a solution to a problem at hand. In a way, the repartee is sort of like the admonition about meeting people: "You get only one opportunity to make a first impression!" If you execute the repartee well and do it with good timing, you can achieve great respect among your peers.

But more effective than the repartee is the seizing of an opportunity to address a situation in a way that gets you what you want in tangible benefits. I did this sort of thing with good effect occasionally but not often—infrequently because the appropriate occasions are scarce, and besides, I, like most of us, am only occasionally adroit enough to use them to advantage. This memoir is a story about an opportunity dropping into my lap. It was the type of chance that required dexterity and imagination. Would I be up to the challenge?

THE HEILIGER HUEGEL Ski Club was a big part of my family's life. The club operated the best ski hill in southeastern Wisconsin, and Kathy and I had skied there long before our children were born. We had in earlier years been active participants in club affairs, and in the course of events I had won their annually awarded trophy for the most contributive member. After living full time at Pine Lake during the seventies, we bought a small house in Fox Point in which to live during the school year so that our children could attend University School.

I had played hockey at the Winter Club at University School for years, commuting on Sundays and Wednesday evenings from Pine Lake, but that had not interfered with my skiing. However, with the move to Fox Point, Rich and Alby took up organized hockey, and I took up coaching. Five years later, Kathy and I were looking at a dues statement from the ski club with dues at $500. We realized that we had not used the club since we had moved to Fox Point, and after a brief discussion in which we agreed that in the future we were not likely to use it more than once or twice a year, we decided to give up our membership.

Heiliger Huegel had always had a somewhat arbitrary policy stating that if your annual dues were not paid by October 1, your membership would be forfeited, and your place in the limited membership would be given to one of the current applicants, of whom there was no shortage. We understood the policy, and we effectively resigned by not sending in our renewal. It was on September 30th that Kathy mentioned our defection from HH to her sister, Judy. Judy was surprised, particularly because the club had a policy that allowed members to "go on the county," meaning to pay dues of only fifty dollars, when the sum of their years of membership and their age reached 75. I was only a year away from this objective. Kathy and I huddled quickly over this idea and decided to pay our dues for the current and the next year to establish our lifetime privilege.

That was not to be. It was two weeks later that we got a written notice from the secretary of the club informing us in singularly frigid language that our dues had not been received on time and our membership had therefore been "terminated in accordance with published policy." This was a club to which I had belonged for thirty years? And I had been once received that most "valuable playerl," trophy This had to be a bureaucratic mistake.

I told Kathy not to worry, the club's president was Jim Barry, a good friend of mine, and he would rectify this mistake. I called Jim, told him what had happened, and he allowed that adhering so closely to this policy was a tad capricious. He said that the next board meeting was in a week, and he would use that opportunity to fix the situation.

It was just a week later that Jim called me back, opening the conversation with, "Boy, you have a couple of real enemies on this board!"

Even as that revelation was a surprise to me, I knew where this conversation was going. Nevertheless, I really did not care much about staying in the club, so notwithstanding this personal rebuff, I ended the conversation by saying that it was okay, and I was not going to dispute the board's position. I did not even bother to find out who my enemies were.

These events occurred at the end of September and early October. It was six weeks later, early December on a Sunday morning, that I received a call that roused me from a deep sleep. As I fumbled for the phone, I glanced at the bedside clock. It was precisely 5:00 a.m.

A voice came to life from the phone. "Hi, Dick, it's Jim Barry, and I'm so sorry to be calling you so early, but I just couldn't sleep, and I had to talk to you."

Pause. Jim was looking for a response, which shortly I acknowledged by saying, "What in the world could be so important?"

"Well, I was at a cocktail party last night, and I learned that you had bought the hill (the leased property on which Heiliger Huegel operated) and that you are planning to evict us when the lease is up next year."

Another pause. This time I let the silence be my ally, giving me time to think and allowing Jim's fears to gestate. They did, and before I got around to responding, Jim blundered on, "Is this because you're pissed because we kicked you out of the club?"

What an opportunity! My mind raced. In the space I had made for myself, I began to formulate a plan, recognizing that I wouldn't even have to lie to get what I wanted. I replied, "Pissed may be a little strong, but it was annoying to get kicked out of a club I had belonged to for thirty years for being one day late with the dues."

Another silence which I just let hang.

"Yeah, I agree, but you said you really didn't care."

Now for the coup: "Would you like to have me back in the club?"

There followed a pause, one that was just a tad too long. But, hey, it was pretty early, Anyway, he came up with the correct answer, "Oh yes, of course, we would."

"Do I have your word that you will get me back in the club?"

"You won't evict us from the hill?"

"You have my word."

That is the way the conversation would have gone if I had had my wits about me. However, it didn't go quite that way. When I heard Jim's rumor and heard that he was up all night worrying about my exercising my newfound power, I found myself empathizing with him. Needing to relieve his anxiety, I let my opportunity pass, reassuring Jim and acknowledging that the entire rumor was false speculation. One might say that I showed a compassionate side of myself, but that's just an easy out. With the perspective of time, I have to admit that it was not compassion that motivated me. It was that I did not think fast enough. I needed more time to come up with the scheme I outlined above.

I wonder why I remember this incident so vividly. This entire episode was not important to me, but it would have been satisfying to turn the opportunity handed to me into a personal victory. Being quick on one's feet with the rapier repartee is a skill devoutly to be wished; unfortunately, a skill that I possess in insufficient amount. Nevertheless, even if one is not as quick as one would like to be, then knowing how to play for time should be the weapon of choice.

CHAPTER XXII

Ballet Is Not for Sissies

My interest in the ballet was kindled on a business trip that took Kathy and me to London for the International Amusement Game Show. We were there for a week; and while we really were busy with the games show during the daytime, our nights were free. In retrospect, it is difficult for me to believe that I didn't find some other way to fill those evenings in London, but it is a fact that we went to three performances of the Royal Ballet. I thoroughly enjoyed those evenings. The experience sent me off on a side trip that was to assume real importance in my personal life over the next seven years of my life. It was the beginning of a truly enjoyable adventure in the arts.

EVEN THOUGH HE was about to become an important part of my life, I didn't know who David Halling was. When I saw him across the McGinn Lounge, he looked familiar but beyond my recollection. So I asked who he was, and my companion said, "Oh, that's David Halling. He's president of the ballet!"

Since we were at the Performing Arts Center sipping Coca-Cola between acts of *Coppélia* as presented by the Milwaukee Ballet, being president of the ballet gave David Halling an aura of importance. Little did I realize that I was destined to have his job in less than a year!

I had not been interested in dance at all until about a month before this event, when I had been traveling with my wife, Kathy, to London on business. We had been in London for a full week and had attended the Royal Ballet on our first night there. It had been a grand affair. Then because we had such a good time, we returned twice that week. I would admit that what I liked about the ballet in London was the grand scene that these events offered: attractive people, the buzz of conversation, spectacular architecture in the theatre building, champagne served between acts, all of this sensory abundance accompanying, for me at that time, a completely unfamiliar dance performance. It was a romantic scene, one of which I liked being a part. It was this perspective that had brought me for the first time to Milwaukee's ballet.

Because I had picked up a few ideas about ballet as entertainment from my London experience, I introduced myself to David Halling. David, walking with a cane, was a tall man with a debonair manner, seeming to have nary a care in the world. His persona would have been aptly described by the expression, "A hale fellow, well met."

After an introductory exchange, I suggested casually that the Milwaukee Ballet might do well to adopt some of the embellishments we had enjoyed in London—with particular emphasis on the intermission ambiance. The Milwaukee plain suit-and-tie routine, together with plain black dresses, and even pants suits, did not help to create a sufficiently glamorous aura. And what about champagne? David gracefully took my suggestions in stride and opined that a little champagne might go a long way in mitigating some of the more egregious dancing faux pas, of which he acknowledged there were many with this ballet.

That was on Saturday. On the Monday following, I received a call from David in which, after some pleasantries about the Saturday's performance, he asked whether I had any interest in serving on the board of the Milwaukee Ballet. I was flattered by the offer but resisted, dispassionately and objectively pleading ignorance of everything about the business of ballet. David was persistent, though, and after a brief conversation, I agreed to sit down to discuss the possibility with him.

In a meeting a couple of days later, I learned that a ballet directorship was to be no sinecure; the ballet, like most performing arts organizations, had significant financial problems. In addition, it had an artistic director, John Paul Comelin, who was difficult to manage and had a healthy appetite for spending. The administrative head was Roberta Bourse, the woman who had founded the ballet ten years earlier, but whose business skills had not kept pace with the growth of the organization. There were no financial reserves. Nevertheless, even with these problems, David had put together what appeared to be a good board of directors, having many people I knew and respected. What seemed more important, the product on the stage had seemed to be quite acceptable to the audience.

We talked about what I might be able to do in this environment. David described the board committee structure, and I noticed the absence of a planning function. I mentioned that planning was a discipline in which I had some background. Understanding that there was value in having a plan, David jumped at this idea and agreed to establish such a committee if I would chair it. With his beguiling enthusiasm, he had enticed me into this troubled organization. While he had told me of the problems the ballet was facing, I would learn later that things often are worse than they appear. With my eyes tightly shut, I joined the board in late October.

As I got to know the board, I found to my gratification that some of the ablest members were interested in long-range planning. I was able over the next few months to lure the best of these directors onto my committee, persons who knew a lot about ballet and some who even understood the business of ballet. By April, the committee was functioning well, and we were beginning to pull together the elements of a long-range plan. The main problem we faced in getting any plan in place was that the short-term plan was not working. As we approached the end of the ballet season, that being late spring, the company was running out of money. My initial concern for the elegance of the intermissions had given way to the need to address the real problems of ballet, which, as in all of the performing arts, are always about money.

At our May committee meeting, the Long-Range Planning Committee, rather than writing a plan, was deeply involved in coming to grips with the current financial plight, which, in this case, was meeting the biweekly payroll. We were becoming a shadow board because the board was not confronting the real problems faced by the company.

Actually, the situation of the ballet was not complicated, but our financial problems seemed intractable. The artistic director had gone well over the budget allotted for the last performance of the season, and the revenue had fallen short of expectations. We were out of money, even without considering the current payroll. Nevertheless, the artistic product was okay, and we were getting reasonably good reviews. Our bank line of credit was overdrawn, and our bank had already turned down our request for an extension. How in the world did I get myself in a position where my committee was talking about meeting a payroll, maybe out of our own pockets?

We were discussing the possibility of looking for money from a few loyal supporters, preparatory for a fund drive later in the year when the door opened. David Halling burst in, and without any ado, announced that he had a couple of announcements. *Bravo*, I thought, *David has a contribution to make here! He surely has been thinking about our predicament.*

David didn't bother to hem or haw; he came right to the point and declared confidently, "I have been grappling for my entire presidency with the financial plight of this company. We just don't seem to be able to fill enough seats to pay for the expenses that our productions cost. After considerable thought, I came to believe that most of the problems we have at the ballet are caused by our artistic director, John Paul. Mainly, he has always refused to budget reasonably, and, even with budgets that we can't afford, he exceeds his spending projections. So I met with him an hour ago to have it out with him on these issues. Getting absolutely no place with him, I decided to fire him and did so on the spot."

He was right. That was just how we saw the problem.

David paused for a long moment to let this news sink in. Then he continued, "I recognize that this action was a major undertaking, a decision that I probably shouldn't have taken alone. I should have at least cleared this with you guys. But I did it, and I think it was the right thing for the company. Anyway, after John Paul stormed off, I reflected on what I had done. I realized that I had only addressed half of the problem. It was clear to me that Roberta was not up to her job either. She just is not strong enough to deal with the ego of any artistic director. It came to me that I might as well clean house, so I called Roberta and fired her over the phone. I realized then that I should inform the leadership of the board of these actions. Knowing that you were meeting here at the University Club, I came directly, and here I am."

There was an uncomfortable silence during which we all waited for another shoe to drop. "How is he going to pull this all together?" was a thought that had to be running through everyone's mind.

Finally, David went on, sounding a bit less confident and even somewhat apologetic, "On the way over, I started thinking about the magnitude of what I had done. I did some stuff that had to be done, but this job is just too big for me. So, I am resigning as president. I hate to leave you guys holding the bag, but I'm sure that you can figure out what to do next."

Without another word he wheeled around and left!

There were eight of us in the room. It did not take us long to realize that we were now, as David had suggested, holding the bag. Someone needed to be the leader. It might have been anyone in the room, but it soon became clear that as chairman of the committee, I held the short straw. After a brief discussion, during which no good alternatives emerged, I accepted this responsibility, not because I had naive confidence in my ability to restore the company to health, but because my companions on the planning committee had that confidence in me, and they were very persuasive. Besides, I liked running things.

During the next few days, a little digging turned up a lot of stuff that I had missed as I had set up my committee and had failed to learn in the intervening period. The situation was worse than I had guessed. It wasn't just money and artistic leadership, although those deficiencies were daunting. Just as important, among the various stakeholders in this enterprise, there was no common view about the present problems and none for the future. There were diverse opinions about the discharged employees and the role of the board and its leadership. All the major participants were at war with one another. The dancers saw the board as the enemy, and there was a National Labor Relations Board labor union election immediately in the offing, with the Actors Guild (AGMA) being the organizing body. There existed a hostile relationship between the administrative staff and the board. Neither the board nor the administration got along with the ballet's auxiliary, called, incongruously in the prevailing circumstances, "The Friends of the Ballet." These "Friends" were withholding from the board funds which had been raised in the name of the Milwaukee Ballet because they believed the board to be incompetent. The community performing arts funding group, the United Performing Arts Fund (UPAF), was threatening to do the same because of the mounting problems.

Halling had created one more obligation just before he abandoned ship . . . that of taking on a new long-term lease. The lease placed the company in an old Schlitz beer garden facility called Tivoli Gardens. It was a beautiful building, being remodeled at the time to serve the ballet's needs, but it would double the outlay for rent. To make things worse, I received a call from Charlie Trainer, who wanted to have lunch to talk about the ballet. I had learned that the Trainer family was the owner of the Tivoli Gardens. Upon my first consideration, I was planning to walk away from this commitment, so I knew it was going to be an unpleasant meeting with Charlie. But after giving our situation a little thought, I welcomed this confrontation as an opportunity for me to face our economic issues and begin the process of restraining expenses. If I agree to honor the lease, I should at least be able to get them to waive the rent for a year or so.

The meeting didn't go quite the way I hoped. Charlie opened the conversation saying how relieved his whole family was that I had taken on the responsibility for the ballet, starting with his charming step-mother-in-law, Sharin, an older lady whom I had known well. According to Charlie, she and her husband had been terribly uncomfortable with the situation that existed with Halling as president. Charlie professed, almost believably, that they were so relieved when they heard that I was in charge, yada yada yada. He carried on in this vein for an interminable couple of minutes, and when he finally wound down, I just accepted his sycophantic praise and accepted the faith of the Trainer family as an additional burden. Having seen the possibility of some upside in the situation, I did take the opportunity to describe the swamp in which we were immersed and tried, without success, to get a contribution from Charlie and his family.

"Maybe later, when your financials look a little better." In a cowardly mode, rather than pursuing this opportunity, I acceded to this artful dodge. Even as we bailed them out of their bad investment, the Trainers were never, to my knowledge, to compensate us in proportion to what we eventually did for them.

The entire plight of the ballet was severely aggravated because, with John Paul gone, we had no artistic product. That meant that the community would not be able to see any value in what we had to offer. Indeed, there was next to nothing of value in the organization other than a determined leadership of the board. The final indignity came from the local newspapers who were feeding without mercy on our turmoil. And our antagonists, those who had been summarily discharged by Halling, together with their allies, were not going to go quietly. Our press was uniformly negative.

At least the company wasn't to dance again until the fall, so the payroll requirements were easing for a while. Nevertheless, all of these issues came to a head immediately upon my election to the presidency in May.

But I am a lucky guy! Our first stroke of good fortune was engineered by one of my committee members, Pat Van Alyea. She invited an acquaintance of hers to interview for the artistic director's job. He was Ted Kivit, who had just retired as the principal dancer of the American Ballet Theater. Ted came to Milwaukee for an interview, and when it was offered by our hastily assembled search committee, he accepted the position of artistic director. While I didn't fully grasp then how great a coup this appointment was, it was, for the Milwaukee Ballet, a critical step in the right direction, one that was magnified by the fact that with Ted came his wife, Michelle Lucci, who had been the prima ballerina with ABT. She could have continued in that role for at least a couple of years, but upon Ted taking the artistic director job, she chose to take her chances with her husband and our shaky company. These two hires were to put us back in the game artistically, and that accomplishment was going to be an essential element in attacking our financial problems.

The NLRB union vote came too soon. There was not enough time to persuade the dancers that they would be fairly treated in a new regime. I did meet with the them once before the election and had made some progress in reducing the level of hostility; but a few days later as I stood next to the labor department official who was recording the vote, even without counting, I sensed that the last vote recorded was critical, and that one went in favor of the union. Sure enough, we lost the election by one vote. I dreaded having to negotiate with a union representative alongside of all of our other problems.

By the time I met with the AGMA's bargaining agent, I had come to the realization that we had a strong negotiating position, that of bargaining from weakness. Weakness in this case meant that it was clear that we could not afford to offer much. If they did not accept something reasonable, we would be out of business, and AGMA's new members would be out of work. That put the union and me in the same boat.

As we met, the union rep and I both knew that I held the key to the dancers' future in Milwaukee. The currency of negotiation was going to be the number of weeks of work and the dancers' pay scale. I needed to cut back materially on both. It did not take the AGMA representative long to understand we had a confluence of interests. He eventually agreed to my proposed terms, while expressing deep skepticism that, even with these drastic cuts, we could save the ballet and the dancers' jobs. Of course, being a union rep, he had to go home with something. He demanded one condition in exchange for his agreement to my terms, this condition to protect the dancers from providing services for which they would not get paid. Under his counterproposal, any time we began a pay period without money in the bank sufficient to meet the upcoming two-week payroll, I would meet with the dancers and explain how we expected to deal with the next payday. I agreed to this condition, thereby initiating the most rewarding activity of my entire ballet experience, that of meeting with the dancers on a regular basis.

Next, it was on to tackling the major financial problems, starting with the Friends and UPAF. With both of these organizations, I found that abject obsequiousness was a truly effective approach: When you want something that someone else controls, even if it is rightfully yours, it is better, as dogs know, to lick than to bite. By means of groveling, I got, on a reasonable schedule, the money the Friends held for us. Similar servility got our UPAF funds not only restored but also accelerated. With these favorable results and only skeletal payrolls during the summer, we had breathing space into the fall, perhaps all the way up to our first performance of the season in late September.

I used this time to take the first steps toward a major fund drive. The first act was to hire a consultant to guide us in this activity. Joan Urdan introduced me to an arts-oriented fund-raising consultant in Minneapolis, who had good Milwaukee connections. This relationship led to my learning a lot about fund-raising as we considered hiring the firm. During the late summer, with professional help, we got through some of the initial procedures of a major fund-raising campaign, including a survey of potential donors. My planning committee constructed detailed budgets for the next three years. In the process, we learned that we needed to raise as much as four million dollars to adequately fund a ballet company that could survive for even a few years. That seemed like a tall order, but we were reassured by our survey that if we got our act together, we could raise the money.

For ameliorating our UPAF relationship, I had formed a committee of board members to be known appropriately as the UPAF Committee. Its first goal was to repair the relationship with the board of UPAF so we could get the money we had coming, an objective that had been achieved by midsummer, then to get a fund drive permission which would allow us to run a drive to "Save the Ballet," and finally to improve over the longer term our allocation from the umbrella organization. At this time, the ballet was receiving only 4 percent of the total money raised by UPAF, although its earned revenue had been close to 20 percent of the total of the five groups supported by UPAF, a fact that had not been considered important by UPAF, probably because of the fledgling status of the ballet. Nevertheless, as the summer ended, we knew that our most pressing job with UPAF was to look good enough on stage to deserve continuing community support.

Against the advice of our public relations experts on the board and in contrast to the prior ballet administration, I made myself available to the press. I found that if reporters trust you and find value in the relationship, they do not go out of their way to hurt you. They are only a big problem when you are trying to conceal something.

Having absolutely nothing to hide, I could afford to be an open book. We were building a story that was interesting but controversial, controversial because the friends of the disaffected parties were not silent. In the skirmishes that ensued, the press came fully onto our side. Their criticism of the artistic product was always fair, even more than fair, and their commentary on our restructuring and management was singularly favorable.

Because Ted Kivit had his own ideal body image for dancers, his were not the scrawny ballerinas so typical in the ballet of this era. They had beautiful, not quite fleshy bodies, sculpted by the demands of their art . . . quite breathtaking, in fact. Further, Ted had a selectively aesthetic eye for the face as well, and so Milwaukee dancers reflected the accepted facial beauty standards of the day. Even in their youth, the women of this corps were, as is the case with dancers in general, possessed of extraordinary poise. So perhaps I had not been relegated to purgatory in having to suffer my bimonthly briefings.

When the dancers had returned from their summer layoff, together with Kivit's new hires, I began meeting with them every two weeks to tell that we had no money in the bank. Then I would go on to tell them how we expected to pay them. At the first of these meetings, these young women, always in their tutus, were reserved and quiet, paying attention to my explanations without venturing any comment at all. They sat with their legs crossed in front of them and, to a woman, chain-smoked their filter cigarettes. As the weeks ticked by, they gradually began to warm to me and would even engage in light banter. Soon, I was sitting on the floor with them and puffing away on my own cigarette. The meetings, which earlier had lasted maybe ten minutes, stretched out delightfully for as much as forty minutes. Virtue is its own reward!

The season began with the presentation of *Carmina Burana*, a ballet that incorporated a professional chorus and did not strain the dancing skills of an almost entirely new company. The production, while not a commercial success, achieved critical acclaim, and the local press began to warm.

By late fall, things were looking up. The internal strife was on the mend. The little old ladies of the "Friends" were becoming friendly. The monthly meetings with them were gradually transformed from inquisitions to celebrations, and I was the celebrant. Further, the dissonance within the administration had disappeared and the attitudes of the company toward the board were improving.

Because we were coming out of the doghouse, I was invited to make a presentation to UPAF, a twenty-minute talk about our progress and goals, a talk which I ended with a plagiarized paraphrase from the movie *Love Story*: "Being part of UPAF means that you don't ever have to say you're sorry." They loved it and gave me a warm ovation. One director, Sue Dragasec, admitted to shedding a tear at my closing. We were back in the good graces of UPAF.

Enthusiasm at the board level was high, what with all we had accomplished; and monthly board meetings were honored with almost perfect attendance. I kept the agenda crisp and required committee reports to be brief and straightforward. We had a pleasant social hour after meetings, which became increasingly popular as our success grew. It had become possible to draw to the board influential community leaders, who came aboard even knowing that we faced a fund drive.

We had hired the Minneapolis fund-raising firm in the late summer, and by December, they were earning their keep. The survey that we had undertaken uncovered latent support for the ballet, support that had gone untapped for years.

Jackie lived in Minneapolis and could not direct the day-to-day management of our fund drive, so we considered looking for a resident manager. As we discussed this issue, Joan Urdan, who was a member of our executive committee and had had considerable experience in arts management, offered to fill this position. After a difficult salary negotiation with Joan, she took the job. Then she volunteered her entire salary as a donation. The salary negotiation had been about assuring Joan that we valued her services as highly as she did.

With Joan's strong presence in the community, we were able to triangulate well on some of the deepest pockets in the community, starting with the president of Briggs and Stratton, Fred Stratton Jr., even though the only dancing Fred had shown any previous interest in was strip tease. Peter Banzhaf invited him to have lunch at the University Club. Peter and I met him on the second-floor landing. When Fred saw us together, he turned around and tried to leave saying, "I'm not having lunch with you guys."

He knew what he was talking about and wanted no part of what we were up to. Nevertheless, we succeeded in collaring him for lunch, and afterward he agreed reluctantly to go to the Tivoli Gardens, the new home of the ballet, to "have a look." Unbeknownst to him, we had our beautiful and smart ballerina, Deborah Ridley, lying in wait for him, working at the barre outside Ted Kivit's office. Ted's office opened up onto the main studio, so there was easy access. Soon Fred was talking to Debbie. They became friends and have remained so ever since. Fred agreed to cochair our fund-raising campaign. His participation put the "good housekeeping seal" on the ballet and gave us important access to major donors and foundations.

By spring, the pieces had fallen into place. The artistic product under Ted Kivit was recognized to be an order of magnitude ahead of that of his predecessor. Michelle Lucci shone upon the stage and gave Milwaukee an icon to adore. The company under the direction of a new business manager, Carolyn Stevens, was running within a budget. The fund drive was underway, and we had achieved significant leadership gifts in keeping with the dimensions of the campaign goals. The Friends were warming up to the board, and we were becoming the darlings of UPAF. What more could you ask? Well, maybe one memorable moment, perhaps one of the best I have ever had:

As the success of the fund-raising campaign became apparent in April, so did the financial position of the ballet become secure. Suddenly, there was money in the bank. At my biweekly meeting with the dancers in late April, I was able to announce that this meeting would be the last of its genre because there was going to be money in the bank for the foreseeable future. Without a word and without a sign between them, they, as a group, uncrossed their legs, leapt to their feet, and gave me a standing ovation. That one euphoric moment made the entire effort worthwhile.

Of course, there were a few other great moments with this organization while I lived out the rest of my presidency. One was our performance of *Swan Lake* in my last year as president. This fine production received critical praise even in Chicago and capped the achievements of Ted Kivit and the Milwaukee Ballet up to that time. *Swan Lake*, which I had first seen in London five years earlier, had been an ideal that I had been told *not* to hope for. I still cherish Steve Laughlin's poster for this production . . . it featuring a beautiful Michele kneeling at water's edge with a swan as her reflected image.

During the fund-raising campaign, which continued for another year or so, we played poker with several prospects who later became some of our most generous individual donors. The original game, which always included Ted Kivit and music director, Danny Forlano, was hosted by Pat Van Alyea's husband, Tom, and still survives in 2018, with a few of the donors of forty years ago still in attendance.

One of my favorite duties as president of the ballet was to attend to Michelle's tantrums backstage when she thought she was putting on a bad performance or whatever else might bother a great prima ballerina. On these occasions, she would tear at her hair, weep torrentially, and throw shoes and other objects . . . fortunately, mostly at the wall. And it seemed on occasion that it was only I who could calm her down and get her together to go back on stage. In the process, she might cling to me desperately, literally crying on my shoulder. I felt needed, and I liked this dramatic role.

I served as president for three years because it was not easy to find a replacement. There existed a recognition out there that being president of a ballet company is a bit like playing Russian roulette. As it happened, when I persuaded Hans Moede to take on the task, his odds were not even that good. As he careened down the path toward another wreck, Hans was said to have said about me, "Gallun didn't know anything about ballet; all he knew is how to raise money."

At least he was surely right about the first part.

During Hans's run with the ballet, he benefited from one other vestige of the prior administration. After running with Bo Black the annual UPAF campaign in 1984, I had moved on to the presidency of UPAF, and independently from me, the members of the Ballet UPAF Committee had insinuated themselves into the leadership of

UPAF. Not only did this group have a serious influence on dividing the pie more fairly, bringing the ballet's share to around 20 percent, but they were important in helping UPAF to double its take over the next three years. Over the entire period of my involvement with the ballet and then UPAF, a period of six years, the annual allocation to the ballet grew from $80,000 to an amount approaching $800,000. Toward the end of my presidency of UPAF, a disaffected UPAF board member, who represented the symphony, was heard to complain that the ballet was completely in control of UPAF. He argued, almost accurately, that ballet people chaired all of the UPAF committees.

It is accurate that the ballet was a special beneficiary of my leadership at UPAF, and while I did have an ax to grind, my bias favoring the ballet was only that the ballet, as a latecomer to UPAF, was being shortchanged significantly in proportion to its size. I had chaired the UPAF fund-raising committee after completing my term as president of the ballet (and, understanding my potential conflict of interest, severing my relationship with the ballet), and it was this committee that determined that, rather than basing allocations on history, they would better be based on the size of the organization adjusted in accordance with the expected cost of each art form. The fairness of this proposal was endorsed by a unanimous vote when it reached the board.

That same year, 1984, my fund-raising committee introduced a process for motivating the member groups to encourage their members to participate in the UPAF annual drive. The process revolved around measuring each group's participation in the drive and scoring favorable behaviors (rather than outcomes) in an infamous summary report called "the scorecard." The discipline introduced here brought about the easy recruitment of campaign volunteers from all of the boards and their auxiliaries and motivated them to make their calls on a timely basis. While the scorecard was reviled for years by almost all participants, it did breathe new life into UPAF, leading to several years of double-digit growth of contributions, and it survived as a management tool for almost thirty years.

Time passed, and my connections with the Milwaukee Ballet faded away. I had other fish to fry, and my focus had shifted to politics. Nevertheless, in the early nineties, I was having lunch with my wife Judith on an opening day of V. Richards under the new ownership of the Neerys. After we had eaten, our waitress, who turned out to be the new owner of the store and restaurant, asked if I was Richard Gallun. I said I was, and she introduced herself. She was Anne Neery, nee Anne Finch, who had become Milwaukee's prima ballerina in the mid-eighties. She recalled being part of the tutu-clad entourage who listened patiently to my promises of payment in 1980.

For me, a guy who is laughed at on the dance floor and who is the original source for the deprecating saying, "He dances like a Gallun," my adventure with ballet had been one of the most rewarding diversions of my life.

CHAPTER XXIII

My Introduction to Weimaraners

Stella, our first Weimaraner, taught both Judith and me a lot about love, assuring that dogs were to be an important part of our lives. It had been twenty-five years since I had been truly involved with a dog, that having been Hornburg. Stella not only reintroduced me to the canine world but ensured that Weimaraners would become Judith's and my breed of choice.

STELLA CAME TO me with my midlife marriage to Judith, who had rescued Stella a month before I showed up. Stella, clever already at six months, inveigled her way into my life during my first stay over. Soon after our introduction, she shyly crawled into my lap and was generous with her affection, all the while exuding that delicious puppy aroma. When Judith and I, hand in hand, headed for the bedroom, Stella, sensing the initiation of an important challenge to her prerogative, dashed ahead, jumped to the bed, lay down on her side of the bed, put her head on the pillow, and immediately began to snore. It was a small bed. There really wasn't room for the three of us. She was displaced only after much gentle persuasion. Judith and I reached a compromise with Stella a couple of nights later that allowed her to have the top of her body on the bed as long as she kept her rear feet on the floor. That lasted for three days or so. Eventually, we got a larger bed.

Judith and I shared a great deal with Stella for ten years, all of that time accompanied by Stella's adopted brother, Max, an opinionated Shih Tzu.

In our first winter together at Pine Lake, we had a long period of black ice on which we played hockey with my children and their friends on this smooth surface. Stella loved the game and, like a Gallun, always went for the puck. In doing so, she would always career past it, completely out of control, her body contorting wildly as she tried to seize the elusive prize. Sometimes as she slid over the puck, she would attempt to grab it between her legs and would do a somersault in the process, ending up sliding helplessly on her back. She accepted her lot cheerfully and always was ready for more. Hockey with Stella provided everyone, but most particularly my son, Alby, with many laughs. Alby missed the coup de grâce, which came in the spring when Stella mistook the black water under a darkened sky for the black ice she had known, and she jumped confidently onto it—only to find that it wasn't there. She looked at me quizzically from the shallows where she then stood, frozen with surprise, as if to ask what had changed her world so radically. In the entire canine world, only a Weimaraner could convey so persuasively the sense of devastation that such a change in nature's laws engendered.

Stella had a few peculiarities, maybe more than all the rest of our Weimaraners put together. The first and perhaps the most charming was that she loved her stuffed animals. They were always with her; and if we went on a trip and forgot to bring at least one, her well-communicated unhappiness would precipitate a trip to a store to buy one. Unlike our other dogs, Stella, even as a puppy, didn't chew her stuffed animals, although she did eat sofas, shoes, glasses, and such paraphernalia. As to stuffed animals, she only nursed them, doing so in all her private moments, working their bodies with her paws as she sucked on their heads.

Stella liked to swim but more than swimming, she wanted to be with Judy when Judy swam. Except Judy swam too much, doing forty or so laps between our pier and that of our neighbor's. Stella would do a lap or two, then get out of the water to sun herself on the pier. A lap or so of rest and sunny warmth, and then she was back in her accompanying role. And so on until Judy had had enough.

Above all, Stella loved to run. On any day that she didn't get a long run with Judy, you might find her circling the outside of the house, doing so at her absolute top speed, careening around the corners, barely in control, and leaping the steps and bushes that were in her path. It was pure pleasure for me to see her joie de vivre.

My reader might believe that I saw Stella as the perfect dog, allowing, perhaps, for the few chewing transgressions previously discussed; and he'd be close to right. She did have, however, one lifelong habit which we never were able to get rid of. She was a counter surfer of the first order, and she could never be trusted in the kitchen. Fortunately, the two doors to the kitchen could be kept secured. However, occasionally we failed to maintain this discipline. Once, it was on Christmas Eve while we were entertaining family and friends and eating oysters, while the main course, a prime rib roast—a whole one—was resting in the kitchen. I had failed to secure one of the kitchen doors that provided unseen (from the dining room) access to the kitchen.

As we went to dinner, we left Stella in the living room, nestled on the sofa in front of the fireplace. What a good dog! Just before I was to retrieve the roast for carving, Michael MacNeil, one of our guests, walked in carrying in his arms the roast, au jus staining his shirt and running down his pants—a real mess. What was Michael doing with the roast? He explained that he had heard banging at the dog door and went to investigate. He had found Stella with the entire roast in her mouth, the roast crosswise to the opening and too long to get through. Not to worry . . . Wipe the roast down and carve it up!

I've always wondered: Should there not be consequences for these deviant behaviors? The answer to this question, one that Judy had internalized but one that only came to me later: "There are no bad dogs, only bad masters."

During Stella's life we owned a house in Florida. It was on Upper Captiva, and it could be reached only by boat and golf cart. Stella loved to travel by boat. When we set out from the Pine Island Marina with the boat loaded with groceries and other necessities, she would always ready herself to become the bowsprit. On our usual shortcut to Upper Captiva, we needed to cross a long shallows of about a mile in length. To do so, we had to get onto a plane in the deeper water close to the marina to get the propeller above the sand for the crossing. Stella would wait until the acceleration was accomplished before assuming her pose, that of standing erect on the bow, her ears waving in the breeze like semaphore flags, a regal sight indeed and a poignant memory of mine.

Once we flew directly to North Captiva on the Quadracci's Learjet with Harry, Betty, and Stella. Stella quickly accommodated herself to this regal mode of travel. I put her at my feet as we took off and gained altitude, and Stella dutifully held her appointed position until we leveled off at thirty thousand feet. Then she rose calmly, stretched, and inhabited the one unoccupied seat in the cabin, making herself comfortable by sitting erectly so that she could look out the window. She held her viewing position for a long time, just looking at the postage-sized map of southeast Wisconsin streaming slowly by below. What she was thinking I will never know, but what goes on in the mind of a Weimaraner will always be a mystery to me.

Stella liked her life on the island because the four of us, Judy, Stella, Max, and I, went every place together, except that when we went out for dinner, we often had to leave the dogs at home. One evening as we were getting ready to travel to Boca Grande by boat, Stella made it clear that she wanted to come along. We carefully locked her in the house, knowing how determined she could be. Then we left, driving our golf cart the mile and a half to the Safety Harbor Club dock. From there, we took the boat to Miller's Marina on Gasparilla Island, where a favorite restaurant of ours stood above the marina.

By the time we returned later that night, it was fully dark with just a sliver of moon to light our way. We navigated carefully through the shallows at the mouth of Safety Harbor, then docked and tied up the boat. We walked easily down the pier in the pale moonlight, illumination that disappeared as we entered the tunnel of mangroves that guarded the landward end of the pier. As we edged our way off the pier in the inky darkness, we could only grope our way to the golf cart. But when we finally came upon it, a ray of faint moonlight illuminated the cart. As we approached, we could see the shape of our Stella curled in the driver's seat softly snoring. She awakened without alarm and greeted us warmly as if this coming home was run of the mill. We, of course, were surprised that she had escaped the house, tracked us to the dock, and had just settled down to wait patiently for us. Part of this mystery was solved when we arrived home to find a badly mauled double screen door with a hole in it of the requisite size for a slender Weimaraner.

Back home at Pine Lake, Stella was always a great companion for Judy, going along on Judy's daily runs, usually for five miles or so. Stella seemed to enjoy most of the run, but when the two of them ran down Oakland Road on the west side of the lake, frequently, Stella was threatened by George Dalton's predictably vicious German shepherd, Heidi. When they approached George's house, Stella, definitely a lover, not a fighter, would hang close to Judy for protection. If Heidi made her menacing move, Judy would do what was expected of her, threatening Heidi with most unladylike language. Somehow, this angry dog always got the message and slunk off. The next time Judy would see George, he would get the same kind of treatment, she giving scant attention to the fact that George was my boss.

Later we moved to Colorado. There, Stella's biggest problem arose when Judy was working inside, and I was outside in the garden. Stella would not know where she wanted to be, and she solved her dilemma by incessantly racing back and forth between us, wearing out more than one dog door in the process. When we hiked in rugged terrain that required Judy and me to use handholds, Stella would climb with us. In these places, she would follow my instructions to the letter, going to the exact places I pointed out to her with my climbing stick. She trusted me to keep her safe, and I always did.

It was a good run with Stella, eleven years altogether, not enough for such an integral participant in our daily life. Then, like Hornburg thirty-five years earlier, she too suffered a stroke, from which she gained a respite of a few months, which allowed us to take her, once more, to Denver for a last outing. Stella still loved stuffed animals and was always appreciative of another, so we took her to "Build a Bear" to create for her a custom teddy bear. By the time we had filled it with an extra heart and other amulets and talismans, the bear was so heavy that Stella could not lift it; but she nursed it for the few days that remained for her.

CHAPTER XXIV

Life with George

When my mother died in the early eighties, Kathy and I were living in our dream house on Oakland Road in Sauerkraut Bay on Pine Lake. Over Kathy's objection, I bought from my mother's estate my family's house on a point at the north end of the lake, a prized property with an ancient white elephant mansion to live in. A little later, a compromise with Kathy led to our putting both houses on the market on a "whichever goes first" basis. Even with these two excellent properties fairly priced, there were no buyers in this "Reagan-recession" economy. My temporary discomfiture brought into my life an exceptional man, George Dalton, who was going to introduce me to an important phase of my life.

George, at sixty, bore the scars of two and a half failed marriages and a business bankruptcy that had wiped him out a few years earlier. Even with these scars, he carried himself with confidence and evident energy and held a positive view of his future. My ensuing twenty years with him enlightened me to the fact that, while he was a powerful leader, he was also an eccentric human being with amusing foibles.

IT WAS IN 1983 that I first got introduced to this unusual man. "Introduced" may be the wrong word because it was he who telephoned me, opening the conversation by introducing himself. "Hi, I'm George Dalton, and I'm going to buy your house."

That was an unusual opener but great news for me. My house on Pine Lake had been for sale for about six months with nary a nibble. Something about this guy sounded real; he didn't say that he wanted to look at it he or that he even was going to make me an offer. He said he was going to buy it! He sounded like he knew what he was doing. So, I responded sensibly, "Well, why don't you make me an offer?"

"Well," he said, "I don't have any money right now."

What a letdown, very disappointing after such a good beginning. I was quiet for a moment, thinking that at least I was no worse off than before the call, when the caller continued with, "But I expect to have some money in a few months."

Being still something of a smart-ass and having no idea that "some money might be quite a few million," I reposted sarcastically, "Why don't you just call me back when you do?"

I hung up, immediately forgetting the name of the caller.

Some months later, I entered into extended negotiation with another prospect, one who was very businesslike but definitely not a gracious buyer. His style was to point out the defects, of which there were many in our hundred-year-old house. After a good deal of investigation and tire kicking, this guy was about to sign an offer at a price to which I had only reluctantly agreed. I was expecting to meet with him on the very day that I next heard from George Dalton. On that day, the buyer and I were planning to draw up and sign a sales agreement. Nevertheless, because my buyer was bringing his lawyer, even though we had already reached an informal agreement on price, I knew I was in for more negotiation.

That morning, the phone rang. The caller said, "This is George Dalton. Remember me? I'm the guy who is going to buy your house."

I remembered, and right away, I sensed that maybe there was something to this guy. So I responded, cutting, I thought, to the quick, "So, now you have money?"

"No, I still don't have any cash" (pause), "but I have something that is just as good."

Doubting this possibility, I waited for an explanation.

It came confidently, "Credit!"

Even though credit may not quite as good as cash, it did not take George long to convince me that he was a viable buyer. He was the CEO of a new data processing company called Fiserv that he had financed in a leveraged buyout. He took a moment to tell me about himself and the company. In the process, he made a good impression. Not only did he sound credible, but also, in contrast to my other prospect, he was pleasant to be with, and, what's more, he didn't appear to be a nitpicker.

After George finished his introduction, I explained to him that I had agreed to meet with another buyer later that day to finalize a sales contract. Employing his ingenuous charm, George persuaded me to use the intervening time to meet with him at my house and then to have lunch. We did so; and after viewing the house, the lunch went on well into the afternoon. I got to know an archetypical skilled buyer.

George was deferential and captivating, showing his appreciation of the property at every opportunity; he was a delightful companion in every way. At the same time, he deftly explored my relationship with my other prospect, trying, in the process, to figure out what he would have to pay. While I do not think that George yet understood his skill as a buyer, he clearly knew how to handle me.

It wasn't too long after he bought our house that he invited me over to see his auto collection, which was housed in a couple of old outbuildings as well as a new barn that he had added. He had some amazing autos already, and he would continue to add to his collection. But when we entered his new barn, it wasn't the cars that caught my eye. It was a large poster, at least eight by ten feet, presenting a bikini-clad nymph that demanded my attention. The model was a beauty, the image evoking that of Botticelli's Venus arising from the sea. I reacted immediately, asking, "Where did you get that, George?"

He came back, "Don't you recognize her?"

"No, should I?"

"Why, that's Pauline."

Then I came back with a comment not processed by my brain. "That must have been quite a few years ago."

True to his character, George took no umbrage, responding indifferently, "Not too long ago—maybe two years."

Despite my tactlessness, George and I went on to develop a useful friendship, one that developed during chance meetings on his pier or mine. Our relationship grew, and soon, I was advising him informally about Fiserv's early acquisitions. I observed that George, while understanding the downside in all of these early purchases, always emphasized the positive in dealing with sellers. While he was careful to buy only successful businesses, he had to overlook a few blemishes. In some cases, he admitted to seeing significant limitations in the target company. I remember probing his thinking about one marginal property that he was determined to acquire. "Why in the world would you buy this piece of shit?"

He pondered this question, seeming not to have a ready answer. Then he responded thoughtfully, "Dick, I need this acquisition to be in the game."

He was right about that. He was a lot smaller than the major competitors. He needed to bulk up to become a player.

In our casual conversations, I learned a lot about this seemingly simple man. For starters, he was a "mensch," a man of feeling and weltschmerz. He was self-effacing and modest, bearing the scars of two failed marriages and of having recently lost all of his money in an investment with his former employer. Still, he was a positive thinker about almost everything in which he was involved. Every day was a good day for him. He was a dreamer who talked of his vision of the coming business success of the company he had just founded. As early as 1985, when he shared his business goals with me, the mission of this company was to become "the leading provider of data processing services to the financial services industry." Now, that seemed to be way beyond an overreach. His company had come along well, and from its size at the founding, about thirty million dollars of revenue annually, the company had more than doubled in size. Nevertheless, the dominant company in this industry was EDS with financial services revenue well into ten figures. Further, there were at least three other competitors that had revenues that were multiples of those of Fiserv.

Fiserv had been created by the combination of two companies, Sunshine State Systems located in Tampa and First Data Systems of Milwaukee. Both were the detritus of failed financial institutions. Their leaders, Les Muma and George Dalton, respectively, had been acquainted for years and had extensively discussed combining their core software systems. They had even discussed merging the two companies and, in the process, had become good friends. Conveniently, their parent companies got into difficulty at about the same time.

After falling into a financial malaise, the debacle that cost George all of his savings, the Midland Bank, for which First Data was the data processing department, had been acquired by First Bank of Minneapolis, hence, the name, First Data Systems. First Bank possessed its own DP department; so it decided to spin off the Milwaukee facility, which mostly processed Wisconsin savings and loan companies.

Sunshine Systems was being sold for much the same reasons. First Data was larger and on its own had been quite profitable, while the Tampa center had been losing money and would continue to do so for years. Thus, First Data was the apparent survivor in the buyouts and simultaneous merger of the two data processing businesses, transactions that were financed by Welch, Carson, Anderson, and Stowe. Because Sunshine Systems had been operating in the red, George was the natural leader in the merged companies and became the CEO.

It was fortuitous for the company and George that Welsh Carson was involved. They were a recognized force in the financial data processing industry and had a favorable history with a number of major investors. Just as important, they insisted upon establishing good management systems in the companies in which they invested. Among their requirements, they demanded two things that were critical to Fiserv's success: a business plan and a strong CFO, here, in the person of Ken Jensen.

Ken established one of the great strengths of the company, that of superior financial management. In addition, he himself had a fine analytical mind and extensive experience in data processing from years spent in management at Sun Microsystems. Even with these skills, Ken was viewed as an outsider and a tool of Welsh Carson during the early years of the business. The business plan, with which I had some later exposure, was no great shakes, but it was a plan that laid the groundwork for an industry-wide rollup. It did represent the last formal planning to be done for the next ten years.

So, the company was underway with a couple of additional advantages to help it along the way to its eventual industry supremacy. Those advantages included a reserve which George had established over prior years, either to help stabilize the banks' earnings or to give him a cushion when he took the business private. More important, in the long term, the bank data processing industry was one which was consolidating, and one whose main competitors in the consolidation were managed by assholes; e.g., men with gargantuan egos, few moral scruples, bad personalities, and dominant management styles. It might be said that at least one of them of them was a teensy-weensy bit crooked. It was a good bunch to compete against. In fact, success in business is not entirely different from success at tennis; in both, a major determinant of a favorable outcome lies in how well you pick your competition.

Of course, I did not know any of these advantages in 1986 when, during one of our visits on his pier, George asked me how well I knew Jim Wigdale, the then chairman of the Marshall and Ilsley Bank. Upon learning that I knew Jim pretty well, George asked me if I would try to persuade Jim to talk to him about "putting M&I Data Services together with Fiserv," which really meant them selling the business to Fiserv. I could see no problem in making such an introduction, particularly because George was a good guy, and his company seemed to be doing pretty well. In addition, Fiserv, having made four or five acquisitions, was almost as large as M&I Data, and I had accepted the idea that this combination would make sense. Besides, I had recently purchased stock in Fiserv, so I was acting in my own interest.

The meeting that I scheduled with Jim was premised on a separate banking issue, and I did not raise George's request in advance. After doing my business, I directly confronted the Fiserv interest. Jim was clearly taken aback by my suggestion. After a few hems and haws he suggested that perhaps we should include Dennis Koester, president of M&I Data. Dennis was immediately available, and upon being asked to share his views on the subject at hand, he went into a diatribe about the problems he saw at Fiserv and why the proposed combination wouldn't work. What it came down to was that Fiserv had not consolidated any of its acquired businesses, and they were now maintaining at least six separate and complex software systems. The resulting inefficiency would soon lead to unsustainable operating costs.

I had been aware of the fact that Fiserv had not consolidated any of its systems; and when I had asked George what he was planning to do about this problem, his answer was, "Well, something will come along." Nevertheless, Dennis's comments hit home with me, and George's earlier response seemed a bit too casual and perhaps evasive. My meeting with Jim and Dennis lasted about half an hour, and try as I might, I could not persuade them even to talk with George. I went home and called George to tell him that the M&I would not talk with him. Then I did a really unfortunate thing. I sold my Fiserv stock. I never told George about that.

A footnote to the M&I's and others' view of the need for consolidation;

Fiserv got along pretty well running many of its acquired processors on their existing systems. All of its competitors in the rolling up of the industry, including M&I Data, did consolidate their acquired operating systems, bringing them onto a central system. In the process of consolidation they had to release their customers from existing contracts, throwing them into the competitive market for data services. They would always lose a portion of their acquired clients and many of the lost clients would gravitate to Fiserv. In addition, the management of these companies would often be discharged to capture greater efficiency. and the loss of customers, so the management-owners were chary of their future under the aegis of our competitors. These actions helped to make Fiserv the preferred acquirer in the industry. More importantly they made me a white knight! And George was right about something coming along. When it did some eight years later, Fiserv could persuade a large number of its users to convert to a clearly better system and to pay for the privilege.

The weakness at Fiserv that Dennis Koester had identified for me turned out to be one of Fiserv's greatest strengths. It may have been the decisive reason that Fiserv emerged from obscurity to industry leadership in less than ten years.

CHAPTER XXV

Pauline's Peril

It was two years after George bought my house that he asked me to join Fiserv to help him with acquisitions. In the early years of this job, I was going to learn that George was a man of many parts, most, but not all, useful to him. One of his most charming characteristics was his independence from the usual strictures of social convention. George did not care much what people thought of his candid sincerity or of the public persona he wished to present. He knew who he was and was proud to be that person, even with his warts in full view. To wit:

IT WAS SUPPOSED to be spring, but this was Milwaukee. It was also George's wife's birthday, so I arrived at Klemmer's Hall in the midst of a driving sleet storm at five sharp, that being the appointed hour for the party. The parking lot was already filling, and it was quite apparent that it was to be a big bash. The lot had its share of Buicks, those being the standard company car because of George's loyalty to Wally Rank, who had been an early investor in the company. However, the array of Lexis, BMWs, and Mercedes-Benzes, etc., told me that in addition to our own management cadre, the hoi polloi of the community was going to be in attendance. It turned out that, in addition to George's entire family, the guest list included many company employees but also customers, vendors, investors, and even the governor of the state.

Finding a place to park, I got out of my car, bundled my coat around me and pushed through the inclement weather toward the main entrance. Then I saw it. A silver Cadillac DeVille parked conspicuously next to the front door! This car, topped by a largish red velvet bow, evidently was Pauline's present du jour. Nevertheless, with the rain pouring down, there was no opportunity to ogle. Hurrying to get out of the cold, I passed a small gaggle of guests who were admiring this phenomenon of generosity and forged into the comfortable atmosphere of Klemmer's banquet hall.

Now, Klemmer's is a nice Polish restaurant with an attached great hall for events like this one. For today, there were three bars set up around the perimeter of the big hall with a tarmac of dance hall proportions in the center. George and Pauline were greeting their guests in the center of the room. It was a loud group, and the conversation seemed to center around the birthday gift. Knowing that I could greet my hosts later, I resisted the urge to partake of this ceremonial activity and looked for a more fulfilling diversion.

The bartenders were not yet under pressure, so I sidled up to the closest bar and asked for a martini. I might say that Klemmer's make a mean martini, which I had previously discovered on lunch forays with George, who occasionally liked to have a pop at noon. Per my request the bartender gave me a few extra olives. As I turned to join the party, I heard the bartender calling me back, "Sir, sir, that will be eight dollars."

The party was a great success, the cash bar notwithstanding. The conversation was good, the hors d'oeuvres were delicious, and the atmosphere took on the aura of a good drinking party. But suddenly, out of the blue, the lights were dimmed. Next, I heard the clinking of silverware on glass. Clearly, there was to be a speechmaking break, perhaps one of some duration. Then, as I rushed to get another drink, even the cash bars were shut down. More clinking of glasses. As the hall began to grow quiet, Kevin Kasper, the company's head of public relations, stepped to the podium to initiate the formalities. After a few brief remarks and a toast or two, he introduced a slide show highlighting the romance of George and Pauline in their interconjugal period. The entire proceedings were a real downer for the party, particularly for those who, like me, held an empty glass.

The atmosphere was not greatly helped when George got up to add some color to Kevin's rendition of this middle-aged romance. George, never a public speaker, droned on about his and Pauline's personal histories, their travels, and their travails, and eyes throughout the room began to glaze. George was not only losing his audience, but he was also wrecking a pretty good party. Finally, when he had the audience tightly in the grip of ennui, he said, and I quote verbatim:

"A lot of you will remember that when we all worked in the Midland Bank data processing department, Pauline and I, who were at the time married to other people, were suspected of playing around together."

Barely audible gasps from an awakening crowd. George continued, unabashed:

"Well, now, it's time for me to set that rumor straight for once and for all."

Then, after a dramatic pause—a pause that brought the assembled crowd to full attention—he dropped his bomb: "We were."

You could have heard a pin drop. Total silence punctuated perhaps by a bit of throat clearing. Eyes were mostly on the floor, but when I looked at Pauline, she was staring straight ahead and had become devoid of color.

Happy birthday, Pauline!

CHAPTER **XXVI**

King of the Island

My brush with royalty started innocently enough. In 1987 I rented for the season a house on North Captiva Island from a local realtor, Gary Walker, who proceeded to make himself my new best friend. Gary loved to show me property, and together we speculated about what I might do with the properties he showed me. There was little happening on the island. That was part of its attraction, and with little to do we had plenty of time to spend together. In the beginning it had been just life on the beach away from civilization that had attracted me to this remote Island. Little did I know that like Yertle the Turtle, I was destined to become the center of a struggle for control of all that I could see.

AT THE TIME the island was at an early stage of gentrification. The Safety Harbor Club dominated the real estate scene with a development which reached across the center of the island from an excellent harbor on the bay side to the beach on the gulf side—with a lake surrounded by houses and unsold lots lying in between. To its resident members, the club provided electrical access, sewerage service, dockage, tennis courts, a pool, and a clubhouse. Interior lots in the club, those on the lake, of which there were many yet unsold, were priced at about $45,000. With the value of the sewerage amenity at $20,000, the electrical connection at $15,000, and the dock facility at $10,000, the land, the club membership, and the natural beauty were, more or less, free. What a deal!

During my first stay at Sam Weinstein's house, which I had rented for the season, I saw and evaluated every available property on the island. I began to understand the hierarchy of value that existed. The top of the market was that of gulf front properties, which could be had for around $80,000 to $100,000 for a 100-foot lot, followed by property on the Pine Island Sound, which, while having good water access and nice sand beaches, sold for only 25 percent or so less. Interior property had practically no value, unless it had views of the gulf, was on a canal (which gave it access to the

207

ocean), or was in the Safety Harbor Club with its extensive infrastructure. Without these amenities, interior quarter acre lots could be had for less than $10,000. One of the key issues on the island was the availability of a place to keep a boat. With several hundred interior lots still unsold and regulations limiting waterfront development, dock space was going to get dear. As my reader can appreciate, there were many obvious ways to make a profit on real estate in 1986.

Looking to the future and wanting to make a buck, I decided to make an offer on a commercially zoned property that included a dozen boat slips, my bid falling just short of the asking price of $90,000. Having discovered that his property had value, the seller immediately withdrew that property from the market, so I missed a good opportunity. Boat slips became valued at twenty thousand each in less than two years. You do the math.

Late in the spring, I negotiated for a harbor front property that was inside of the Safety Harbor Club, and had a private dock and was entitled to all of the club infrastructures. The seller had been asking $80,000. After extensive negotiations, I agreed on a price of $72,500. A year later, I listed the property with Gary asking $99,750. A member of the island gentry, a Mik McMicken, took the bait and offered ninety and, recognizing that I was making a good return on investment, I accepted. That was fine . . . until McMicken failed to show up for the closing. I called him wondering how he had missed our closing date, and he informed me curtly that he had changed his mind about the property. When I suggested that we had a contract, he said, as if to dare me, "Sue me."

I proceeded to look into that possibility and discovered, unsurprisingly, that I had a good case. A year later, with interest, legal costs, and taxes, McMicken paid $115,000. Although I often walked past his big house on the beach, I never met the man until two years later, when I was introduced to him at the "Over the Waterfront" restaurant. As I proffered my hand, he extended his, but when he heard my name, he withdrew his, whirled around, and walked away. Apparently I had offended him.

My next acquisitions were two adjoining lots off the beach, one of which provided the only access to the oceanfront house, a teardown, it appeared, in front of it. By owning both of the lots behind this teardown, I had the property hopelessly landlocked; i.e., the owner could not get to his property without traversing mine. Shortly after I had made this purchase, I called the landlocked owner and he, not seeming to recognize his precarious access problem, indicated only a mild interest in selling. He wanted an excessive price—excessive, at least to me. I let him cool his heels, planning to raise the landlocked issue later if I had to.

The owner was a private pilot who occasionally flew off and onto the airstrip that crossed the island immediately south of my new property. I had watched him occasionally practicing takeoffs and landings, he seeming to do a good job at both.

He appeared to be an adequate pilot. But appearances don't count for much in pilots. One day when I was back in Milwaukee, I learned that he had taken off in his airplane with an empty gas tank. That's hard to believe; pilots always check their tanks as part of a routine checklist. Nevertheless, he had no gas at all, and his engine was sputtering as he became airborne. He tried to turn around, but the engine died, and the plane stalled as he began his turn. He crashed into the ocean just off the end of the runway, killing himself in the process.

Not wanting to be a ghoul, I bided my time in approaching the new widow. By the time I talked with her, she was anxious to get rid of this inherited property; and, perhaps recognizing the weakness of her position, she proposed a very favorable price. I never had to raise the issue of access.

The three, actually four, lots I then owned gave me an opportunity to have two beach houses, both on double lots. An unexpected bonus emerged in that the house I had purchased was quite salvageable. The combination of the two adjoining properties for personal use and rent made an attractive investment proposition, and needing money for construction, I used it to entice my two sons and Richard Weening to join me in developing the property.

Our development plan was straightforward. First, we moved the existing house to the south, moving it from its center position on the property, thereby creating a second beach frontage lot to the north. Then we remodeled the beach house, turning what had appeared to be a teardown into an attractive beachfront cottage. After we completed the remodeling, we built a four-bedroom house next to it, with both houses to be rented when we were not using them. We bought two memberships in the Safety Harbor Club, which gave us docking rights and access to the clubhouse, pool, and tennis court, not only for ourselves but for our rental guests as well. While ours were nonvoting (class C) memberships—the voting memberships were attached to properties within the Safety Harbor development—they, nonetheless, entitled us to attend club meetings and, more importantly, to participate in club affairs; i.e., to serve as a director or as an officer of the club association.

The annual meeting of the Safety Harbor Club followed soon after our purchase, and having a growing interest in what was happening on the island, I attended. That decision marked my entry into island politics. I saw right away that there were a few issues upon which the membership was divided, including the control of children and dogs, the admission of outsiders to the club property, the use of the Safety Harbor roads and beaches for nonmember island residents to transit the island, and the existence of the Over the Water Restaurant in the main village of Safety Harbor.

While I was bothered by the excessive control issues, it was this last matter that caught my attention because it was a nice restaurant and the only one on the island at the time; it served good food and provided a service not only to members of the club but to tourists who were passing through in boats. The directors wanted to keep the riffraff out altogether, and they put no value on the support to the restaurant provided by outsiders. They wanted to break the lease and run the restaurant for the benefit of members only.

No shrinking violet me, I volunteered, thinking I would make a point that would impress them with my wisdom, that from my experience with restaurants, they would be making a big mistake in trying to run one. What's more, I pointed out that they did not have the critical mass to support a restaurant; and with only members attending, it would surely fail. The directors were not looking for advice. My advice was not well received.

The restaurant issue stayed alive for the next number of years, and I listened to the debate on this subject without getting further involved. Other issues came to light that began to annoy me more than the potential termination of restaurant lease, starting with a condescending attitude of the board to me and other members who did not live in the club development and friction that existed between the "insiders," those members who were allied with the board, and others who did not want to get involved in island politics. Finally, I realized that the composition of the board was inappropriate, with two of the nine positions filled by a vendor and the paid manager of the club. The coup de grâce came when the assistant manager was to be added to the board in 1991.

It was upon this election that I began to think about trying to influence the affairs of the club. My thought process was accelerated when, from disaffected members, I learned that the manager, Jack was his name, had accosted and treated members rudely when he did not like their behavior. Not the role of a manager, in my opinion! Further, it was general knowledge that he had regularly threatened transient tourists who wandered off the main road in the club property. In one case, it was reported that he was seen ousting a tourist while screaming, "Get off my island!" Because of the conflicts that these issues created, there was a growing rift between the Safety Harbor Club and its members and the other residents of the island. And I began to see that there was an undercurrent of disaffection among many of the members. An important consideration motivating me was that none of the directors wanted to hear my point of view.

After considerable discussions with Judy, talks in which she definitely took the other side, I decided to lead a change in the board of directors and, picking among my small cadre of political allies, found appropriate confederates who were willing to stand for election on the platform materializing in my brain. Nevertheless, this task was going to be more difficult than any of us could imagine. My objective was further complicated by the fact that the club had only three members up for election each year, promising that my takeover would take at least two years.

There were eighty members eligible to vote. That meant that we would need perhaps as many as forty votes, but that only if all the members voted, a prospect that seemed unlikely at the outset. In prior years, only half of the members had voted. While initially, I had about a dozen allies in my rebellion, about half were class C members like me and had no vote in the prospective election. I went to work ten months before the next election date, with confidence but only about six votes in my pocket.

Safety Harbor was mostly a vacation community, with members who visited for short periods on their own schedule, so I did not know many members, and there was little opportunity for face-to-face meetings before the next annual meeting. I was lucky that I had, as a member, a telephone list of all the members. Nevertheless, I did face difficulty in soliciting votes, since many, perhaps a quarter, of the members, had intermediaries, like their lawyers or business assistants, or phone numbers that failed for a variety of reasons. However, working alone much of the time, but with some help from my accomplices dealing with their acquaintances, over the next ten months, I was able to make contact with all but about a dozen members.

Contact is one thing, but persuading people who are uninvolved and naturally suspicious of interlopers is another. Even so, with the annual meeting in April, I had thirty votes in my pocket by the beginning of the year. In an ordinary Safety Harbor election, such a count would have been sufficient to carry the day, but the board was on alert, and the club management controlled not only the election machinery but also the access to the more obscure members. With an identified opposition about equal to my year-end count, just locating uncommitted members became an arduous task. The remaining members that I did locate, to a man, had already been contacted by Jack and were prepared to be skeptical of my arguments for change. A few were totally unreachable, as with owners who were estates and trusts, and their representatives could not be found, at least by me. With carefully crafted arguments emphasizing whatever issue seemed to be important to the target, most often the inappropriateness of having employees and vendors on the board, I did bring a good number of these recalcitrant voters to my side. In any case, by the eve of the meeting, I had thirty-nine votes in my pocket.

I was confident that this vote would carry the day, but not confident in the voting process. I was certain that the management and the board had something up their sleeve; so I hired a lawyer who had had prior experience with homeowners associations. Before the meeting began, he verified the process of counting, reviewed the proxies for apparent appropriateness, and made sure that our thirty-nine votes were all counted. They were all there, but in the final count, the management slate had forty votes. Having viewed all the ballots in advance, my lawyer did not know of any way to challenge that tally. Neither did I. My tortuous road to Camelot had abruptly hit a detour. The winners exulted in their victory, disparaging me and my associates as *gallunatics*. Not such a bad epithet, really!

In the aftermath of this outcome, Judy provided me with needed comfort, reminding me of the pain that attending in the minority four tedious meetings over the next year would entail, particularly as we had to wait for another year to receive the crown. Those meetings would have been deadly and so would have been the fight over the next election.

My partners in the property, who had been supportive of the struggle for control of the club, had been losing interest in the island, Rich and Alby because they never could get enough time to enjoy the property and Weening because he had other fish to fry. And about this time, Judy and I were starting to think about living in Aspen. I guess we had all had our fill of North Captiva. For these reasons, not so much because of our loss in the election, we decided to sell and did so easily.

It was in the spring less than a year after our sale that we revisited the island, staying with friends. The annual meeting fell during this visit, and there was to be a celebration that evening because a new group had ousted the old guard. We were invited to attend the event being held at the clubhouse with our hosts, and as we announced ourselves at the table of name tags, "Richard Gallun and Judy McGregor," the lady with the name tags emoted, "Mr. Gallun, you must be the man who gave us our name. We are the *gallunatics*!"

According to my old friend, Gary Walker, the *gallunatics* did take over, and the paranoid faction dispersed soon after this election. The island became a better place. I had not become king, but my effort did not come to nothing.

CHAPTER XXVII

No Politics at Fiserv

According to Webster, business politics are "activities within an organization that are aimed at improving someone's status or position and are typically considered to be devious or divisive."

That definition seems somewhat bland even as it includes the words, "devious" and "divisive." While leaving room to fill in the blanks, it runs short of describing the array of bizarre behaviors that make up the reality of organizational politics. Politics is a tool to which any skilled executive will avail himself in everyday interactions.

Courtesy and reason almost always held sway during my twenty years at Fiserv, but even in this collegial environment, politics often interposed itself. It was a factor in most discussions and negotiations at all levels of decision making in this company. Even so, George Dalton so fervently believed that he had eliminated politics at Fiserv that in his PowerPoint presentation for acquisition targets, he had a slide that stated: "No Politics at Fiserv." And George loved to dwell on this subject, doing so for as much five minutes in a ten-minute presentation.

IN THE EARLY days of Fiserv, say through 1990 and even up to 1995, all of the executives of the companies acquired by Fiserv tended to stay on after the acquisition, often for many years. It is a fact that in the early nineties, I was able to refer any potential acquiree to our list of prior acquisitions, and with one exception, that being in the case of a death, the principal owner was still running the business that Fiserv had bought. Fiserv had a plethora of skilled executives. As is the case with most business leaders, their skills were much about manipulating the people within their organizations and without. Ergo, politics had been a way of life for them and was a skill that was not going to be easily exorcized—even in the benevolent environment of Fiserv.

In my earliest conversations with George Dalton, he had liked to talk about the culture he was shaping at Fiserv. The essence of this culture emerged from the company's motto, "People make the difference," a statement that a company highly values its employees, not a unique corporate principle, but one that is usually given not much more than lip service. When I later became an employee, I found this value to be sincere to an extent rarely seen in corporations of any size. From it and George's leadership grew an environment that nurtured collegiality and respect, a combination that made the company a great place to work.

In those dialogues with George, he talked about his dislike of politics in business and waxed eloquent that he had eliminated politics from the Fiserv scene. I came to understand that one tool he had been employing in this effort was that of never allowing associates to talk behind one another's backs, doing so by forcing their issues out into the open. While I did not doubt that confronting backstabbing was a reasonable tactic in maintaining peace within the organization, even with my then limited exposure to the company, I knew that there had to be other political discord lurking in the background. George surely had missed something here.

Another subject, one that George talked frequently about in our informal discussions, was his previous experience working for John Kelly, the founder and CEO of the Midland Bank. George was repulsed by the symbols of authority that are typical among bankers and are not unusual in many businesses. These symbols included titles, private secretaries, and perks assigned according to status, which might include assigned parking spaces, office size, and company cars.

By the time I came to Fiserv as senior vice president for acquisitions, a time when there was still only a small executive cadre, I was differentiated as the only vice president with "Senior" in front of his name. A great effort was made to make certain that, given my august title, I had a larger office than the Milwaukee data center manager, an ordinary vice president. I was allotted an appropriate model Buick to fit into the hierarchy of Buicks in a company where everyone drove a Buick. I was assigned the fourth-best parking space, right next to that of Pauline, George's wife. Pauline, an ordinary vice president, had the third space. A hierarchical structure was already apparent, and it was to grow to a dimension that would challenge even most banking organizations.

I had been with the company only for a short time when I was invited with the leadership group to attend a "strategic planning" meeting in Houston, Texas. Much of this meeting was led by a consultant, whose assignment was to disseminate the strategy of the executive management and the board of directors into the minds of the operating groups in the field. It was presented as an opportunity for the senior corporate staff and the field hierarchy to influence corporate strategy.

The consultant, a Dr. Cleaver, who had a long-term relationship as an advisor to our HR department, had a strategy for the meeting, one that would fill time and perhaps achieve his objective of extending this particular consulting assignment.

Before the meeting, Dr. Cleaver polled the directors and executive officers, George, Les Muma, and Ken Jensen, for the key values or goals of the company. Then he had them, acting together, put these principles in order of their importance to the company.

At the meeting in Houston, Dr. Cleaver spent an entire day getting the management group to identify what they saw as the key values and another day in ordering them. Amazingly, the list of values, seven of them in both cases, were identical, ranging from responsibility of the company to its employees, to sales growth, to customers and community, and finally, to profits before taxes and shareholder interests. However, when these values were ordered in Cleaver's arduous process, those of management were in the precise reverse order to that of the executive group. Dr. Cleaver had felt good about the uniformity of the lists but found this difference in ordering to be somewhat disquieting. He delivered the news of this dichotomy at our final meeting.

I am not able to recall the hierarchy of the values identified, but I do remember that George's group had named profits before taxes as its seventh and least important corporate value, while the management group opined that it was first. Similarly, George's group put employee welfare first among their values, while the management put this value seventh. And so on down the line.

At the concluding meeting, Dr. Cleaver discussed with us this anomaly, as well as the ordering of the other five values, and it was concluded and agreed that we would have more meetings to gain an understanding of the differences in viewpoint. On the surface, it was an amusing perceptual dichotomy, not a critical misunderstanding, because all the perceived values were complimentary to Fiserv and were actually seen as genuine by all participants. Nevertheless, a week later, back in Milwaukee, I learned that the company had severed its relationship with Dr. Cleaver, not just this planning relationship but his other functions as well. There was a warning here, one that Machiavelli would surely have understood: the lesson is not to deliver undesired news to someone who possesses the power of your execution.

—◦∞◦—

Frank Martire came to Fiserv with the acquisition of the financial service data processing business of Citicorp in 1990. He left ten years later, shortly after George retired to be succeeded by George's erstwhile "partner," Les Muma. I visited Frank in his office to wish him well as he was cleaning out his desk. He shared with me that he was leaving because Les had told him that he, Frank, had no chance for the top job because he was "George's man." An amazing declaration even as it may have represented the truth. Even at Fiserv, you needed to be on the right team!

Frank indeed came with his own political baggage. It was from Jim Welles, president of Sommerville Data Processing, an item-processing center that I had courted and purchased in the early nineties, that I learned about the political environment at Citicorp where Frank had learned the ropes. Jim told a story about his son Charley, who had just graduated from Bowdoin College with a degree in human relations. Charley, looking for the big world in Gotham, got an interview with Citicorp, and, while talking with one of their high muckety-mucks in HR, was asked by his interviewer why, with his background, he was interested in going to work in HR at Citicorp. Charley responded ingenuously, "My college work was oriented around making the work environment a better place. I want to help people succeed in their jobs."

This response was punctuated by silence, an interlude finally broken when the interviewer sucked in his breath and stated definitively, "Son, you have come to the wrong place. This is Citicorp. Here, we don't help people; we stab them in the back!"

I hadn't done a lot with Frank during his tenure at Fiserv, but two or three years prior to his departure, he came to me with an acquisition idea for his business unit, the Large Bank Group. He was interested in acquiring a small company in Dayton that had a software product that serviced the tellers and the loan platform. In our discussion of the target, Frank confided in me that his organization had almost completed the development of just such a product but that he had decided that the cost of completion, developing an organization to sell and service the product, and entering the market were substantial. Indeed, he thought that the cost of buying the target company, appropriately named Teller Systems, would not be much greater than Frank's completion of development and market entry costs, but more importantly, that it would not be a drag on his business unit's profitability. I accepted his analysis and was glad to have a target that I would not have great difficulty selling internally.

I headed for Dayton a couple of days later, meeting with the Teller Systems owner, and learned that company could be for sale at the "right price." After a visit or two, it appeared to me that their own value assessment, $10,000,000, was not badly out of line with our pricing parameters. All the stars were aligned. Nevertheless, it took a few days of negotiation to get to an agreeable letter agreement. It was a month after Frank had brought me the idea that we started our due diligence. In our letter of intent, we had reached an agreement at eight million, but as we approached closing, the seller had decided, based on improving performance, that he wanted nine. It was unusual for a price to change from that which had been set out in a LOI, but the seller had a point, so I agreed to meet with the management committee to defend and get approval for the increase.

That meeting was run by Don Dillon, who had joined the company recently with the acquisition of ITI, of which he had been a principal owner and who, as a by-product of that purchase, had become the largest shareholder of Fiserv with commensurate influence. At ITI, of which Don was still president, there resided a barely adequate teller system which, adequacy or lack of it notwithstanding, earned significant revenue for ITI. That set the stage for some unavoidable controversy over whether we needed to buy another such system. During the meeting, it came to light that Frank's group had an almost fully developed teller system. Don pounced, opining authoritatively that he couldn't see any reason that we would want a third teller system. Expecting to get strong support from Frank, I started to respond, arguing the underlying economics of this "buy vs. make" decision. Frank, understanding Don's power and knowing who buttered his bread, remained tactfully silent. My (really Frank's) arguments fell on twelve deaf ears, and the deal was dead. The meeting ended, and Teller Systems was never mentioned again. No politics perhaps, but then . . .

All's well that ends well. Even with his weak-kneed posture on the Teller Systems deal and his unseemly banishment, Frank did all right for himself in the long run. After spending a long time in the wilderness after his exodus from Fiserv, like five years, he eventually became president of Metavante, formerly M&I Data, and from that vantage point engineered what amounted to a reverse takeover of Fidelity Systems, which, after that transaction, supplanted Fiserv for a time as the leading data processor in the financial services industry and remains an annoying competitor to this date. Upon completion of that transaction, Frank became its president. Even losing politics can yield rewards!

—⊶∞⊷—

Political activity at the top is a lot about getting the organization to do the right thing, at least right in the mind of the political initiator. Because he held a fertile and persuasive intellect, Ken Jensen didn't lose political disputes very often. A major part of his strength was derived from the fact that he didn't make a lot of mistakes. Ken worked from the data and generally tested his assumptions before taking a position on any important matter; nevertheless, he did make one mistake, and it was a doozy.

It was in the late nineties that an elderly couple was seen several times in the Fiserv boardroom. The word spread that these two were the owners of an electronic teaching system that taught continuing education to life insurance salespeople. The company was Life Instructors Inc.; and, if acquired, it was to become a resource for a new insurance data processing division. Ken had initiated the transaction, and no one at headquarters other than George or Les knew much about it. That wasn't unusual. Acquisitions were confidential. What was unusual here was that Howard Arner, who headed the insurance division, seemed to be in the dark. I learned from Howard that the due diligence was being done by Emerald Financial, a Fiserv West Coast unit that touched on teaching in its general business, doing the diligence without Howard's participation.

It was only a short time later that I learned from an angry Howard that we were buying the business at a price that was way outside of our usual parameters, even though the due diligence team had nixed the transaction, and he had strongly objected to the transaction. This was the only time in my entire experience at Fiserv that we made a purchase without the endorsement of a due diligence team or without the approval of the man who would be responsible for the management of the acquisition.

This tale might have ended here but for the resignation of the ownership couple a month after the closing of the transaction. They had gotten more than enough from the transaction so that they would never need to work again. Apparently they had not signed an agreement to continue to run the business. Management was thin, and we were left with a sales manager, a vice president to be sure, but one who, unfortunately, would prove to be not up to the task of managing the business. The disaster turned eventually into a total loss. There were a bunch of lessons here, but the biggest one was that Ken Jensen had established some good procedures that even he should have followed religiously.

Speaking of big mistakes, it was about six months before he retired that George asked Tom Neil and me to look into the business of running call centers. That seemed like a reasonable assignment because Fiserv generated a lot of call center activity in the normal course of business. George suggested that we might consolidate our small call centers around such a venture and sell this service to outsiders, doing so efficiently by increasing the scale of the business.

Tom and I added Dick Fitzgerald to our team, and the three of us looked at the major operators in the business. We gave this study a lot of time over the next three months and concluded that not only would this business be an unattractive investment for Fiserv but also the entire call center business was laden with risk. George accepted our report without comment and seemed to understand our conclusions.

It was just three months later that George retired. Then we learned via the grapevine that he had purchased a call center business for himself and was getting his friends and neighbors to invest in it. When one of my Pine Lake neighbors tried to duck George's aggressive sales pitch by claiming a temporary cash shortage, George loaned him the money for his investment, a loan that was dutifully repaid later as the business was slowly descending into oblivion.

A new level of intrigue was launched with George's departure from the company in the spring of 2001. As it turned out, it seemed that George hadn't been as eager to retire as Les was eager to have him retire. Apparently, the friendship of these two had been stretched as the tug-of-war over George's retirement date had progressed, and even with his departure from management, George remained an irritant to Les from his position on the board of directors.

Later that year George invited me to have lunch and to visit his new business in Waukesha. As he showed me through the office in the early afternoon, he did not have to introduce me to his employees because I had known most of them when they had worked for Fiserv. One of them, Eddie Albert, the former controller at Fiserv, was sprawled in his traditional after-lunch position, leaning back in his reclining desk chair, feet on the desk, mouth agape, and snoring while the game of solitaire on his computer awaited his next play. We did not disturb Eddie, and, as we passed the next office, George commented casually that he was saving that one for me.

It was not too long before it surfaced that George had been soliciting Fiserv employees to join his company even as he remained on the Fiserv board. I had not made anything of his devious invitation to me, and no one had taken particular notice of the other Fiserv employees whom George had hired because, for the most part, they had left Fiserv well before George had started his new company. It was a different story when Tom Hirsch, then controller and later CFO, acknowledged to the Fiserv board that George had openly approached him. Offended by this deed, the board demanded—and got—George's resignation from that body. This unseemly affair seemed to have further hardened positions among George, Les and members of the board.

Upon George's departure as CEO, Les had maneuvered to make the company his own. At the time it was not so shocking that Frank Martire had left, even as Frank's description of his reason for leaving was off-putting. However, after Frank's exit, it was felt that Mike Gannt, who was brought in by Les to run the Insurance Division, seemed to be the strongest executive in the company and had become Les's heir apparent. It was generally believed that he would become president when Les surrendered that title to become chairman and CEO. Apparently Mike thought so too because when Les proffered the presidency to his longtime associate from Tampa, Norm Balthasar, Mike, surmising that he had been taken out of the line of succession, resigned. It appeared to me that Norm's appointment was based on loyalty and an old alliance, rather than on his credentials for the job. Les later explained that the Balthasar elevation had been an interim appointment and that he and Norm planned to exit together three or four years hence, leaving the top spot for Mike. It should have been easy for Les to make that point to Mike at the time Mike was leaving. Apparently, if such an elucidation was offered, and it seems likely that it was, that explanation was not acceptable to Mike.

As he took up the reins as president and CEO, but not chairman of the board (under the circumstances a position of arguable power then occupied by Don Dillon),

Les continued most of the management philosophies of the past. There appeared to be no great changes in the offing of strategy or culture. Despite the Martire flap, there was no purging of George's people. Les did institute some important new tactics, one being that of establishing an operation in India to "offshore" extensive data processing activities at a considerable benefit to the company. To Les, it was a necessity of the competitive environment. To George, now out in the cold, the exporting of Fiserv jobs was an act of perfidy and a violation of the revered "people make the difference" philosophy. It launched a deadlier level of political warfare, marked by George sniping at Les from his position as a stockholder and exploiting his long-term relationship with the board chairman, Don Dillon. Indeed, political infighting, now orchestrated by George, the antipolitician, was reaching its dramatic denouement.

The Muma era was marked by Les's growing absence from the Milwaukee office as he began to spend an increasing amount of time in Tampa, where he was building his retirement home. The directors noted his truancy and a level of hostility to Les arose within the board, probably abetted by George. Then in 2004, Mike Gantt rejoined the company at Les's behest, returning as the designated heir apparent. This move was received well by those members of the management team who had not envisioned themselves in the top job, those who did aspire to this post being, however, not an insignificant number. Mike Gannt took over the recently consolidated banking unit, which comprised more than half of the company's total business, and set about preparing himself for his expected elevation.

However, during that summer the clouds began to gather. The board announced the initiation of a search for a CEO to replace Les, stating that, even though they had their man in Mike, a search was "good practice." By the time the announcement came in the fall that the new CEO would not be Mike Gannt, it came as no surprise. It was to be Jeff Yabuki, who came to Fiserv from the presidency of H&R Block.

Up to this point, the politics at Fiserv had been deadly serious and was effective in influencing important decisions and policies, but the political intrigue was almost always carried on in a discreet and genteel manner. While there had been winners and losers in internal disputes and negotiations, damage from these controversies had never amounted to much. With the advent of the Yabuki era, that all changed. The values of collegiality and trust were early casualties on the altar of efficiency. No longer were doors and ears opened for easy communication among the levels in the organization. Relations between bosses and minions became oppressive and unpleasant, with cursing and browbeating present even at the highest-level meetings. Political battles were pitched more openly, and politics as a method of projecting power became de rigueur.

Of course, it is arguable that the circumstantial environment surrounding Fiserv during the period of George's governance had provided an unusually favorable opportunity for adherence to lofty values. As this era wound down, the competitive environment was worsening, leaving work to be done to maintain Fiserv's leadership in the industry. One competitor, Fidelity Systems, had achieved market share equal to Fiserv's, many services of the company had become commoditized, and customers increasingly shopped for price. In sum, there was emerging pressure on margins. While cost control had always been a Fiserv competence, it became increasingly important in the new century. While I tend to be critical of Jeff Yabuki and his cronies for their discordant behavior, this new management did address well many difficult organizational and strategic issues that had been left untouched for many years. They did so with insight and determination but without grace. The price of these changes was the end of a unique culture.

Before leaving the subject of no politics, there are a few interesting side notes about Fidelity Systems's rise that bear on this story, to wit:

We had two opportunities to buy the forerunner of this company. The first chance arose out of the failing but not insignificant bones of Systematics Inc., after that company had executed a number of ill-fated strategies that had resulted in significant losses. That opportunity surfaced in the early nineties. We demurred then because the price was too high. The company was offered for a second time after the turn of the century, again a somewhat distressed sale. On both occasions, we at Fiserv failed to recognize the importance of putting an important, albeit weakened, competitor out of the market. We refused to pay the necessary price. Enter Fidelity Title, a company with very deep pockets. After Fidelity bought and funded the business, the company, by then Fidelity Systems, acquired Metavante and after a few missteps, began to challenge Fiserv for industry leadership. Eventually, they became our peer and actually took over from Fiserv the mantle of leadership in the financial data processing industry, the objective so avidly sought by George Dalton almost twenty-five years earlier.

George Dalton may have been wrong in believing that there were no politics at Fiserv, but he had created and sustained for more than twenty years an environment that encouraged trust and collegiality while providing a record of financial success almost unrivaled in the United States during my lifetime. He did so with a conviction that he was doing the right thing, not only for the company but for all the participants in the business: employees, customers, vendors, and shareholders. Because he was human, he failed to live up to his own high ideals once or twice as I have observed here; but his steadfast adherence to his basic values shines as a road map for business and personal success.

Les Muma put the final cap on the "no politics culture," doing so in 2014 when he, for reasons about which I cannot even speculate, joined the board of directors of Fidelity Systems. It is odd that the position was offered to him at all given his earlier advice to Martire, but even more surprising that he took the job. It may have been an act taken to return the spite shown by George and the board in Les's last year as Fiserv CEO. He who laughs last laughs best.

CHAPTER XXVIII

Life Is about Learning

As a child, I learned nothing about sexuality at home, either hetero or homo. I remember classmates, indeed close friends, who demonstrated female characteristics as early as first grade, but even as we later entered high school, they were not identifiable to me as homosexual. They were just effeminate. By the time I entered Williams College, I had realized that there were homosexuals among us, but I cannot remember knowing any "queers" at Williams. The idea of real people being gay just had not dawned on me.

It was only after I entered the business world that I had any exposure to this then confusing issue. I had several brushes with men who befriended me and, early in our acquaintanceship, tactfully, and even ambiguously, propositioned me. I, equally tactfully, demurred. I initially found these advances to be disturbing, even at the age of twenty-five or thirty, but I had adjusted enough to reality that I did not let this new knowledge interfere with the continuation of these relationships.

Little did I know what the future held for me; some of my best friends would be gay.

IT WAS ON Judith's and my first dog trip that my eyes began to be pried open. For us a dog trip was an adventure that was centered around exploring the out-of-doors and the wilderness in interesting places, sharing this time with our dogs; it was to consist of hiking, swimming, and other activities that one can do in the company of dogs. We had put this inaugural trip together using a book that identified superior inns and hotels that allowed dogs. The time was about 1995, when most good hotels would not allow dogs; so it was worthwhile to plan carefully around the availability of accommodations.

With our dogs, Stella and Max, we headed south from Aspen to begin our exploration of the Southwest. Our first stop was to be in Santa Fe, where we had reservations to stay at an inn called the Turquoise Bear. Santa Fe would be a new experience for us. It turned out to be a difficult city for us to find our way around because of its random street layout, a consequence of its venerable age, and its location in the foothills of the Sangre de Cristo Mountains. I got disoriented as soon as we left the interstate and shortly was completely lost in a not quite urban maze of narrow streets and foreign-looking buildings. But with help from our guidebook and after only one major misstep, we found our inn, just off the historic Santa Fe Trail. It was certainly a prominent location, only a few blocks from the state capitol, and one that, despite the winding and dead-end streets, should always have been easy to find. Its neighborhood was residential, and like the rest of the city, all the houses in it were constructed entirely of adobe, dressed in a soft brown color and built in what I would call the Northern Mexico style. Even though the private properties were walled, there was enough visibility to see that, despite their monochromatic uniformity, the houses were attractive, some quite impressive, and all tastefully landscaped.

The Turquoise Bear fit right into the neighborhood, both in its adobe architecture and its elegance as well. It looked like the kind of place that was going to reinforce our confidence in our guidebook. We entered its walled compound through a modest gate, coming into a small parking area that couldn't have handled more than ten cars. It turned out that the Turquoise Bear was a bed and breakfast, having only about a dozen rooms. But, as we were soon to learn, it was a B&B with a few surprises.

With the dogs on leash, we walked to the front door through a well-maintained garden. We entered into a vestibule where a lady was sitting behind a writing desk, clearly the owner. She rose to greet us—so I thought—but more importantly, she wanted to greet our dogs. She addressed them for a minute or so before acknowledging us, apologizing to us for this slight, but we saw right away that she knew how to deal with dog owners, that is, by paying attention to their dogs. She spent the next few minutes admiring the beauty of Weimaraners, a conversation that I had come to enjoy. After Judith had registered, we started to leave for our room, and as we reached the door, the lady declared, "You know, we are having a small cocktail party in the living room tonight. Would you like to come?"

Being loyal to the purpose of our trip, I inquired, "Can we bring our dogs?"

The answer came back without hesitation. "Of course, you can. I'm sure the other guests will enjoy them."

We had come to the right place.

That idea was reinforced when we got to our room and found a roaring fire waiting for us. But that was not the end of our surprises. When we got to the cocktail party accompanied by Stella and Max, who facilitated our introduction to the other guests, it became quickly apparent that the inn was not only dog friendly but was gay friendly as well. As it turned out, we were the only heterosexual couple in the place. We met a lot of nice people that evening and even exchanged a few business cards, thinking, as we often do, that we would see them again. In any case, it was an enjoyable evening, and it fit right in the idea of the dog trip. Most importantly, we had made some good friends.

Over the next twenty years, we returned to Santa Fe about a half-dozen times, always hoping to stay at this delightful inn, but we had misplaced our dog book; and we had forgotten the name of the inn. Despite what I knew of the location but because Santa Fe is such a confusing city, I never found this jewel again. That is, until we bought our Santa Fe house and found the Turquoise Bear a block away at the end of our street!

It was a short time after that first dog trip that Patsy McGregor, who had settled in Aspen, fell into managing "Gay Ski Week" after the prior manager had left in a huff just a week before the event was scheduled to commence. Because Patsy's predecessor had done little to prepare for the event, there was a lot to be done. Patsy threw herself whole hog into a difficult situation, and pretty soon, there was a lot of the preparation going on at our house.

With Patsy running Gay Ski Week, Judith and I ended up hosting a group of volunteers who were helping to coordinate the event. Several of these volunteers were also working on their own project for participating in a "drag race" to be held toward the end of the week. The drag race was to be a ski contest with the contestants in costume or "in drag," skiing down past the audience at Little Nell. The volunteers were building a float for this event in our garage.

Two days before the kickoff of Gay Ski Week, there was a hubbub in the living room where Patsy was working with the volunteers. When I confronted her, wondering what the uproar was about, she explained to me that the "drag queen," who had been hired for the occasion, had become indisposed and would not be able to come up from Denver for the event. There was no time to hire another queen, and she didn't know what to do. It seemed that the drag queen was an important position in the week's agenda because it was he who would be the focus of many of the activities, acting as an entertainer and as MC for events like the drag race. Finding a replacement was not going to be easy, particularly on short notice. Everyone's, including Judy's and my, lives were in disarray for twenty-four hours while Patsy and the event promoters occupied our house, agonizing over how to fill the void. After a considerable search, they found a drag queen that the event could afford. The only problem was that this queen was in Orlando and there was no money for his transportation to Aspen.

Now *that* was a problem I could get a handle on! I had about two million United Airlines miles at the time. It was provident that United was the best connection between Orlando and Aspen. So I volunteered my miles, and Patsy wrapped the deal up with the queen right away. Patsy's big problem was resolved; my involvement with Gay Ski Week was about to begin.

The hook was set two days later when there was no one else to meet the queen at the airport. I was destined to get the nod for this task. As he got off the plane in bib blue jeans with a Grateful Dead sweatshirt under his suspenders, George didn't look like much of a queen to me, but it was he whom I was to meet. On the way to town, I found him a pleasant, amusing, and slightly shy man. Right away, we got on well, so Patsy asked me to drive him to the opening dinner that evening. Driving him wasn't a hardship; nevertheless, I had been set up well, and even as I did have a day job, I had become his chauffeur for the duration.

The week culminated in the aforementioned drag race, which started at the top of the first rise at Little Nell and ended in front of the bleachers at the bottom of the mountain. George was the MC and in charge of the program—including the responsibility for selecting the judges for the race. When we arrived to view the race with an old B-School friend, Hugh Eaton, and his wife Gay, I introduced them to George. Thereupon, George asked the four of us, including Judith, to be the judges. I thought he was just paying me back for squiring him around, but George had a sharp tongue for sexual innuendo and may have been just looking for props.

The program, which was broadcast over loudspeakers to the attending crowd, began with an interview of the judges. It is difficult to imagine how much mileage George was able to get out of "Dick" and "Gay" at a drag race. Hugh, particularly, and George engaged their wits intellectually, and together, they kept the crowd in stitches for an extended period. While these preliminaries ran on, the competitors gathered at the halfway point on Little Nell and awaited the long-delayed signal to begin.

Finally, Hugh and George finally ran out of material—that was after twenty minutes of off-color banter—and the drag race began in earnest with about ten competitors. All were in elaborate costume—solo or teamed up. Every one of the competitors showed some talent: skiing skills, acrobatics, or dramatic or humorous antics. However, *the best performance* was that of the serpent that had been fabricated in our garage. However, instead of the five reticulated segments to be carried by six individuals, they had only finished three, which required only four participants. Even with this shortcoming, the three segments worked well together, and as their float glided sinuously down the mountain, the crowd roared its approval, and the judges never needed to cast their votes; it was a victory by acclaim.

That evening, the final dinner was held at the Aspen Mountain Club, the province of the rich and superrich atop Ajax Mountain. Access was by gondola, which, while enclosed, did not give much protection from the weather. When I picked George up, I did not comment on his low-cut evening dress even as I thought he was overdressed for the occasion and underdressed for the ascent up the mountain. We got into our four-seater gondola, George, Judith, and I. At first, we were all warm enough, but as the three of us ascended the mountain on an eighteen-minute ride, the temperature dropped precipitously. I noticed George's teeth starting to chatter; so, as any gentleman would, I offered him my blazer, putting it around his shoulders. George accepted it graciously and drew it tightly against his bare skin. My chivalrous gesture visibly moved him.

We were soon at the top and were among the first to arrive. As the guests drifted in, dressed to the nines, I realized that George wasn't overdressed at all; but more importantly, there were a bunch of really good-looking chicks at the party. I mingled for a while, taking note along the way that Judith too was having a good time. But then I saw that George was alone at the bar looking a tad lonely and forlorn, so I went over to be with him. For the rest of the cocktail hour, we had a good conversation about our new friendship and the difficulty of growing up gay in an era of identity hostility.

When dinner was announced, I got my reward for my week's attention to the needs of Gay Ski Week. I was seated between two beautiful lesbians who enjoyed tormenting me as I tried to lead them onto the true path. Maybe my real reward came later. When we dropped George off at the airport the next day, he said to Judith. "I really like your husband; he is a truly good man." I too liked George and had enjoyed the week of our relationship. His approval was important to me.

CHAPTER XXIX

The Eye of the Beholder

When I was courting Judith McGregor in the early nineties, we spent our vacation time together at North Captiva Island. It was in the early days of the regentrification of this island, and there were a few houses that cried for replacement, either because of their state of dilapidation or their atrocious architecture. As Judith and I walked the beaches, I held forth on the bad taste expressed in many of these structures, and Judith, at least at first, would absorb my aesthetic critique and remain silent. However, as she warmed to our relationship, she began to object to my "intolerance." She argued not that the houses in question possessed any artistic merit, but that they expressed a point of view different from mine, and it was not necessarily bad taste that they revealed. I contended that in aesthetics, there is an absolute, partly stemming from such mathematical truths as the "golden mean" as well as other dimensional ratios that are intuitively acknowledged by the sophisticated eye. More important, I continued, was the subjective processing of experiential information that led over time to aesthetic maturation. I was speaking in this connection, not of formal education but the wisdom that is achieved through observation and participation. I did not say so, but I thought I had achieved that maturity.

What I have expressed here is a reasonable thesis, but it was not a winning argument with Judith. Few are. Even after the houses in question had been torn down and replaced by better ones, Judith persisted in her opinion; I was beginning to learn that her next change of mind would coincide with the next arrival of Halley's Comet.

IT WAS AT an early age that I had started to appreciate the influence of design in both landscaping and construction. The genesis of my appreciation rested with my parents, both of whom had artistic talent and an eye for beauty; they were always making changes to their houses, most of them positive, but they did some pretty bad stuff themselves.

Then in 1969, when Kathy, and I bought the Vilter house at Pine Lake, I was at the beginning of an excursion into my architectural education. This house was an old, then a ninety-five-year-old, farmhouse to which the Vilters had added a Greek facade and a large veranda embellished with Ionic columns. It reflected its age with complete integrity: the roof sagged, the paint was peeling off in large chunks, the chimney was on the verge of collapsing, and the area around the house was a jungle of weeds. Nevertheless, the house had a character that shone through the ravages of time. Even considering its dilapidated appearance, my in-laws, who had introduced us to the house, said it had "great bones," whatever that meant.

Strangely, I could not find an architect that wanted to do remodeling, so I hired a designer, Al Sternkopf, who was a neighbor on the lake. He agonized for a couple of weeks and in due course brought us drawings that promised extensive change. He did allow that it would be expensive to execute his plans, and when we went out for bids, the cost came back at more than $130,000. "For that," Al said, "I can build you a new house. Let me show you what I did for a little less over at Pewaukee Lake."

Kathy and I went to Pewaukee, knowing at the outset that $130,000 was well beyond our budget. We looked at the house, which was okay but not what we had in mind, being sort of the fifties in style. So we returned home, and in the process of contemplating our next steps, thought of Howard Patterson, my friend and hockey line mate from Williams, who had directed his near genius intellect towards architecture.

When we called Howard, he seemed excited by our project; and he agreed to come right away to help us with our decision, willing to do so for the price of an airline ticket. We didn't know what to expect from this gambit, but we believed that Howard had three things going for him as a player in our decision-making process: he specialized in remodeling old houses; and unlike Al, who wanted to sell us a house, he had no ax to grind; and he was our friend.

A few days later Howard flew in for an overnight, and Kathy and I brought him directly to the new house. When we pulled up at the front door, Howard got out of the car and walked around for a while without speaking. He seemed to be off in another place, dissociated and sort of out of it, not an unusual behavior for Howard, who had competed with me for several years for the hockey team vagueness award. Then suddenly, he burst into laughter with an expression on his face that suggested that he had fallen into Rapture. Not understanding why he was laughing and becoming concerned that he had finally gone over the edge, I asked, "What in the world are you laughing at?"

Having difficulty getting his laughter under control, Howard finally responded, "I just can't believe that you would tear this house down. It's an unbelievable treasure! Back in Connecticut, people would give *anything* for a house like this."

Not yet understanding, I asked, "What in the world is so special about this house?"

Howard responded with passion, "I can't believe my eyes; this is amazing! What you have here is a pure Wisconsin farmhouse with a neo-Greek façade, and the combination actually works! The architect who did this was a genius!"

My eyes had been opened; I had heard what he had said and could grasp the sense of his words. For me and for Kathy too, it was a moment of epiphany. The house was to become "our Wisconsin farmhouse with a neo-Greek facade."

We returned to our house in Milwaukee after eating dinner at the Red Circle Inn. Howard and I stayed up most of the night, talking about the house, working with Al's plans, and doing sketches of all the elements in the house. Howard showed me how we could preserve what we had and save money in the process. It was stuff like saving the windows when you make changes in the elevations and using those windows elsewhere on the house. Because fenestration is such an important architectural feature, and windows are expensive as well, you need to be careful about what changes you make. Al's replacement of traditional nine-foot-high farmhouse windows with modern picture windows was not going to happen.

When Howard left the next day, I had almost a hundred individual sketches. Ahead of me was significant work conveying these changes to Al, who possessed major ego issues that would impede that conveyance, so I had to present Howard's ideas piecemeal. Al and I spent many evenings together adjusting the plans. I would present Howard's ideas orally, or if I needed to, I would sketch what I wanted. I took frequent recesses to refer to Howard's drawings. Al was not happy about this process, and during one evening that he found particularly stressful, he blurted out, "Look here, Dick, I'm in charge of aesthetics!"

I got around his pique on that occasion and on many others by arguing that we just had to save money. I never saved quite enough until his drawings fully reflected Howard's ideas. Eventually we got the remodeling cost down to $80,000, and that amount covered not only the cost of taking the entire house back to the studs, but it also included an attached garage and a fourth bedroom as well.

When completed, the house was superb. Al proclaimed until his death that it was the best remodeling job he had ever done. With Kathy's permission, he regularly brought clients through to see "his work." This remodeling was the foundation upon which I began to fashion my own sense of aesthetics. I think that it was placing myself in the middle of the creative process, between the architect and the plan, that allowed me to begin to internalize the complex issues of tasteful design. In study one can gain knowledge, but it is in working in the real world that one gains the experience needed to elevate one's personal taste.

Kathy and I lived in that excellent house for fourteen good years. Then, after my mother died, we moved to my family's property on the other side of the lake. It was a magnificent estate, even though the house, a white elephant at best, encompassed nine thousand square feet of living space, much of which was in a deplorable state of repair. Nevertheless, the house stood high on a promontory, dominating the north end of the lake with views to the south and west, an aspect that provided excellent exposure to the incoming summer storms as well as to the lake itself. The property consisted of eighteen acres, almost six hundred feet of shoreline, and a half-mile long wooded driveway leading to the first hole of my grandfather's golf course, that of the Chenequa Country Club.

The generally bungalow aesthetics of this house had been aggravated by a major change my parents had implemented in the fifties when they enclosed the porches on the east and south sides of the house to create a useless and tasteless entry hall and a larger-than-desirable living room. It was with Steve Seidel that I often discussed these mistakes, and through his tutelage that I had developed strong ideas about remedies.

After Kathy and I separated in 1986, I decided to undo my parents' alterations and restore the porches that had once been there. In the process, I found the foundations for the pillars that had once supported the upper floors of the house before my parents had replaced their function with steel posts and beams. I decided to restore the old appearance of the original house, taking it back close to a hundred years, allowing the steel to continue to support the upper stories but with faux columns placed on the original foundations. As these sturdy-looking columns were being finished in plaster, I could see that they didn't look right with straight sides. Then I remembered learning in Art I at Williams about parallax. I thought that that might be the problem. Checking this issue out, I discovered that to avoid the illusion created by parallax, sets of columns need to be a little fatter a third of the way up. How much fatter wasn't clear, but that was an issue for trial and error. After a couple of tries, we got it right.

The house at the time had been an ugly gray color, and while I could remember it in several other colors throughout my lifetime, I could not remember it ever looking good. One day, after playing tennis with Richard Weening, we sat next to his tennis court admiring his house, which was dressed in a new paint job. With a house similar to mine, similar in that it had an exterior mostly of stucco accented with occasional wooden framing and decoration, he had created a modified painted lady. It looked good to me. A few days later, I hired a painter and told him to copy Weening's house. He did as instructed; and in its new clothes, our house had never looked better. After some initial carping, Richard accepted the idea that imitation is the greatest form of flattery. He gave me a hard time for my plagiarism, but I took this criticism in stride, knowing that one need not improve on the good just because you can't come up with the best.

With the new porches on the house together with the new paint job, the appearance and feel of the house were better. Nevertheless, since the first floor was four feet above the ground, I still had a problem, one that arose from its great height. With the foundation and basement windows showing, the house, rising almost four stories, was too tall for its volume. Additionally, even with the open porch I had created, there was still limited access and egress, a "feng shui" issue, which resulted in an interior sense of confinement.

My single solution to all of these problems was to raise the level of the ground on the east and south sides of the house, giving ground-level access to the new porches and then to create egress from the living room to the porch. Between these new French doors in the living room and the front door, the entire porch facilitated access to outside spaces. The feeling of the house was transformed; the downstairs rooms felt open, an invitation to the out-of-doors.

I had no problem raising the ground on the south side of the house. It was just a question of fill, about four feet of it, to be blended into the slope running twenty feet down to the lake. The only real problem was to the east where there was limited space between the house and the driveway, and the drop to the drive was all of five feet, a height that cried to be addressed with a wall and spacious stone steps. I took on this project personally, building a one-hundred-foot wall, a job that took me most of the summer. I learned in the process that wall building is, rather than physical exercise, which it definitely is not, a contemplative activity, more like meditating than working. Just as important, it made me much more sensitive to the basic nuances of landscaping.

Thoroughly enjoying my newfound stonemasonry skill, I got the itch to build a garden in the depression east of my grandfather's English garden. What was appealing about this area was its interesting terrain, with slopes that dropped ten to fifteen feet together with lush existing vegetation. On the eastward declivity, there was a substantial field of royal ferns, abutted on the adjacent northern incline by an expanse of lilies. These two slopes could be employed to frame the central feature of the garden, a pond, which I set out to dig forthwith, having the assistance of my new stepson, Skip McGregor. While we were digging this pond by hand, it occurred to me that this land already presented many of the features of an Oriental garden, in the slopes, vegetation, and interesting rocks. This habitat spoke to me in Japanese.

What was surprising to me in building this garden is that I did it without plans, only with a vague idea of what the garden would contain. It was the formation of the land that guided the development of the garden. As I installed stone paths, walls, and river courses, I often copied details from the many landscaping books I had recently accumulated, many of them about Japanese gardens. As with my earlier borrowing from Richard Weening, I was not shy about taking particular components from these sources; good design is good design, and a good job of copying an effective design deserves a gold star. Some fifty years earlier, a Country Day report card had announced that "Dickie gets most of his ideas from the other children." To this day, I am not sure whether that was criticism or praise.

Nevertheless, there was some ingenuity and originality in establishing the infrastructure for the garden: shaping and laying the pond and river liners so that edges did not show and so that no water escaped; creating drainage away from the rivers and ponds so that rain would not introduce debris into the waterways; designing overflow receivers to carry away excess water; and building an underground water recycling system and underground electrical wiring to run the pumps and lighting. With the help of my caretaker I did all these things and did so without the use of outside contractors.

One of the highlights of finishing the initial phase of the garden was selecting the boulders that were to line the pond, to edge the rivers, to create an illusion of cliffs on the slopes above the pond, and to simulate islands in a dry sea. I chose about twenty massive boulders; they were huge river stones that had been molded by the abrasion of water over a few eons. These rocks, weighing between a half ton and a ton and a half, were delivered to our site on skids. I surveyed my rock collection for a few days, deciding where each one should go, then preparing the ground to receive each rock, and finally asking my friend, Glen Price, to bring a crane from the Price Erecting Company to move them to their destination. Along with the massive crane that could reach up to six stories, Glen brought two men to operate the machinery and guide the stones to their resting places. Without requiring any instruction beyond where each stone was to go, they started to move these boulders right away upon their arrival, and I was amazed at several outcomes. First, I was surprised that I knew from my planning, without any notes, exactly where and how each stone was to be set. Second, the stones were moved into place quickly and needed no adjustment at all after being placed, and third, the placement was completed in less than an hour. The result was immediately pleasing; at this point, the garden had taken a semifinal shape.

The final piece was planting. Judy and I invested the late summer and fall in this task. We started with a natural environment superior in plant materiel, but trees and bushes are crucial elements in a Japanese garden. To the extent we were able, we bought Far Eastern trees like Oriental birch and Korean lilac and, of course, Japanese maple; but we planted a number of Scotch pine, obtained as crooked as we could find them. While they are not usually found in Japanese gardens, Scotch pine worked well because it grows fast, adding a considerable volume of wood each year. In addition, it is easily trained into unusual shapes with splints and weights. We planted these trees sideways or, at a minimum, leaning steeply. The idea was to shape the trees so that they would appear to have been sculpted by the wind. This work kept us busy well into October. While a Japanese garden is never done, phase one, at least, was complete by late fall.

That garden may have been the diamond in the crown of my landscaping career, but I did have at least one more act. When Judith and I bought our one-half acre, almost treeless lot, in Aspen, I knew I had a landscaping chore ahead. Two ideas made our plan the winner in 1998 of the award from *Sunset* magazine for best new spa garden in the West.

What we did with the limited space available was to create a mountain stream across the south side of the property and a sunken garden between the house and the western property line. The two features worked well together as we used the earth from the excavation for the sunken garden and from the downstream collection pool of the river to raise the elevation of the river's header pond at the southwest corner. By raising the header pond four feet above the grade and by dropping the pumping pond two feet, we attained an eight-foot drop over the hundred-and-forty-foot length of the stream. That ratio created a sufficient grade, one that, with a strong flow generated by a large submersible pump, provided a background melody of cascading water. We bestrewed the streambed with mountain river stones and achieved a realistic appearance for it, realistic enough so that when visitors first saw it, they occasionally exclaimed, "I didn't know there was a river back here."

A Japanese garden principle that I especially honored in Aspen was that of using borrowed scenery, a principle that I may have carried out to excess. I not only made good use of the neighbors' plantings as a backdrop for our landscape design, but where they abandoned the use of part of their property with their own screening, I expropriated that property for our own use, if only visually. In doing so, we greatly expanded the sense of space on our small lot. The areas separating us from one of our neighbors and that between the house and Shadow Mountain, which is the right shoulder of Aspen Mountain, seemed to become ours, as did the mountain itself.

This effort might have been my last real gardening attempt because our next move put us in a condominium at the University Club Tower. Nevertheless, we had, in our purchase there, acquired a large deck, one that I thought was for the dogs and occasional outside dining. I had forgotten that small spaces offer the most elegant environment for creativity. Judith, who, for the years during which she had served as my assistant in the garden, had been lying in wait for an opportunity to reawaken her chartreuse thumb, claimed the deck for herself. She started by telling me early on that this garden space was to be her garden. She was definitive in her limitation of my contribution to her project. I stayed out of her way.

It may be true that an artist's mode of expression is guided by his or her basic character, spirituality and values. Judith's and mine are quite different. Whereas I have had a love for order and formal organization that creates pleasing patterns, Judith is strongly drawn to cacophony and disorder. I am attracted to the big picture, the blending into a whole of the elements of a composition. She delves into the detail, in the process, not caring much about the seeming dissonance that emerges from a riot of incompatible colors. If you take the time to examine her creations, you will find real soul in her work; it is her heart that is invested here with much the same affection that she offers to her dogs and grandchildren. To Judith, gardening is not art; it is life.

It is Judith's love of dissonance and disorganization that may be the key to our long-ago argument about taste. She, like Jean Dubuffet, sees no basis in reality for standards of beauty or ugliness. For her, there are no rules, and her mind is unfettered by convention. Beauty is what she decides it is, and ugliness exists only in my mind. I have internalized the significance of these differences in taste and appreciate her aesthetic sense. Nevertheless, our argument is not over yet. Her ability to create an artistic composition does not negate the fact that there is still plenty of bad taste in art and architecture.

CHAPTER XXX

A Side Trip on a Bike Path

While I liked my bicycle as a child, it was a long interval between bike rides once I started to drive a car. It was going to take a new life in a new place for me to scratch up enough interest to take up as a sport this often uncomfortable activity.

I MET DICK Burke when I joined the board of University Lake School in 1974. We had just entered our oldest two, Liz and Rich, in the school, and Kathy and I were making an effort to stay on top of their education. In the process of managing the affairs of the school, we got to know Elaine and Dick Burke, and they became our friends.

Toward the end of the seventies, Dick confided in me that his business, which was that of a significant wholesaler of appliances, was being disintermediated by the appliance manufacturing companies that he represented, meaning that, rather than using a wholesaler like Dick's, they would sell directly to the retailers and recapture the margins that were being taken by distributors. Dick was philosophical about this bad turn, but he was already on to his next act. He was applying to the MIT business school for the next fall and expected to gain there the skills he thought he would need to start a new business.

My reaction was that he was crazy. He would, with this program, take two years out of his career to learn skills that, based on my experience, he already had. And he was forty years old. I expressed this view obliquely, but Dick paid little attention. He completed his studies over the next two years, and while doing so, he came up with the harebrained idea of starting a bicycle company. Imagine, a new bicycle company in 1979!

I scratched my head and tried to dissuade him from plans that were already well thought out. He knew what he was doing, and to his credit, he didn't pay any attention to my superficial objections. His strategy was to employ superior engineering to make a more durable frame that theoretically would deliver better performance. Given the large size of the companies that dominated the industry, it looked to me like a tough course to run. Shortly, he had started a company which he called Trek, put everything he had into it, and walked a narrow path through a minefield of competitive hazards for almost ten years.

It wasn't until I married Judy that I had much of an interest in bicycling, but when Judy talked me into biking, I called Dick to get two bikes from him. We not only got a good price from him, but we also got good service as well. Dick, on at least two occasions, delivered bikes to us at home and sold them to us at cost. When we moved to Aspen in the middle nineties, Judy called Dick to get some mountain bikes so that we could explore the backcountry together. On this occasion, though, Dick demurred, saying that his best distributor resided in Aspen, and he just could not sell around this agent. What we should do, he suggested, was to tell his distributor, Charlie Tarver, about this conversation, and Charlie would give us a good deal or at least the best deal he could make. I might have worried more than I did over this last caveat.

Our meeting with Charlie was cordial. He was congenial and was eager to get us started, so he put together a package of items that we would need to become bikers. The package included all the biking clothing one would need to enter the Tour de France—and more—including gloves, helmets and special shoes that would attach to the pedals so that when you tipped over, you would stay attached to the bike. And don't forget the cyclist wardrobe, water bottles, bicycle pumps and tool kits to fix things when they went wrong. After showing us all of this stuff and promising us lessons in mountain biking as well, he finally pulled out two nice-looking bikes. I was starting to get a little nervous about the price of all this stuff, but there never seemed to be a chance to raise the issue of the price. Charlie just kept the banter going. Finally, as we prepared to leave, I popped the question. Charlie gushed, "Oh, don't worry about that. I'll be practically giving this stuff away. I want to take good care of Dick Burke's friends."

So we left with the goods, a bit in doubt about what kind of "deal" we had made, but, hey, we had never gone wrong with Dick Burke before, and we had never paid more than $125 for a bicycle. Besides, we would need most of the paraphernalia he had sold us.

The next events were our mountaineering lessons, and they were *not* a piece of cake. The first lesson found us in a downtown park, mostly getting used to having our shoes attached to the pedals. The braking and gears initiated some dilemmas of their own, and neither Judy nor I escaped without some loss of blood. The second lesson was worse, as we rode out to the Aspen Meadows with our instructor; and he instructed us to ride the narrow paths that circle and transect a twenty or so acre field of sage. Now, sage is a user-unfriendly plant at best, but when it grows to shoulder height and has arms an inch thick, it can rip you from your mountain bike, that is, unless your shoes are clipped firmly to the pedals. Then it just grabs you and tears at your skin, leaving you in a helpless heap to await being detached from your bike by the instructor. The paths at the Meadows are perhaps a foot wide, leaving little room for correction of balance through steering. With so little room to maneuver, steering gets to be a fine skill. Judy and I, having not yet acquired these skills, just added to our body scars.

It was awhile after this final lesson that Dan Minahan, father of my stepson Skip McGregor's then fiancée Katie, visited Aspen, accompanied by Katie and Skip and Katie's brother, John, as well. It was a long enough time after our Meadows experience so that when Dan suggested mountain biking, Judy and I, having forgotten about the pain we had experienced with this sport, thought we were ready for a mountain adventure. The proposal was that we take Government Trail, the bike path running from Snowmass to Aspen, as of our virgin trip. This trail was deemed as relatively easy in the Snowmass to Aspen direction because it is mostly downhill, and because the hazard rating was adjudged modest. We would learn that the hazard ratings were calibrated for bikers more experienced than we were.

As we left Aspen for Snowmass, it was one of those beautiful late-summer days with the shadows lengthening and the crisp cool of autumn hanging in the early-morning air. Turning up the Brush Creek Road, we could see the first evidence of Jack Frost's work toward the top of the ridge that is Snowmass Mountain. I was impressed by the colors at the top but awed by the knowledge that we would be pedaling almost all the way to the top before we began our descent to Aspen. The day was perfect for our bicycle adventure, but I was beginning to feel apprehensive about the challenge of this virgin trip. I realized I had not biked in challenging terrain since that ugly day at the Meadows.

Reaching Snowmass Village, we searched confidently for a sign designating Government Trail. Finding none, we finally surrendered to that odious and unmanly way out: asking directions. Dan spotted a bicycle shop and opined that that might be a good place to seek advice. As the proposer, he got the right to follow up in the bike shop.

"Hello," Dan said as he entered.

"Can I help you, sir?"

"As a matter of fact, you can. We're looking for Government Trail."

"Hmm, Government Trail, eh?"

"Yes, Government Trail."

"Hmm, you guys experienced bikers?"

There was a short hiatus in the conversation here. Dan didn't want the truth to be known, but the taciturn shopkeeper knew how to wait out an unsophisticated tourist. Then Dan, always tuning in on the subtle implications of interpersonal communication, queried, "Why are you asking that?"

Taking just a second to contemplate whether he might be out of line, the bike shop proprietor responded deferentially, "Well, sir, it's just that you've got your helmet on backward."

A good sport, Dan reported this exchange verbatim, and we all laughed at his faux pas. Then we checked our own helmets.

While we all enjoyed Dan's discomfiture, his visit had been propitious in that we found the trailhead practically next to the bicycle shop. The problem was that the trail started where we were in the village, and we were faced right away with biking up one of the residential roads for a rise of almost 2,000 feet in a little more than a mile. That makes for tough pedaling, and Judy and I quickly ran out of gas. Fortunately, so did Dan, and he, always a problem solver, flagged down a delivery truck driver with whom he shrewdly struck a financial deal to get us to the top of the road. With the children out of sight ahead of us, we threw our bikes in the back and hunkered down in the truck bed, concealing ourselves from the young people, whom we soon passed as they labored their way up the steep grade. After arriving at the top of the residential road, we were amazed at how quickly the children arrived; that steep mile had taken them less than fifteen minutes.

Although we were at the top of the road, we were definitely not at the top of the trail. We labored along an upsloping trail which led for a mile or so across ski trails and through some dense forests. An hour later, we found ourselves at the top of the trail, and we were looking eastward down a declivity toward Aspen. We stopped for a moment of breath catching, and then our leader, Dan, having earned this post through his prescient decision making, headed down the mountain.

It wasn't very long before Judy and I were standing alone watching Dan and the children fade into the forest below. We both knew our time had come. Without a word between us, I started down the trail. I realized in an instant that this one was dimensionally a clone of the trails we had suffered on at the Meadows. It was about a foot wide with bushes that rose almost to the height of the handlebars. Only there was one difference that was disturbing to me: the slope of the trail was dropping off swiftly.

I rode about a hundred yards and began to think that even though the path was steep, narrow, and rocky, I probably would be able to do it. "Probably" was a key thought here; and thinking particularly about the likelihood of a fall as well as the jutting rock formations, I pulled over to unfasten the pedals from my feet. As I got my heart rate under control, I wondered what had happened to Judy, who had been right behind me. Then I heard a faint voice complaining, "No way, no way!" Of course, it was Judy, and I was not surprised. She had not yet gotten used to the kinds of conditions mountain bikers face. For that matter, neither had I.

When she caught up with me, it was not very hard for her to persuade me that we should abort this folly. Somehow, we communicated our decision to the others, and we walked back and steeply up for a distance, and then, as the grade flattened out toward the top, we got back on our bikes and rode to the takeoff point. Just as we reached the apogee of the trail, we encountered a group heading for Aspen. Of course, Judy and I felt embarrassed in front of this bunch, who were facing the trail fearlessly. Nevertheless, before we could explain, one of them volunteered, "Boy, you guys did it the hard way. Almost no one ever takes Government Trail from Aspen to Snowmass."

We just let that statement stand, acknowledging it with a nod, and continued back toward the trailhead in Snowmass.

When we met up with the rest of our party in Aspen, we learned that we had made, for us, a good decision. While the group was exhilarated by their adventure, all of them had suffered serious falls, several over the handlebars. They each sported at least one apparent injury, a cut, a wicked scratch, or a darkening bruise. I think Judy and I would probably have done worse.

Soon, it was the end of summer, and it was time to settle up with Charlie. It took a couple of visits to elicit the tally from him, but when he put it together . . . It was a doozy. Seventy-five hundred dollars! Most of it was for the bikes, which were top of the line Treks. Charlie couldn't even think of taking the bikes back for something cheaper because they were used, and he couldn't discount them to us either because "They are my best bikes, and I just can't mark them down. It wouldn't be fair."

He explained that all the clothes were discounted by 50 percent and so were the lessons. Those items came to about $500 after the reductions, so overall, he was offering us a 6 percent reduction from full price. I might have pursued a very different ending to this transaction, maybe just returning the bikes, which still looked almost new, putting the burden of collecting or compromising on him, but I didn't. I caved and paid what he demanded.

By no means was this the end of our relationship with Charlie Tarver, however. An aggressive cyclist himself, Charlie was personally deeply immersed in bicycle speed record making. The fastest bike rides had been achieved on steep ice sheets. So that's what Charlie did for fun! He rode a bicycle down the steepest glaciers he could find. In Charlie's final effort, it was reported in the *Aspen Times* he was going well over 100 mph when he lost control. When he woke up in the hospital, his wife and his girlfriend were at his bedside fighting over his allegiance. Months later, when he got out of the hospital, they had both lost interest and left him to his own devices. Somehow, that drew him to Judy, who, providing counseling, spent much time trying to reorient Charlie to his changed condition. Therapy continued for several years, and Charlie did achieve an ability to manage his life. He compensated Judy by taking up the cause of breast cancer in Aspen and doing so generously.

Dick Burke became a legend as an entrepreneur, not just because Lance Armstrong rode a Trek bike to victory many times on the Tour de France but because Trek made the best mountain bicycles in the world. The company became the largest bicycle manufacturer in the United States, and I expect reaching annual sales of well over a billion dollars.

Dick died prematurely in 2008 from complications of heart surgery. His son, John, a longtime friend of Rich Gallun, has run the company since 1998. Charlie Tarver was back for a while managing Aspen Bicycles. He has never regained his jaunty repartee. Judy McGregor has given up all forms of bike riding. Dan Minahan still leads bicycle tours and always wears his helmet correctly. I still cling to my $5,000 bike trying to get my money's worth out of it, but at the moment, the tires are flat, and this objective is becoming increasingly remote.

CHAPTER XXXI

Do Something Stupid, Stupid

During my second year at Harvard Business School, I took a course called Manufacturing, not so much because I thought that I would become a manufacturer, but more because this course was viewed to be the most important learning experience at the B-School. Even though I ignored much of the valuable advice that came from Professor General Doriot, the course worked out to be a life-altering experience for me.

Although this course was focused more on the general's life philosophy than on manufacturing, it did nurture my interest in making things as an objective of my life work. The general quickly made me believe in the superficiality of the financial career that had been looming in my future.

Nevertheless, the guts of this course was not predominately about the issues facing manufacturers; rather, it was in the nuances of living one's life in the business world. There were lessons in how to read the newspaper, how to adjust your standard of living as you became successful, how to determine the value of information based on its source, and even how to deal with the nerds around you, particularly the ones that might become your boss-- —all issues that we were certain to face. But when we were led into subjects like how do you select your board of directors and how much should you rely on your banker, the subject seemed a little remote.

It is this last question—should you trust your banker—that made a lasting impression on me. The general's answer was a clear no. The banker, while not really evil, is just a tool of his environment. He is your friend when money is loose, but when it gets tight, he needs his—and yours—as well. When the going gets tough, not only is he going to get his money back, but he is going to blame you for his inconvenience in having to press you for it.

THE MARSHALL AND Ilsley Bank was founded in 1847, just ten years before the formation of the Trostel and Gallun leather partnership. Both Samuel Marshall and

Charles Ilsley, having had German origins, it was natural for the tannery, like many other German-owned businesses, to bank with the fledgling Marshall and Ilsley Bank. The relationship was destined to last for one hundred and fifty years. During that period, both parties, being the M&I and the Gallun family, prospered and loyalty grew between them.

The Gallun family had the earlier great success, and by the mid-nineties, my grandfather, Albert I, had become a director and, according to my father, our family's ownership interest became the largest in the bank. Whether this happened all at once or over the years, or, for that matter, at all, is lost to me, but it was clear that my family was to have a great influence during the next hundred years or so.

By 1950 the Gallun family interest in the bank had declined to about 10 percent. Even at that late date and modest ownership, I believe ours remained the largest ownership share. Ted Gallun, as the eldest son of Albert Senior, had taken the Gallun board seat after his father's death in 1936 and would hold it for much of the rest of his life. My father had opined that his father, Albert Sr., and then his brother Ted, were the power behind the Puehlicher era, which ran from the twenties until the nineties. Without ownership control the Puehlichers ran and seemed to control the bank in a period when bank and corporate executives, for the most part, behaved like employees. (That role changed after World War II, when, thanks to the outrageous ability of chief executives to select the board, the top executive became more like the owner than an employee.) Nevertheless, the Puehlichers, John Senior, Albert, and then Jack, ran the bank successfully for three generations, 1920 to 1990, much of it under the patronage of the Gallun family. It was a rewarding alliance for both families.

My business relationship with the bank was a long one and I, having had, even before I attended the B-School, an understanding of how bankers can influence one's life, purposefully attempted to cultivate my image with my bankers. Nevertheless, General Dariot provided some additional guidance here, teaching about an invisible tape that records all of your deeds and follows you inexorably for all of your years. I particularly remember his caution about drinking with your banker, an unmistakable proscription: "When he is considering your worthiness for the loan, all he will see is your wasted visage, and he will forget any favorable attributes you possess." I, from the beginning, watched my p's and q's and attempted to create an unassailable, invisible tape.

My relevant history with the M&I began soon after I graduated from college. Casting around for a job after an unsuccessful attempt to get into medical school and an abortive try at graduate school in chemistry, I thought that, given the Gallun influence there, the bank might be a good place for me to land and get my feet on the ground. I had no qualms about nepotism; I wanted to be a beneficiary of it. I spent half a day with various people at the bank and got my assessment at the end of these interviews from Jack Puehlicher, the then new president. I guess I should not have been surprised when the exit interview went something like this: "Well, you passed muster in your interviews. You can come to work at the M&I. But young man, understand this: The reason we are offering you a job is because of your family's importance to the bank."

In fairness to Mr. Puehlicher, he did make a few references to my mediocre academic record at Williams College and my negligible and unrelated (to banking) work experience. But hey, I had just graduated from college. What could he expect? In any case, I could take a hint—so I joined the army.

That was my first personal encounter with the M&I, but they were my family's banks, and I banked only with them until the early seventies. It was in 1970 that I bought Electriwire, and with this business, I started banking at First Wisconsin. I did so only because a First Wisconsin banker had helped me find and finance the business. That relationship lasted two years and ended when my second First Wisconsin banker, as he returned for my signature on my unsigned personal financial statements, gave me the wrong answer to my naïve and probably unnecessary inquiry: "What? . . . Don't you trust me?"

My question was in mild jest. His response, a simple no, might not have been serious. It sounded serious to me, and I was soon back banking at the M&I.

During this interval and for a few years thereafter, the bank and Jack Puehlicher were having an epiphany: They learned a lesson that they and their successors would not forget until the next century. That lesson was at the hand of Francis Schroedel, a successful real estate developer who was to bet it all on an ambitious resort near Mukwonago, of all places. To my calculation, Mr. Schroedel put in more than fifteen million dollars of his own money, and the M&I loaned him something more than six million. When Schroedel went down, the M&I came into possession of the property and other collateral. The bank's lesson, which I first heard from Steve Seidel in 1975, was, "Don't do anything foolish."

This lesson was to become a mantra for the bank and its leaders, a mantra that I heard repeated often for the next thirty years.

I doubt that this lesson was really learned then. First of all, the bank had always been cautious; in addition, I believe the Schroedel affair turned out to be a bonanza for the bank as they resold the property several times, each time recovering a major part of their original loss. Nevertheless, the bank skillfully dodged the bullets that came in the seventies and eighties—third world lending, REITs, asset-based lending, and the like—that hounded most of the other major banks in the country. The M&I, avoiding these minefields, continued to grow while others were licking their wounds and retrenching. The bank looked at the turn of the twenty-first century like an emerging national power in the banking business. But that success for the bank was to come later; my history with the bank was just beginning in the early seventies.

My first real banker at the M&I was Jim Wigdale. Jim was to have a long relationship with the bank, and he had the stuff to get to the top. In fact, he was a rare bird among bankers. He was one of the nicest people to grace Milwaukee, and he was smart enough, perhaps not smart enough to get into Williams College, but he did graduate from Stanford, and that is a qualification—at least for becoming a banker. He worked hard, learned the business, and he knew how to lose gracefully to Jack Puehlicher at racquetball. He gained a significant credential when he joined the Gallun family through his mother's marriage to Ted Gallun.

Most importantly, Jim had humility—and a sense of humor—both unusual attributes for a top banker. To wit, after Jim had become chairman, Patsy McGregor, then living in Paris, was unable to close her account for which she was being service charged at a rate that was quickly consuming her balance. Judith tried to rectify this situation, but no one would help her. It seemed that to close an account, the owner of the account had to appear in person. Within the bank's bureaucracy, there was apparently no way around this impediment. Judith called Jim Wigdale. He cheerfully agreed to look into it, and in short order, the account was closed, and the fees for inactivity were credited to Patsy. When Judith thanked him for his service, Jim retorted, "No, I should thank you. You gave me something to do today."

Now *there* was a chairman who knew the dimensions of his job.

Throughout my Wigdale era, Jim was accommodating to me, money was available, and I was able to finance a variety of speculative ventures without much hesitation on the part of the bank. Jim got a little nervous about a risky and sizable uranium investment of mine and was uneasy about the leverage it created (he called it a speculation—maybe a gamble). But the uranium deal eventually worked out for me, and I paid off this loan, Jim moved on to bigger jobs, and I inherited Tom Lathrop as my personal and business banker. Tom was a great guy and a good banker, but he, like Jim Wigdale, was on his way up, and I would eventually lose him to promotion. During the period that EWC and I were banking with Tom, Jim Cerny had gotten our company into "best management practices." After one of the bank's annual operations audits, Tom asked if we would allow the bank to use EWC as a manufacturing system model for their new small manufacturing customers. We were flattered and glad to comply. We did so for many years. We were writing our invisible tape.

Then came Gina Peters, and she saw us through a period that was pleasant and unchallenging in my relationship with the bank. Like our previous lead bankers, Gina was destined to move up the ladder, but she was with us until we sold the company to TYCO. Upon the sale, we paid off a loan of a little more than two million dollars, a loan that had grown with the business and never been completely eliminated but not ever a source of a problem for the bank.

I recount this history mainly to assure my reader that I had spent time and worthwhile effort to build this relationship so that there was confidence on both sides, not just theirs in me but mine in them, as well. To this point, I was sixty-five years old with forty of them pretty intensive with the bank, and I thought my invisible tape looked pretty good. But I had forgotten at least one of General Doriot's precepts: "When the going gets tough, they want their money back."

After I went to work for Fiserv and during the next ten years, I had an occasional lunch, always at the University Club, with Dennis Koester, then president of M&I Data, later to become Metavante, to talk about the acquisition by Fiserv of this business. The deal looked more attractive to the M&I than it had in my earlier visit with Dennis and Jim, what with Fiserv's bona fides having been established. Nevertheless, there were tax considerations that kept getting in the way of this transaction. These meetings were always cordial but were more conversational than they were aimed at making a deal. At every meeting, Dennis reiterated his belief in the M&I mantra, "Don't do anything stupid." A few years later, when Wigdale passed the baton to Koester, I judged that the bank was going to be in good hands.

Well, it's been a long story getting here, but bankers are bankers, and I was bound to learn what that means before the end of my life. As George Doriot had said (much more colorfully than I say it): "When they want to make a loan, they are your best friend, but when business turns down, they will be the first to jump ship. Moreover, when times are bad or you are in difficulty, they will disclaim their relationship with you and, claiming fiduciary responsibility, cash in your collateral and go after whatever else they can get, saying all the time that you are a bad, or at best, an imprudent, person."

In 2006, Judith and I sold our Aspen house for a very good price and bought our University Club Tower condominium for two point two million. We took an eight hundred thousand-dollar mortgage, mostly because I had places to invest most of the extra proceeds of the Aspen sale. Our then M&I personal banker, following General Doriot's rules for bankers, suggested that we take a second mortgage of seven hundred thousand, which would support a line of credit, available whenever we needed it. Money was loose and they were hoping to put more of it out at interest. I did the paperwork required and reserved this availability for a future opportunity. It was not long after, in 2008, that I wanted to raise a lot of money for son Rich's young company, bswift, which was a black hole for cash because of its rapid growth. I cashed in all of my investments, and I mean *all*, and took down the entire line of credit, investing this money in convertible notes of bswift.

Of course, it was only a short time before the crash of that year came along, and for the first time, M&I, having ignored their well tested mantra, did more than one stupid thing and was fast becoming one of the biggest losers in the game. Well, perhaps not the biggest but certainly one of the most catastrophic. And they would soon be scratching for liquidity.

The first sign that they were in trouble that would affect me came upon me a couple of years later, with the arrival, in 2009, of a real estate appraiser from Appleton to appraise our condo on behalf of the bank. I didn't take this to be an alarming event, and we showed him around our unit and the common areas. While he was pleasant enough, he did not really seem to understand what he was looking at. When we saw his appraisal result (eight hundred thousand), we were taken aback. His report had no comparables from our building; his comps were solely from the adjacent Kilbourne Tower, which had original units still unsold and where many units had been sold at distress prices. Somehow, he could find no comps in our building even though several units had been resold in the depressed market of the day, at prices only a little less than original cost. We talked to a local appraiser who thought a reasonable valuation for our apartment would be a million six to a million seven. That was in the range of contemporary sales at UTC. This information, when provided to them, made no impression on the bank. What they possessed, and what I had not realized, was that they had a demand note from me and could do as they pleased. Nevertheless, even though this appraisal would barely cover the first mortgage, I was not immediately alarmed because I was a long-term client, and besides, I held a couple of million dollars of notes in bswift, and it was doing well. They wouldn't think of touching me.

The next of the general's predictions was upon me right away. An unfamiliar bank officer unceremoniously demanded payment, and then when I protested, refused to talk to me; with this act, I was cut off from contact with the bank . . . I mean, *totally*. No one from the bank would have any interaction with me. Despite my long and amiable relationship with the bank and excellent credit history, I had become pariah! Following prescribed procedures, I'm sure, the bank next refused to accept payment of interest—interest that had always been paid on time—rejecting my attempts to keep the account current. I was in arrears because I was not willing or able to respond to their demand for full repayment. Their refusal to accept interest seemed odd to me because they had me on the hip with their demand note anyway; it seemed to me that collecting what interest they had earned was in their interest. No doubt there was logic to their refusal.

Somehow, I kept the M&I at bay, but pretty soon, they were gone, and the BMO was in the act. Nothing much changed, but suddenly, we had a collection officer in Arizona, a Mr. Kyle Keen, who threatened immediate foreclosure and was unwilling to discuss any approach to resolving our situation other than me paying off the entire loan. He was there to collect the bank's money.

It had taken me a while, but eventually, I found a lawyer who did not have a conflict of interest. (The M&I did or had done business with every significant law firm in Milwaukee.) My new lawyer was able to forestall foreclosure and held the BMO at bay for several years, a feat that seemed almost magical to me as I had been unable to get anyone to discuss the issue at all. He arranged for me to pay off not insignificant amounts of principal in exchange for withholding action. Fortunately, I could meet those amounts by selling convertible notes in bswift to friends and relatives, but, unfortunately for me, at prices that were not greatly above my original cost. The fact that I had more than two million dollars of these notes at face and that they were providing me with over $200,000 of annual income, made no impression on the bank. They wanted their money. All of it!

Well, we bobbed and weaved with Kyle for two years, my attorney effectively deflecting the BMO's foreclosure efforts. In late 2013, I had visibility of a liquidity date for bswift in the next year. My attorney negotiated forbearance until the next June; and in April, thanks to bswift's sale of a quarter interest to Great Hills Partners, I was able to retire the remaining debt.

This entire debacle lasted for Judith and me a little more than four years. Having suffered under the sword for this term, Judith had difficulty believing that we were out of trouble until the money was in the bank. I had a bit of fun with her the morning the deposit from the bswift sale came in. I asked her to check the bank balance to see if I could write a check. She did and had difficulty believing her eyes but finally was ecstatic. The BMO did not know whether they could apply the check to the loan that day because Kyle Keen was out playing golf. The bank clerk who conveyed that news to Judith got a good piece of her mind. In the end, they accepted the payment as in "immediately."

All is well that ends well. For me, anyhow.

However, the M&I's failure did not end well for many customers and most shareholders. The outcome that haunts us losers is that the perpetrators of this disaster, the top officers of the Marshall and Ilsley, walked out with immense financial rewards. In addition and in spite of their failure to comply with their time-tested mantra, some of them were entrusted by the BMO to continue in the top management of their successor company. Maybe the BMO's mantra is: "Let's do something really stupid."

CHAPTER XXXII

Being There

I HAVE OFTEN been accused of being overly competitive in my various arenas of sports and games. I indeed loved competition; and, like most of my descendants, gravitated to competitive sports. But while I loved winning, it was really more about the game itself, mostly the heat of the competition. I think Vince may have been right for the Packers; but, in general, winning is not the only thing. For me, being there was the real thing—being there and rejoicing in the contest!

In a recent conversation with my son, Rich, I was reminded of one of the great values of competition in learning, particularly for the young. Rich reflected that early on his son, Henry, wasn't too good at math but was pretty good at fantasy football, at which to excel, you need to have a good understanding of statistics and probabilities. Henry became facile here, and as a result his math performance blossomed. Rich observed as well that in his own experience, the best training for a sport is not in repetitive exercises but in actual competition. Confirming this view, I attribute my own success at hockey in college, despite the limited ice time and instruction that I had encountered relative to my Williams teammates who were, to a man, raised with extensive coaching on artificial ice, to the significant exposure to competition that I experienced in pond hockey at Pine, Beaver and Mud Lakes.

Here I present a few vignettes of contests that linger in my memory, lingering not because they were memorable victories but because they amused me.

Sailing

Without question, sailing was my favorite lifetime sport. It wasn't just sailing a boat that was my passion, though; it was the race. I loved the aesthetics of the sport, but I sailed more because I reveled in the contest. I could lose myself totally in the race, forgetting the world and any troubles that were bothering me at the time.

I realize that, when I was in my teens and twenties, I was an unnecessarily aggressive competitor, using combative tactics and the racing rules as a bludgeon against the opposition. I had some success in those years, like finishing fourth in the National "E" Championship in 1960, but in those early years I didn't make many new friends on the race course. In retrospect, I did not have much fun sailing. I became increasingly unhappy with my results and with my own conduct on the boat.

When I returned to Pine Lake after graduating from business school, I gained two new crew members, Susie and Richard Sternkopf; and after our first confrontational—and unsuccessful—year together, I decided, and we agreed, that we would sail for enjoyment and fun, not having a concern about our finishing position. The next season was a new experience. We never quarreled on the boat, and we laughed at our mistakes, however they occurred. We narrowly missed the Pine Lake Championship that year, and we began a long period of relative local dominance. In the ensuing years, various crew members and I won many races; and even as I had unrequited ambitions for success in the Inland Lakes Yachting Association (ILYA), I had a ball against some really good competition on my home lake.

One Inland race stands out in my memory because it involved an exciting battle with Mother Nature, as well as a dramatic finish of the race. It was as close as I ever got in my E-Scow to winning an Inland race. I was sailing then with Tom and Chris Beda in the annual championship regatta at Green Lake.

The wind was light, and the day was gray with an overcast of low clouds. As we were milling around with eighty or so competitors before the start, Chris remarked that there was some ugly-looking weather on the northern horizon. We looked at the approaching but still distant black clouds that portended a summer squall, a common occurrence in August in Wisconsin, and reasoned that those storm winds, while potentially dangerous, would give us an advantage if we could be the first to get to them. As the clock wound down to the start, the black clouds were fast getting closer, and we assumed that others would be competing with us to get into this new weather. To our amazement, no one seemed to notice.

The wind at the start was wafting lightly from the northwest, and with the first windward leg headed directly into this light breeze, we planned to take an early port tack and go directly north, straight into the approaching weather. When it arrived, we would certainly be among the first beneficiaries of the winds generated by the storm.

We started at the judges' boat in the uncompetitive second echelon, not needing to be the first boat across the line because we planned an immediate tack. We just had to see that we were next to the judges' boat as we crossed the line so that we could tack without interference. As we expected, the boat ahead of us relished his position atop the fleet and continued on the starboard, holding hostage, for a while, the entire rest of the fleet. Passing the judges' boat right behind him, we tacked to the right. We sailed completely alone in the undisturbed wind for maybe ten minutes, heading directly at the approaching storm. A few boats had followed us after they cleared the congestion at the start, but the closest of these was ten boat lengths back. We reached the lay line, the point at which we could fetch the mark, and we could see the wind on the water just ahead of us. Suddenly, we ran into the storm wind, a header right on the nose, and the boat was knocked flat. On this knockdown, we tacked, helped in doing so by the new wind direction. After recovering from this maneuver and adjusting to the changed conditions, we found that the storm winds, then about twenty-five knots, were manageable but barely so. With the new wind direction, we were on a broad reach into the mark. It was an exhilarating ride to that mark, but because the new wind quickly filled the course, and because the boats behind us had a faster angle of sailing, our lead on reaching the buoy was only about ten boat lengths, a good lead but no sure thing.

With a windward leeward course, two-and-one-half times around, there was still a lot of race ahead of us. The stormy weather persisted for the balance of the race with gusts reaching over thirty knots, and we, thriving on this tempestuous weather, extended our lead, getting to the final windward mark with a forty-yard lead over the two boats that had stayed with us. The fleet was back another hundred yards. On the final downwind leg, we held our lead, all of it, until we approached the finish line, when both of our competitors, behind and just a bit to leeward, caught a major gust that we could not reach and, both of them, going almost directly downwind on a full plane, dissolved our lead and passed us to leeward—right at the finish line.

We finished third that day, certainly a disappointing result under the circumstances. Nevertheless, I will always hold dear the excitement of reaching those storm winds ahead of the fleet and the exhilarating ride into and around that first mark.

Hockey

In his second year of Bantams, Rich, playing with his line-mates, Tom Beda and Billy Zito, won the tournament for the Bantam State Championship. They returned to Milwaukee with swelled heads. A week later they were facing a very weak team from Zion, Illinois. The team was so weak, having not only poor skaters but, in addition, only seven of these. Recognizing that he was playing the state champions, the Zion coach, within my earshot, asked Rich's coach if he would lend him a player for the day. Despite my age, I jumped at the opportunity and volunteered for this chance. It seemed appropriate to me since I had been mixing it up with these boys in "old men's" and pond hockey and at forty-three, was no longer completely in control. Besides, the boys didn't object because they were confident that the three of them could keep me under control. Without much consideration on the part of the coaches, my offer was accepted.

From the time the first puck was dropped, it was evident to me that the state champions had drunk the Kool-Aid of hubris. Each of them wanted to win the game by himself, and no matter what impediment was in front of him, he was going to carry the puck to the cage and score. As it turned out, that impediment was usually me, and I was able to steal the puck more often than not. Not always, though, and before the final whistle, the three of them were able to amass six goals among them. That total proved to be insufficient as I scored six goals too, and the rest of the Zion team scored one. Can I be blamed for holding that double hat trick as a memorable accomplishment of my life?

Tennis

Rich Gallun won the State Open tournament for ten year olds when he was ten; at twelve in the Chenequa Men's Championship, he was runner-up to Loren Spires Durand, the best player Chenequa had ever had up to that time. Again, facing Loren in the finals the next year, Rich won this tournament. Twice Chenequa Men's Champion at thirteen! He appeared to have a bright tennis future ahead of him. Nevertheless, Rich's state ranking, which had been three when he was ten, declined a little every year until, at sixteen, it bottomed out at twenty-six! Rich hung up his racquet and did not play at all for the next four years. Not even once.

After graduating from college, Rich returned to Milwaukee. When the championship tournament rolled around, he decided to enter and somehow, perhaps based on muscle memory, or more likely a weak lineup of competitors, found himself in the finals. There, however, was a real barrier to prevent him from claiming another championship. That obstacle was in the form of Danny Schaefer, who was to be his opponent, and at the time, was ranked number one in the state for the sixteen and under. Remember, not only that four years earlier Rich was ranked twenty-sixth in the same arena and that he had not played since, but also that the level of play among juniors was advancing rapidly in the eighties. Danny had a good tennis résumé, and the finals looked to be a blowout.

When the day of the finals match rolled around, I, certain that Rich faced an ignominious defeat, decided to support him by showing up. I drove out from Milwaukee that day, arriving about a half hour after the match had started. The match was being played in the "pit," where the most important matches were played because there were bleachers there for the tennis fans. I noticed right away that the bleachers were empty even though I could see that Rich and Danny were still going at it.

There was only one spectator in the stands, so I asked him what was happening. He reported that Rich had lost the first set, six love, but surprisingly, after the audience had lost interest and left, was competing well in the second. The score in the second set was five four in favor of Danny, who was serving. It looked like the match was about to end anyway.

But Danny double-faulted on the first point that I saw; and then, in a voice dripping with annoyance, announced the score as add out. Next, he muffed his overpowering first serve, the ball going off the top of his racquet and landing in the next court. On the second serve, this time being more cautious, he hit a soft ball that set up an easy overhead winner for Rich. But, Rich, rather than trying to put the return away with a shot that he didn't have, let the ball bounce and dinked a lob to the deep center of the court. Danny set up for an overhead smash, but again, hit the ball over the fence. Five all! As they changed ends, Rich stopped in front of me and wiped his face with a towel. As he did so, he looked up at me and winked, giving me a confident grin. Rich knew he had him right there.

As I watched the next seven games, I could understand what I had missed. From my viewpoint, Rich had only two strokes—a forehand and a lob—no backhand, no serve, no net shot, and no volley. But he used the strokes he had effectively. Apparently, he had the patience to get through the first set while setting up the psychology for the undoing of Danny's game. Rich had reached the denouement of his strategy just about the time that I had arrived. In all the tennis I saw that day, he ran around every backhand while using the dink effectively—almost always getting all but his opponent's most difficult shots. He was never tempted to make a hard shot. Danny was having difficulty getting the ball past Rich, and his frustration mounted as Rich proved unwilling to give up an error. The last seven games, all to Rich, took less than fifteen minutes. The last two were love games.

My own interest in tennis arose from the beating that Kathy used to give me early in our marriage. My competitive nature led me to bring my game to a level where I could compete with her and eventually beat her. Then I set a goal to beat her sister, Judy, a goal that matured into a major life objective. Judy and I played only occasionally over the years, but I never got close.

I reached the pinnacle of my game in my early sixties after quite a few lessons, lessons that were aimed mainly at beating Judy. Finally, I thought I was ready, and Judy, always confident, was glad to take me on again. The game started as I hoped it would. We exchanged hard baseline shots with long points that were usually won by forced errors. I was at the top of my game as I found myself ahead four to two. Then, suddenly, the game changed; no longer were we playing a baseline game but instead, coming at me were a mix of short shots, lobs, and cuts, no more hard hits at all. I tried to adjust, but in short order, I was toast. The score ended at six-four.

That was a life objective that I abandoned. Judy and I never played again, not because I knew that she had my number, but because I wasn't willing to spend the time to develop the skills that I would need to defeat her. Maybe I am not as competitive as some think.

I played many times in the Chenequa Country Club annual championship tournament; but because I played a marginally okay game of tennis, I never reached even the semifinals. Except for one time. It was at age fifty-seven that I, for the first time, found myself in the finals of this tournament. Not just the singles but with my partner, my son-in-law, Todd Krieg, the doubles, as well!

I admit that in this year, 1992, the competition was not at a peak level. The traditional winners were someplace else that year. After working my way through the initial brackets against mediocre competition, I was pitted in the finals of the singles against Dick Burke, a longtime adversary who usually played me about even. For both of us, it was our first time in the finals.

With the tennis dinner that night, we had come up against the last day for playing this match, both having had conflicts which had prevented us from getting it off earlier. The same complications had delayed my doubles match too, so I was facing two matches on the same day, singles at nine, doubles at two. And the weather report was for sunny, ninety-five, and humid. It was not a good day for tennis, but we were not permitted to reschedule.

When I stepped on the court at the appointed hour, it was already ninety on its way to one hundred degrees, but I was prepared with a case of Gatorade—that would be nine quarts. The fans were sparse, considering that it was the finals, but there were a half-dozen spectators, including my daughter, Liz, and her husband, Todd, my doubles partner.

I got to serve first game; service was my long suit, usually a winner against Dick, at least when I had all my strength; but despite my service advantage, the game dragged on for ten minutes before I finally won it. That one game took a greater toll than you can imagine. By the end of the last point, I was sweating profusely and was winded. As we changed ends, I watched Dick toweling off, and I could see that he paid the price for his defense. I remember the first set progressing slowly from there, partly because we were evenly matched, partly because we had some long rallies, but mostly because we both shuffled slowly back to the service line when serving. Neither of us complained about the increasingly slow pace of the game. By ten thirty, we had just completed two sets. The score was one apiece. Both of us were dripping wet; our clothes were completely soaked. At least I had a dry shirt to change into. Six bottles of my Gatorade were gone, and I was dead on my feet. I got to sit down for the five-minute break before beginning the playoff set, but that respite gave no relief. My opponent appeared to be suffering too, but his determination was apparent when he declared assertively, "Well, the five minutes are up. Let's get on with it."

An hour later, the heat had taken an additional measure of both of our stamina. We were tied at 6-all, and the pace of the game had continued to slow, but neither of us had given up chasing the ball on good shots—not that there were many of those because we were no longer making good shots. We just didn't have the strength.

At 7-all, I broke Dick's serve and could see a path to victory. I was determined to end this contest, but Dick was just as determined to stay alive. That game went on interminably with each of us having ad a half-dozen times. Finally, having ad in, I hit a good ball to Dick's backhand and stumbled to the net. Dick bravely retrieved the ball and managed a deep lob over my head. As the ball came down behind me, I, not being able to reach it, understood that if it were out, I would win the match; but if it were in, I would not have enough strength to toss the ball up for the next serve. I was truly done! No matter what happened, I was finished. It was out by six inches, and the match was finally over!

It was twelve fifteen. We had played for more than three hours. Dick dragged himself over and shook my hand, then limped off. My only remaining fan, Todd Krieg, helped me off the court. Even with this assist, I could hardly walk.

The rest of the day was a nightmare. During the hour and a half before the next match, I took in liquids (no more Gatorade was available, and besides, I had lost my taste for it), got rubbed and coddled by my Liz and Todd, ate a little but never regained any real mobility. Todd understood that and that I was going to be just a fixture on the court, and he was going to do the running.

Fortunately, the opposition, although fresh and energetic, was short on skills. It was a very slow game from the beginning. Everyone had to wait while I got into position after the completion of each point. One of our opponents frequently complained about my slow movement between points and even called on the referee to encourage speeding up the play. I did not respond to these complaints, and the referee did not press me on my movement. The match went to three sets and lasted almost three hours. By the end, Todd was flagging a bit, having covered most of our end of the court for the entire duration, but he played skillfully and made good judgments about when to chase the ball and when to save his energy. We won the third set, and I had my first two tennis championships!

I had not had much of a role in the doubles match; nevertheless immediately upon leaving the court, my muscles began to cramp and spasm painfully. Todd got me home and put me in the lake to cool me down. He and Liz attended to me for the next two hours, feeding me their prescriptions for muscle cramps, mostly beer and bananas but some other bad-tasting potions as well. For the first hour of this therapy, my muscles in my entire body cramped painfully, particularly in my legs, arms, chest, and stomach. I was personally very concerned that the cramping would go to my heart, and I protested that my attendants should call a doctor. They encouraged me to be brave and let time do its healing.

It did.

My moment of glory should have been the tennis dinner that night, and perhaps it was. But I don't remember a thing after getting out of the lake.

Canoeing

It is hard to believe that a group of men could turn canoeing into a competitive sport, particularly on a trip to the peaceful boundary waters in Western Ontario. I took such a trip on an invitation from my lifelong friend, Bruce Beda. It was a men's trip and was intended to include all of our sons, who were all close friends. The only defector here was my son Rich, who didn't like to canoe except on white water, of which there is little in the Quetico. Perhaps it was a good thing that we didn't have Rich because that left us with an even number, which is good when you are pairing up in canoes. Alby and I became a fixed team in the approaching competition.

The downside of this adventure was to be the limitations on food, and we all were big on our meals. Because of extensive portaging, we carried only dried food, plus two one-pound cakes of lard and two salamis per person. Our daily catch was to supply the protein. We did always have plenty of fish, but you would be surprised about the body's requirement for fat, particularly when you are paddling and portaging for eight or nine hours a day. Four ounces of lard and a couple of slices of salami don't go as far as you might think. By the end of the week, there was competition to see who would do the dishes because the cleaner got to lick the lard residue from pancake and fish pans.

But this memoir is about canoeing competition, not about eating and doing dishes. It all started on the second day when Bruce spotted our prospective campsite about a half-mile distant at the end of a lake we were traversing. He opined, "Boy, look at that peninsula next to the mouth of the river. That's going to be where we camp."

Well, the decision had been made, and that's where we were going. So we kept on paddling, but with no comment from anyone, the pace, almost imperceptibly, started to increase. As we moved across the smooth surface of the lake, the sound of the canoes slipping quietly through the water became muffled by the noise of the gradually increasing pace of the sloshing of paddles. At first, the race was a subtle and undeclared contest, but as the campsite grew nearer, the reality of the competition was out in the open. In the end, there was no prize for the winners. The losers did not even acknowledge that there was a victory . . . but we all knew who had won.

For the remaining evenings of this expedition, the day's competition began in the same way, but always at a greater distance than it had on the prior day. On the final day, we sighted our destination, a pier at least a mile away, at which we would meet the plane that would take us back to Ely. We all knew that this pier would be our destination, and this final race moved quickly into high gear. The exertion was intense for the next fifteen minutes, and the lead changed hands several times. Alby and I hit the pier first, but the Beda canoes swept past us and hit the beach together.

Two hours later, we were still arguing about where our final race really ended; but we were doing so as we revelled at Ely's Pizza Hut, each of us with his own pitcher of beer, six large pizzas being snarfed, and everyone who smoked smoking a cigarette, the first he had had since we had run out of smokes two days prior.

Skiing

When I was fifteen, my sister, Carol, was a competitive skier, the runner-up to Kit Sherry in the Midwest Championship for sixteen-year-olds, then going on to the nationals, where she was five seconds ahead of the field at the midpoint of the downhill . . . just before she crashed.

I did not get into competitive skiing until I was sixty-five. It was my granddaughter, Katharine Krieg, who tweaked my competitive nature as it related to skiing. I was taking a leisurely run down Silver Bell on Ajax Mountain with the entire Krieg pack when we ran into a NASTAR course that started next to the outrun from the top of Bell Mountain. We watched the racers for a while; then suddenly, Katharine, then ten years old, challenged me to be her opponent on the NASTAR course. I accepted her challenge with pleasure, feeling confident that no ten-year-old was going to beat me in a race. In this first race, I, giving, as was usually my wont, no quarter, blew her out. She was a piece of cake! Not only Katharine, but also her siblings, proved to be easy meat, and I did enjoy this soft competition for their entire stay. The next year, Katharine and I had fairly even races, but I kept a slight win-loss edge. What made it close was that I eased up a bit pursuant to Judith's counsel, that I should let my grandchildren win every now and then. Nevertheless' the following year my ascendency over Katharine was finished; in fact, I could never beat her. After a couple of my losses to her, she avoided me when we were selecting opponents. It seemed that now she preferred to race with her father rather than with me. What I learned from Katharine was that no one wants to race with a loser!

Well, when Katharine no longer wanted to race with me, that was tough enough, but this loss was aggravated by the fact that Gretchen was pressing me already. But worse, I could tell that pretty soon, I would be relegated to Sam. I discussed my concern over this problem with KK and Doug Neimann, not entirely an ego issue for me . . . but maybe a little. I would maintain that it was more about staying in the game than needing to win.

KK found a solution for me: for Christmas that year, she and Doug gave me a year's pass to the Aspen racing school. That gift was one of the best gifts I ever received. The course was taught by recent Olympians and gave me a few skills that kept me in the game—if only for one extra year. The most important thing I learned was that slalom is much about carving the turns around the gates-- not allowing the skis to skid at all. However, carving requires getting your knees majorly into the hill, a difficult posture for me, and a skill that I never was fully able to assimilate. What I did absorb allowed me to compete for a while with Gretchen and it held Sam off for a while.

What I learned was that all of my grandchildren seem to carve their turns intuitively; and so, as more of these intuitive skiers came along, they were beating me at younger and younger ages despite my acquired skills. But at least I no longer have to listen to Judith saying, "Maybe you should let them win!"

Stratego

With the decline of my physical capabilities, I decided to revert to my mental prowess. I had come to wonder about even my intellectual competence when Sam Krieg was regularly able to demolish me at "Four Across," at age six. Not only did he beat me regularly at this simpleminded game, but he was a bad winner—at least when he was six—with his jeers defining the word "obnoxious." I listened to his taunts for hours after his victories, but he could always lure me into another game, if only because I wanted to beat him.

As I could see the handwriting coming at me, I needed a new game, if only to keep Sam in his place. I hit on "Stratego," a game that required the use of memory and strategic thinking as well. Sam had not gotten around to strategic thinking yet, but his memory was excellent. My memory had already begun to flag, but I had a huge advantage in strategy and tactics. So, after I taught him the game, I won easily; but by the time he was sixteen, he had become wise to my strategies, and my dominance was gone. And I was losing at Stratego more than I was winning. Sam went to college the next year and I missed my competitive forays with him.

After Sam graduated from Williams, I knew I had my hands full to hold his interest in intellectual games with me because he had become a genuine intellectual. Nevertheless, I decided to upgrade my Stratego game and developed a number of new strategies, doing so in private, and trying the new ones out on Rich Gallun. I was successful with Rich and took my new skills to Sam. To this day, neither Rich nor Sam have figured out how to beat me at Stratego!

You, my reader, can be the judge! Am I overly competitive, or do I just want to be there?

CHAPTER XXXIII

Living on the Edge

In earlier memoirs, I have talked about the dangers that lurk in the clouds just behind the horizon, addressing in the telling, nature's destructive power on a global scale. While nature's power is awe-inspiring even in a thunderstorm, with wind velocities in local cells occasionally reaching hurricane force, it is possible to resist this incredible force with knowledge, strength, and experience. In this recounting of a poignant memory of a summer storm, I recall the joy of challenging nature at a personal level.

IT WAS AN ordinary summer afternoon. Although the sun shone brightly in a cloudless sky, there was a somber heaviness in the air. The burden of the atmosphere, dense with humidity, portended a summer storm. Nevertheless, the lake presented a glassy veneer reflecting almost perfectly an image of the opposite shore as well as the blue of the sky. The only blemish on the surface of the lake was to be found in the occasional catspaws that were beginning to show on the water, moving briefly from south to north, then evanescing as quickly as they had appeared. It was a beautiful afternoon for swimming, but swimming was not on the agenda. We were planning to compete in a sailing race that was supposed to start in twenty minutes. It did not look like a promising day for sailing.

My boat was rigged and ready, floating listlessly at the pier, tethered there on a sagging bowline. My crew lolled on the pier, dangling their feet in the water and taking an occasional dive to relieve themselves from the heat in the tepid but still refreshing water. The crew consisted of my son, Alby, and our friend, Chris Beda. Both were strong, athletic young men in their midtwenties. The three of us had sailed together for many years, and my competitors acknowledged that I had had, in recent years, the most skilled crew on the lake. Not only did these young men know how to set the sails properly, but they knew better than I how to shape the sails for best efficiency by bending and raking the mast.

As race time approached, the weather seemed to be improving, at least for sailing. The catspaws were consolidating, and as we looked to the south from our pier at the north end of the lake, we could see the signal sparkle of blue and sunlight dancing on the water a mile away. The wind was beginning to rise, wafting softly from the south. We would have a race after all. I noticed, without taking note of its significance, that the day was dimming a bit; the intensity of the sun was subsiding, and a halo had formed around it. Presently, the light wind we had seen as ripples in the distance arrived. Meanwhile, the judges had set up a starting line near the opposite shore less than a half mile away. We raised our sails, setting the boat up for the light wind that seemed to be in prospect for the afternoon. However, by the time we reached the starting line, the wind had risen to about ten knots and looked to be still rising, so we adjusted our settings for medium wind.

The course was a windward leeward running the length of the lake two and one-half times. The judges went through the routine procedures for starting a race, and quickly, we were off in a stiff breeze almost at the regulation starting time. I got a poor start and found myself in the middle of the fleet "eating" the bad air bouncing off the sails of boats ahead of and next to me. For the next ten minutes, I was totally occupied in attempting to get clear of the boats around me, without much success. When I finally got a chance to look around, I realized that conditions had worsened considerably. Already, the water had lost its sparkle and was metamorphosing into a steely gray. The wind continued to rise, and we made what adjustments we could to accommodate the heavy winds that were upon us.

It would normally take fifteen minutes to complete the mile and a quarter that made up the first leg of this course. But the conditions were rapidly deteriorating and soon, had gone way beyond normal. As we approached the south mark about twenty minutes after the start, the sky, even as the sun still shone dimly through an eerie haze, had become a grayish brown. The water had taken on the color of creamed coffee, this color the reflection of the sky mixed with a dense profusion of white-capped waves. Later, we were told that the wind at this point was touching, in the gusts, 35 knots.

The only way you keep a scow upright in such circumstances is to point the boat closer to the wind, but there are limits here. If you sail too close to the wind, you slow the boat to a standstill and lose steerage. Then the wind takes over, forcing you broadside, and you have no way to avoid capsizing. It is a fine skill and an exhausting effort to keep an "E" boat upright in these conditions, requiring intuitive steering and considerable coordinated working of both sails. Even with a prodigious effort and exacting skill, forward progress almost ceases. Although no one had yet capsized at this point of the race, the fleet was making little headway up the lake. It was evident that it was going to be just a matter of a short time before the entire fleet would capsize.

Recognizing the gravity of the situation, the judges signaled the abandonment of the race, doing so by firing their canon and raising the abandonment flag.

Now my problem was how to get turned around and head for home without going broadside to the wind and capsizing. Well, we waited for a brief lull, one which came only after what seemed an eternity. In it, we turned quickly downwind, somehow executing this turn without a hitch. To this day, I don't understand how we were able to accomplish this maneuver, even in a lull, but we did, and suddenly we were going directly downwind, a point of sailing where there are no capsizing forces even in a howling storm.

By the time we got the boat aimed for home, the storm had reached its peak; the sky was fully black; the day had turned to night; the water was solidly white with foam; and spray was being ripped from the tops of the waves, lashing us viciously on our bare backs. I quickly assessed our situation, taking into consideration our downwind course leading straight to our house, the skill and ability of the crew, the water temperature, and the joy of speed in a sailboat, all of these enticements offsetting the certain knowledge that no one adds sail in a full gale. I caught Chris's eye and shouted, "What do you think?"

Understanding my cryptic question, he rejoined without hesitation, "I'd do it."

So I called to Alby, "Put up the chute!"

And Alby did.

It was a great ride and truly memorable experience for all of us. Of course, it didn't last very long because it was only a little more than a mile to go, and we were going so fast. What I remember most vividly was the surge of power as the spinnaker snapped, and I mean *snapped*, into place. Several motor craft racing next to us lit up in the darkness by their running lights, engines wide open, and just keeping up. The orchestral music came from the rudders; a high-pitched scream arising arose from their vibration. And most unforgettably of all, the ecstasy of being totally out of control . . . The out-of-control thing was compelling. I sensed its authority the first time I tried to alter the direction of the boat after the spinnaker was set. Just trying to make a minor directional change, as little as a half degree, unleashed a powerful heeling force that demanded my surrender of command. With my hand on the tiller, I sensed with absolute certainty that there was no choice but to follow the wind.

Well, follow the wind we did, and very soon we passed the island in the center of the lake, missing it by a mere twenty yards, not that this ever looked to be dangerous because we had been able to see that we were on a course to pass it in deep water before we raised the spinnaker. After passing the island, we immediately started taking down the chute and got it into the boat as we came near home. Then as we attempted a final necessary maneuver, a gybe that would allow us to approach the pier, the catastrophe happened. As the mainsail whipped across the cockpit and filled hard on the new tack, the rotational energy created by the sudden filling of the sail overpowered my ability to steer. We went broadside to the wind and almost instantaneously capsized. It happened so quickly that no one had an opportunity to counter the loss of buoyancy of the aluminum mast as it filled with water. The mast sank, and the boat went "turtle." Having the boat upside down turned out to be a blessing as we ended up sitting out the storm under the boat with our heads in the airspace created by the cockpit. There we were in the hospitable water, safe from the gale raging above us, laughing and rejoicing over one of the great pleasures of life . . . that of living on the edge and doing so without having to experience real danger!

Then much more quickly than it had arrived, the storm passed. From under the boat, we no longer heard the howling of the wind, and we emerged from the cockpit to see the sun breaking through the scattering clouds. Within minutes, the sky returned to the deep blue of earlier in the day. While the wave action was still significant, the wind had died completely, and it was going to be only a short interval before the lake returned to its earlier tranquility. All of these events and changes had taken place over the course of a little less than an hour.

CHAPTER XXXIV

Bear, the Cowardly Hero

Most of us haven't stopped to think about what makes a hero, or for that matter, what is bravery. Judy and I learned a lot about courage from our dog, Bear, who came into our lives in the middle of his. Before I get into his story, one that is replete with all kinds of his idiosyncrasies, we should take a moment to consider together what the difference is, if there is one, between being a hero and being a scaredy-cat, and what is the distinction between being afraid and being a chicken.

Fear is an emotion that is part of our innate defense mechanism. It stimulates the adrenal glands in all mammals to release the powerful hormones that intensify our capabilities, both physical and mental. In doing so, fear prepares us to face dangers or moves us to retreat from them. Either action, fight or flight, might be the right thing to do, depending on the situation we face. Bear was not a fighter, nor was he without fear, but he knew how to face danger, putting his fears aside when the situation required him to do so. While it was his courage under extreme pressure that made him unique, even without this quality, he was a wonderful dog and a loyal and dependable friend.

BEAR, OUR THIRD Weimaraner dog, came to us as a six-year-old delinquent, rejected from his former home in Idaho Springs for offenses not revealed to us. Judy and I were living in Aspen, when she was contacted by the Idaho Springs Humane Society as a potential rescuer for this errant dog, probably because of her reputation as a kind dog owner and a sucker for Weimaraners. Had we had the opportunity to view Bear's record, we might not have accepted him into our family, but in any case, Judy did not put much stock in pedigrees. Only a meeting could satisfy her.

An agent of the Humane Society met Judy in Vail with the dog, presumably for an "interview." She introduced Judy to Bear and then abruptly drove off from the parking lot where they had met, not giving Judy any opportunity to reject the dog. In any case, Judy had never met a dog that she wasn't glad to bring home, so she probably wouldn't have found anything in Bear's past that would have changed the outcome of this meeting. With the Humane Society official out of sight, Judy immediately understood her new responsibility and gave her full attention to the dog. Feeling secure in this friendly environment, Bear hopped confidently into the front seat with Judy, put his head on her shoulder, shuddered happily, and went to sleep as she headed back to Aspen.

When I returned from a business trip the next day, I was immediately out of sorts to find a new dog in the house, one that had not been agreed upon in advance. It would not be the last time that Judith snuck an unapproved dog into the family. Even so, by the time we went to bed that night, this dog had already worked his way into a corner of my heart. After the lights went out, Bear crawled onto our bed and put his front legs around my neck, sighed contentedly, and easily gained possession of my whole heart.

Bear was a strange dog from the outset. For one thing, he had an unusually short tail. In fact, his tail was so short that he seemed to have no tail at all. He certainly didn't have anything to wag. This peculiarity severely constrained his ability to express emotion, but it did not limit his ability to show affection. It took about six months of well deserved attention before his tail began to emerge, and then, as he began to wag it vigorously to express his newfound happiness, it grew to a length of about four inches. This appendage added an important dimension to his personality.

This dog from the beginning seemed to be very connected to both Judith and me. Even so he disappeared from time to time and we would eventually find him down town, usually at a bar where he had made for himself a number of new friends. Later when he became totally attached to us and had lost his wanderlust, he nevertheless disappeared occasionally and we were desperate to find him. One of these times he was gone for more than a day and we searched for him everywhere. We even had the police looking for him. That wasn't the first time we found him locked in the upstairs closet. One might have thought we would have looked there early in our search since we had found him there previously; but we hadn't yet come to realize that he was in the closet because he liked it there. We finally got wise to the fact that he had figured out how to open the door so that he could get inside. He never learned how to get out. Apparently he had never been locked in long enough to complain about his imprisonment. Thereafter, when Bear was missing, the first place we looked for him was in the closet. He was always there.

Early in our relationship with Bear we learned that he liked to run—in fact, to run for long distances. We would let him out of the car on back roads, and he would lead the way at a full run for several miles. We would go out of our way, sometimes many miles out of our way, to find roads that he could run on safely. Our other dogs of the time, Ruby and Max, would not deign to join him on these marathons. When they were offered the opportunity, they would just cringe in their cushions and look at me fixedly as if to say, "Why would I do that?"

I have a picture in my mind of Bear stopping far ahead on a windswept and treeless ridge atop Ajax Mountain, his ears blowing in the wind, looking back as if to say, "Get a move on!" He looked the part of the heroic dog, scouting the dangerous terrain ahead to keep the way safe for his master's entourage.

Bear's sense of duty showed early in our relationship with him. While traveling with the dogs, Judy stayed at a much-less-than-four-star motel in Denver, there being no good alternatives as darkness fell. As the gloom deepened in this threatening environment, Judy became nervous about her safety. Even as she double-locked the door and put on the security chain, her apprehension increased. Bear, sensing her unease, parked himself on the end of the bed and fixed his eyes on the door, growling softly at any disturbance. He remained so throughout the night, never, to Judy's knowledge, even putting his head down. He knew what his job was.

One evening, when she was home alone, a full-grown black bear entered the house and confronted Judy in the kitchen. Her shriek brought Bear on the double. He went after the large beast forthwith, snarling and baring his teeth, and, as the bear exited, nipping at the beast's legs and feet. Bear showed no fear in this confrontation. When the bear was out of the house, he turned to face Bear, who gave no ground but crouched on his belly and glowered at the bear. The bear too went to the ground and glared back at Bear. They held each other's gaze for twenty minutes, neither of them diverting his eyes from the other until the arrival of the police, whom Judy had summoned.

The police, two of them, looked upon this standoff, and Judy asked, "What are you going to do to get rid of the bear?"

Policeman Number One said, "Get rid of the bear? You know it's against the law for dogs to chase wildlife. I should shoot your dog."

Judy reacted as I would have expected, "You shoot him, and I'll shoot you!"

Number One started to respond angrily at this outburst of disrespect but was interrupted by Number Two, who interjected, "Hold on. No one is going to shoot anyone."

It was about this time that the bear, having been outstared by Bear, decided to make his move and slowly rose, turned away, and lumbered off. Bear held his position until the bear was out of sight; then he went calmly to Judy. As she embraced him, he started to shake and did so almost uncontrollably for the next hour. He had given everything his little heart could bear.

Like most heroes, Bear had important fears, but when the chips were down, he did what he had to do. That is what heroes do.

Judy and I had a good friend in Aspen, Mary Lynn Casper. She owned two dogs, an Australian shepherd named Develin and a poodle named Reba. Our dogs mixed well with hers at both of our houses, at her restaurant, in the park, and on hikes. That is, until one day at Mary Lynn's house, when Develin and Bear had a brief set-to from which Bear emerged the loser with a torn ear. Bear was shaken and bleeding but did not require medical attention.

The next time we saw the Caspers, Bear shrank from any contact with Develin. Thereafter, when we went to Mary Lynn's, Bear refused to get out of the car. The entire rest of the time we lived in Aspen, we were unable to get any consideration of reconciliation out of Bear; in fact, if we took him to Mary Lynn's, Bear would stay in the car and shake intensely, teeth chattering until our visit was over. Bear had become terrified of this dog. Soon, Mary Lynn stopped bringing her dogs to our house, and we would leave Bear at home when we visited her. We did so until Develin died, but even then, Bear refused to go to any of the old places.

We thought we had put these events way behind us when Mary Lynn visited us several years later in Milwaukee. Bear rose with the other dogs to greet her, but when he saw who it was, his tail disappeared, he shrank behind Judy and began to shake uncontrollably. It was not until Mary Lynn left that he was able to regain his composure.

Unquestionably, Bear had an elephant's memory, but more important, his heart was as big as any elephant's.

One day, as we approached the car at the end of our daily dog-walk, Bear's hind legs gave out, and he could no longer walk. Nevertheless, as we came to his aid, he refused assistance and bravely dragged himself to the car, a not inconsiderable distance, using his front legs alone. He died a few hours later, young at heart until the end. He was seventeen.

While Bear's memory was long, ours of him will be forever. We learned from him that courage is something you show when you must. I think it is an acquired virtue, one that grows out of love. Like Bear's tail, it is not something you are born with.

CHAPTER XXXV

Wisdom Achieved

What I have tendered here is a collection of remembrances that amused me as they occurred and then stuck in my mind over the years. Even as I have more stories to tell and much more to say, I know it's time to bring this treatise to an end. It is difficult for me to do that because amusing experiences and people keep popping up in my consciousness. I just might have to do this again. But before I give up this pen, I want to share with my reader some important lessons that I have learned about life, love, writing, and reality.

A FEW YEARS back, as I sat in the restaurant at the Paris Hotel in Las Vegas, watching the light and water show across the strip at the Bellagio, listening to Frank Sinatra belting out, "I Did It My Way," I thought Frank was speaking to the life I was leading, a life that I had uniquely created for myself. But as I look back today with a few more years under my belt, as well as the wisdom gained from writing these memoirs, I realize that I am just a bit player in my own life story. I can see that my journey was guided by interactions with others: family, friends, lovers, mentors, and colleagues. The most important accomplishments that are credited to me were in major part the product of relationships and the efforts of persons who engaged with me along the way. Even my most exciting adventures were largely initiated or facilitated by friends. I, like my appropriately named dog, Stella, was "dependent on the kindness of strangers."

I considered titling this book *Born on First Base*, acknowledging that I had started with significant advantages, while still leaving room for my reader to believe that I had improved my lot through diligence and hard work. Within my own reality and in keeping with the baseball metaphor, I believed that I had, as the years turned into decades, advanced from that favored position on first to second base and maybe even to third. However, when I sought Judith's comment on this titling proposal, she dismissed the idea out of hand, declaring bluntly that I was born on third. As is often the case, she was very convincing.

We both were sure that I hadn't made it to home plate, so I had to ask myself: What did I do with my life? Maybe I have spent my life just amusing myself. I suspect that there is a grain of truth in that reaction. Even if amusement was my main event, I think I was pretty good at it. While I was enjoying life and finding out how to get along in the world, I learned a few things that I want to share with my reader.

First about life itself.

Especially if you believe in an infinite universe as well as the concept of eternity, it is a stretch to put much importance on the meaning of one's personal life. On almost any scale, we are inconsequential, and our lives flash by in an infinitely insignificant span of time. If my life has meaning beyond my own pleasure, it is only as a minor contributor to the evolutionary process on an insignificant planet. This concept may not be exclusive to me, but it is still a reasonable framework for putting my life into perspective. My acceptance of my unimportance takes me back to a central idea of my favorite philosopher, Kurt Vonnegut Junior. If he was right that life is about amusing ourselves, then we might as well do the best job of that that we can imagine. In that regard, I have a couple of thoughts about living, starting with making certain that you have at least one truly significant love relationship in your life.

Love in all of its manifestations is one of the most agreeable facets of our life experience. It is at the core of the best human motivation, it is the bond between friends, and it is at the heart of our most important relationships. In its simplest terms, love is a deep affection complemented by a resolute commitment to one's beloved. Even so, it may take a lifetime for each of us to understand what love means personally. I can only bear witness to what I have learned from those whom I have loved.

The mothers I have been closest to will opine that the greatest love they have felt is for their children before, during, and after birth. This love persists for a lifetime, but, as I have observed, perhaps not always at that early elevated level. I have observed that "mother love" may reach its nadir during the child's puberty. It recovers from this low point when the child leaves home but never to that earliest intensity. So much for the constancy of parental love.

Then there are lovers, girlfriends and wives. Sexual love is definitely a mixed bag. In my life, sex was a considerable force, not one that was within my control at all times. Without my touching the details of my private life, allow me to express how I feel about sexual love, doing so from thirty thousand feet.

For me and perhaps for most people, sex has been a bonus, providing recreational opportunities and spurring creative capacity in many ways: think poetry, music, and literature. And beyond the arts, it has spurred personal development and imagination to great heights. What's more important, sex has served as the foundation of a bond between men and women that often survives the urge itself. It did do all these things for me. Yet, with all the good that comes from the sex drive, it is occasionally the instrument of mischief, often disruptive mischief. Some say that God didn't give man enough blood to supply his brain and his penis at the same time. While I might argue that it takes two to tango, I'm certain that men are more often responsible for inappropriate sexual behavior than are women, but the real culprit here may be God. It was He who gave us these instruments of pleasure that have caused so much disruption.

How one uses these gifts, sexual desire and attraction, is a personal choice, not always an important choice, but occasionally a choice that becomes a significant determinant of one's life trajectory. While we needn't be paranoid about sexual intimacy, there can be life-altering consequences from any sexual involvements. One needs to be careful here, careful but not paranoid.

I had a friend, a consultant with whom I traveled extensively when I was in my early thirties. He was fifty-five. In a conversation over dinner one evening, he reflected, "I am so glad to have this sex thing off my mind."

I never came to embrace this idea, but I can say from experience that love goes on after sex loses its power. After you have built a life together with a partner, it is gratifying to be able to look back and to be content, even pleased, with the life you have built together and to feel the bond of love between you. But even with this success in the rearview mirror, you know that it hasn't been an easy trip. Nor is it for most couples. We all did a lot of adapting along the way.

Maintenance of a loving relationship is a lot of work. Those who have made it through long marriages have worked successfully at adapting to constantly changing circumstances, circumstances controlled by the vicissitudes of one's own and one's partner's personalities, as well as the slings and arrows hurled at us by a sometimes inhospitable world. There is a shortcut here though: While we human beings have to adjust to changes in our partner and circumstances, dogs adapt to us and their environment, and accept us as we are. Besides, they don't argue, talk back, or complain about your tracking mud into the house. They will unfailingly greet you with joy whenever you return from even the shortest separation and will be ever responsive to your moods.

As I said in the beginning of this book, Matilda, the nanny, gave me love at the beginning; Matilda, the Weimaraner, is there for me at the end. Better than I can, dogs define the meaning of love. Even if all else succeeds, get a dog!

As I wind up this collection of memories, I am eighty-three years old. "They" say that old people live in the past, and in that, "they" may be right. But other than the fleeting present and a brief and uncertain tomorrow, what do I have? What we oldsters do have, if we still have all our marbles, is a lifetime of memories, memories that are pleasant to recall and often fun to share. Actually, memory is crucial to our perception of reality. It is a key to our humanity, a partial answer to the mystery of life; its failure can be likened to that of the tree falling in the forest unheard. It might even seem that unremembered events never happened. My own perception of reality is based entirely on what I remember; so is it probably with you.

That brings me to the importance of writing. At a consciousness level, writing can be a useful tool for enriching one's reality by keeping a written record of otherwise easily forgotten events. In addition, the act of recording events refreshes and fortifies one's memory. That said, according to the experts, the act of remembering may have some downside. Research has shown that the process of recall itself can alter recollection, degrading the accuracy of a memory. In that regard, one of my favorite memories, that of a battle of mine with nature, covered in a chapter herein, *Living on the Edge,* may suffer from this phenomenon. The other participants in this vivid recollection, Alby Gallun and Chris Beda, do not recall this event at all, even as every one of its dramatic moments is etched in my brain in precise detail. Be that as it may, their failure to recall this adventure does not diminish the value of that memory as a joyous experience within my own reality. Actually their failure to recall may stem from their failure to keep records of their important experiences.

Writing could have been a more important part of my life if I had used it to nourish my significant personal relationships. Other than during my first military service, where I wrote daily to my then fiancée, Kathy, I have never communicated much in writing to anyone. Letter writing was for me and is for most people today a lost art. Having read in the literature some really beautiful communiqués between family members, friends, and lovers, I am sorry I never developed this skill. Nor did I keep a journal, an activity that I would recommend, the keeping of which would certainly have enriched my memoirs. Eventually, I did take up the writing of creative nonfiction and, if my reader has gotten this far, he might agree that I have learned how to write in this mode. But most importantly, for me, writing makes me think clearly about what I am writing about. The expression of a truly coherent idea in a sentence or a paragraph is a demanding activity that exercises the brain. Good writing requires clear thinking.

As I was putting the finishing touches on this tome, I became aware of a defect in my thinking. It was my son, Rich, who awakened me to the thought that I might have misconstrued the baseball metaphor employed above. When I told him of my concession to Judith that I was born on third base, he agreed with that concept. But when he heard the next sentence about not reaching home, he reacted instinctively and passionately, asserting that I, together with Judith, had clearly reached any reasonable definition of home plate.

On thinking over what he said about our lives, I had to agree with Rich; we made it to home plate. It was about six months ago that Judith and I were talking together about the course of our lives. For Judith, it was about the things she loved (in no particular order): our families, particularly our children, our friends, her house, her bedroom, the people at Planned Parenthood and the Conservatory, her dogs, and even her husband. It was pretty much the same for me. And together, we have done our share for our communities. We both have made mistakes that we would admit to and regret; but as we lay together in the fading light, we were both contented and even pleased with the course of our lives, together and previous; neither of us would want to give up any of the experiences we have had, or at least the ones we remember.

To paraphrase the queen: We have been amused.

www.ingramcontent.com/pod-product-compliance
Lightning Source LLC
Chambersburg PA
CBHW050403110426
42812CB00006BA/1783